REPERCUSSIONS OF THE KALAM IN JEWISH PHILOSOPHY

REPERCUSSIONS OF THE KALAM IN JEWISH PHILOSOPHY

BY

HARRY AUSTRYN WOLFSON

HARVARD UNIVERSITY PRESS
CAMBRIDGE, MASSACHUSETTS
AND LONDON, ENGLAND
1979

Library of Congress Cataloging in Publication Data

Wolfson, Harry Austryn, 1887–1974.
Repercussions of the Kalam in Jewish philosophy.

Includes bibliographical references and index.
1. Philosophy, Jewish. 2. Philosophy, Medieval. I. Title.
B755.W64 181′.3 78–9798
ISBN 0–674–76175–8

FOREWORD

Repercussions of the Kalam in Jewish Philosophy is a fitting finale to an extraordinarily versatile scholarly career which began with the publication of Professor Wolfson's *Crescas' Critique of Aristotle*. As this long-awaited, long-delayed monograph is finally, with pride and satisfaction, presented to the public, a few comments about its genesis and gestalt — or, to use a favorite formula of the author's, about its "origin, structure, and diversity" — are in order.

This book was originally conceived and actually constructed as an integral part of *The Philosophy of the Kalam* — a work which unrelentingly preoccupied the author for decades. Thirteen sections of the *Kalam* appeared in various publications between 1943 and 1969; * the writing and composition, in intense, concentrated form, spanned the years 1956 to 1964. In fact Professor Wolfson returned intermittently — it is almost as if he was enthralled, or irresistibly drawn — to the bulky manuscript until his very last days (spring and summer, 1974), revising, re-formulating, re-structuring. While this on-going tinkering with the text was typical — Wolfson regularly reviewed his books *in page proof*, checking for consistency in translation and transliteration as well as elegance of presentation and precision of conceptualization — the delays surrounding the *Kalam* were unprecedented. The problems were manifold, methodological and material, structural and substantive. If I may quote from my foreword (p. v) to the *Kalam*: "This volume, like his earlier works, combines massive erudition with great intuition. This time, however, Professor Wolfson was called upon to apply his method of conjecture and verification to fragmentary, philosophically laconic, and recalcitrant texts; the challenge of fitting these texts, frequently quotations or reports found in late doxog-

* One article, "Saadia on the Semantic Aspect of the Problem of Attributes," appeared posthumously in the *Salo W. Baron Jubilee Volume* (Jerusalem, 1975), pp. 1009–1021.

raphies, into his conceptual framework was great and that accounts for the delay in the completion of this work." Even the baffling allusiveness of Spinoza's *Ethics* and ellipticalness of its style — and the resultant need to unfold "the latent processes of his reasoning" — were dwarfed by the problems of these texts.

Now, in addition to this protracted delay in the publication of the parent book (Fall 1976), its offspring was further delayed for various reasons. Having been excised from the *Kalam*, it lay in limbo for quite a while. When we again turned to it, there was need to review the entire work, revise the footnotes and coordinate all references with the *Kalam*.

As for scope and structure, *Repercussions* treats at length the themes of attributes, creation, causality, and free will, and more briefly discusses Christology and atomism. Some of these discussions are indeed very compressed — close, pointed, laser-type analysis and commentary on select passages. In general, *Repercussions* may be characterized as an exegetical-interpretive work, consisting of a long, impressive series of *explications de texte*. The texts are chosen from a wide variety of Jewish authors who included in their philosophical, theological, juridical, or commentatorial works passages concerning the Kalam: al-Muḳammas, Saadia Gaon, Isaac Israeli, Baḥya ibn Pakuda, Joseph ibn Saddik, Judah ben Barzillai, Judah Halevi, Abraham ibn Ezra, Abraham ibn Daud, Maimonides. Karaite writers — al-Kirkisānī, Salmon ben Yeruhim, Joseph al-Baṣīr, Judah Hadassi, Jeshua ben Judah — are also included. It should be noted that Maimonides (*Guide*, I, 71) mentioned Rabbinite and Karaite philosophers in the same context, cited and characterized them together, and analyzed their teachings concomitantly, for in philosophical terms there is no difference between them.

To be sure, one must read carefully, and critically, to appreciate this textual achievement. Some of the authors are treated in extenso — for example those listed in the table of contents — and some in passing. Sometimes, an illuminating comment or novel interpretation is inserted parenthetically. Smaller texts — for example R. Hai Gaon's famous responsum on the question of the appointed term of life and whether it is subject to increase and diminution — are also subject to re-examination or refreshing interpretation. Inasmuch as the frame of reference is Kalam, the literature of Kalam in particular and early Islamic philosophy generally are cited regularly. This literary range — treatment of ibn Ezra, Halevi, and Maimonides together with ibn Hazm and Nazzam, Abu Hashim, and Ghazali — will surely make this work indispensable for students of Jewish and Islamic philosophy.

It will be immediately clear to the reader that this monograph, while intellectually self-sufficient and intrinsically significant, is inextricably linked to *The Philosophy of the Kalam*. This link is manifest not only in the abundant references to that parent work, but in the very texture of *Repercussions*, which plunges the reader *in medias res*. Adding new dimensions, details, and interpretive insights, the underlying discussion flows directly and smoothly from the earlier analyses. There are no transitional paragraphs, summations, or introductory sentences bridging the works; and I should add that I did not deem it appropriate to provide such sentences or paragraphs. The reader, on occasion, will have no choice but to consult the *Kalam* — and will be duly rewarded for so doing.* Needless to say, even those readers interested only in the Jewish authors must regularly turn to the *Kalam*, inasmuch as extensive sections of Saadia, Bahya ibn Pakuda, or Maimonides are treated there. An outstanding example is the

* Chapter V of the original master plan for the projected two-volume *Kalam* was called "Repercussions in Judaism" and contained all the material presented here in sections I-V. The following chapter on Creation — Chapter V in the printed *Kalam* — began with the lengthy section on "unapproved theories of creation," inasmuch as the framework for that analysis was the enumeration of theories found in Saadia's *Emunot ve-De'ot* (upon which were grafted the corresponding theories enumerated by Baghdādī and those by Ibn Hazm). The remaining three chapters — on atomism, causality, predestination and free will — concluded with sections on "Repercussions."

analysis of Maimonides' characterization (*Guide*, I, 71) of the Kalam itself, which is rife with chronological and conceptual problems; Wolfson's full explication (*Kalam*, pp. 45ff) has many repercussions for understanding Maimonides' conception of the history of philosophy and, indeed, of Maimonides' own place in this history.

Moreover, the *explication de texte* — rich and resonant, always suggestive and frequently speculative — is predicated on the comprehensive review of material and reconstruction of views propounded in the *Kalam.* The monograph is peppered with formulaic phrases which regularly reenforce this connection: "evidently having in mind the statement"; "we may assume that he knew that ibn Kullab." Pithy conclusions such as "Thus Saadia tacitly aligned himself with the Muslim Antiattributists against the Muslim Attributists" are of the same order.

The term "repercussions" deserves special comment, for it reveals Wolfson's conception concerning medieval Jewish philosophy and its relation to the Arabic philosophic literature that provides the matrix and ambience in which Jewish thought was nurtured. Judaism was essentially rationalistic inasmuch as it unqualifiedly rejected anthropomorphism, the reality of attributes, and the denial of free will. In other words, its traditional views were perfectly congruent with what was later to be characterized as rationalistic philosophic views. Its contact with Mutazilite discourse reenforced these inherent traits and provided a philosophic terminology that could be used in recasting them. Thus, in his interpretation of a problematic Maimonidean statement concerning the relation of Jewish philosophers to Islamic writers (*Kalam*, p. 88) Wolfson writes: "by which he means that they all maintain certain traditional Jewish views on the unity and incorporeality of God and on the freedom of the human will which agree with views which in Islam were maintained by the Mu'tazilites in opposition to the Ash'arites, and that they all, in their attempts to support these Jewish traditional views, use arguments which they borrowed from the Mu'tazilites." This coincides completely with his general approach to the history of ideas: "Beliefs and ideas are indeed contagious, and the history of beliefs and ideas is often a history of imitation by contagion. But for the contagiousness of a belief or an idea to take effect, there must be a predisposition and susceptibility on the part of those who are to be affected by it" (*Kalam*, p. 70). Consequently, Wolfson was very careful — and he often commented on this orally — not to speak of influences but rather of repercussions. His concern was not with the influence of Kalam views on Jewish thought as much as it was with the discussion, elaboration, adaptation, qualification, or criticism of these views by Jewish thinkers. This, in fact, reflects a continuous, clearly discernible dialectic sustained deftly and delicately throughout all his works: on one hand, they brilliantly and ingeniously call attention to the interplay of Jewish and general philosophy and, on the other, they underscore that special dimension of Jewish philosophic thought.

Let me conclude with two additional observations concerning the formal relationship of this monograph to the entire Wolfsonian oeuvre. The frequent references — not only to the *Kalam* but to dozens of his articles (see, for example, pp. 3–4) — are clearly not self-congratulatory; they illustrate the cumulative, cohesive nature of all his writing. *Repercussions* is therefore in many respects a microcosm of his life's work, which began with the edition, translation, and annotation of Crescas — a model of what Wolfson used to refer to as "honest scholarship." Wolfson's firm method of philological analysis (minute textual study modeled after the Talmudic mode of study), his original conception of the history of philosophy, and his clear definition of subject matter joined together to produce an impressive, magisterial sweep and extraordinary expertise possessed of great resilience and force.

The philological-conceptual system simplified the fitting together of disparate pieces; it was the core and the catalyst of his work.

This monograph is thus the ripe harvest of a lifetime of untiring scholarship; much study never became a "weariness of the flesh" (cf. *Kalam*, p. 93). Seen from this vantage point, it clearly illustrates the dynamic quality of Wolfson's learning and research: continuous refinement and reformulation of views (see, for example, p. 388, n22, and many others). While he answered critics gently but firmly or offered polite criticism of positions that did not show full awareness of the issues (a particularly instructive example is the long statement concerning the relationship of Maimonides and Averroes on pp. 187–188), he was his own best critic.

As for the importance and originality of this monograph, one need only consult the useful bibliographical review article by G. Vajda, "Le Kalam dans la pensée religieuse juive du Moyen Age," *Revue de l'Histoire des Religions*, 183 (1973): 143–160,* in order to project into bold relief the tremendous advances of Wolfson's study — in clarity, comprehensiveness, and incisiveness of interpretation. As I have noted elsewhere, while some conjectures may be found lacking in full, overwhelming verification, the grand achievement of *Repercussions* will become an enduring, stimulating, scholarly contribution in an area where few historians of philosophy dare to venture.

* This is a slightly reworked version of a paper prepared for the Harvard Colloquium on early Islamic philosophy held in 1971 in honor of the forthcoming publication of Professor Wolfson's *Kalam*.

ISADORE TWERSKY

CONTENTS

REPERCUSSIONS OF THE KALAM IN JEWISH PHILOSOPHY

I. Attributes and Trinity

To the Jews living in Muslim countries and speaking and reading Arabic the view that certain terms predicated of God in Scripture and liturgy indicated the existence in God of certain real attributes was something new. In their own literature, they knew, the terms predicated of God in Exodus 34:6–7 are referred to as God's "thirteen *middot*," [1] from which they could infer that any term predicated of God is a *middah*. But the term *middah*, meaning literally "measure," "that which measures," came to mean "rule," a rule of interpretation, a rule of conduct, and a rule of action, and hence derivatively also the act of meting out something as a reward or punishment. In the Hebrew Bible the verb *middah* was already used in that derivative sense, as, for instance, in the verse "Therefore will I first measure (*u-maddoti*) their work into their bosom" (Isa. 65:7). Accordingly, the ascription of *middot* to God in the Pentateuch could not lead Jews to the belief in the existence of real attributes in God; the *middot* could have only meant to them a way of describing the manner in which God deals with His creatures.[2]

Equally new to the Jews in the Arabic-speaking countries was the Christian doctrine of the Trinity, which was fully discussed by Christian writers in Arabic as well as by Muslim writers. In their own literature, the Jews could only find vague allusions to the Christian Trinity, such as in the passage where certain "sectarians" (*minin*) who claimed that the occurrence of three words for God, *El*, *Elohim*, and *Jehovah*, in Joshua 22:22 and Psalms 50:1, implies the existence of three deities.[3] And if they identified these "sectarians" with Christians, all

[1] *Rosh ha-Shanah* 17b.

[2] Cf. *Moreh* I, 54.

[3] *Jer. Berakot* IX, 1, 12d–13a; cf. *Genesis Rabbah*, 8, 9.

they knew about the Trinity was that it asserted the belief in three deities.

We may speculate what would have happened if, at the time learned Muslims met learned Christians and debated with them the Trinity, learned Jews also met learned Christians, under similar conditions, and also debated with them the Trinity. Would some of those Jews, like some of those Muslims,[4] have admitted with the Christians that there are in God certain real beings, called either "life" and "knowledge" or "life" and "power" or "knowledge" and "power," but have insisted that these real beings are not to be called God? Or would all of the Jews, like some of the other Muslims, have denied the existence of any such real beings in God? The answers to such hypothetical questions would depend upon the kind of learned Jews that would have debated with the learned Christian about the Trinity. If, as is most likely, they were trained on the purely native Jewish literature, Scripture and Talmud, they could have justified the belief in real attributes in the same way as orthodox Islam justified it, on the ground that the attributes, though eternal and distinct from God, are not gods. For, it will be noticed, in the Talmudic allusion to the Trinity, quoted above, the opposition to it is, as in the Koran, only on the ground that the three persons were each spoken of as God. There is nothing in Scripture or in the Talmudic literature which directly and explicitly states that the unity of God meant anything more than external, numerical unity and a denial of polytheism. But if, as is unlikely, the learned Jews debating with the learned Christians were trained on Hellenistic Jewish literature, and especially the works of Philo, they would oppose the existence of real beings in God, even if none of them was called God, for in the works of Philo the unity of God becomes an internal unity and a denial of any kind of divisibility or compositeness in the nature of God.

No such contact, however, and no such debate between

[4] Cf. *Kalam*, pp. 129–131.

learned Jews and learned Christians did take place. It is from Arabic writings of Muslims that they first learned about the problem of attributes, and it is also from allusions in the Arabic writings of Muslims to the Christian Trinity, perhaps occasionally supplemented by Arabic works of Christians, that they first learned of the speculative aspects of the problem of the Trinity. That they should follow the Antiattributists was to be expected. The Antiattributists' arguments that the doctrine of real attributes was like the Christian doctrine of the Trinity predisposed exponents of Judaism against it. Thus from the very beginning they aligned themselves with the Muʿtazilites in their opposition to the reality of attributes. Like the Muʿtazilites, they compared the doctrine of the reality of attributes to the doctrine of the Trinity, and, like the Muʿtazilites, they based their opposition to the reality of attributes on the principle that the unity of God means not only an external or numerical unity but also an internal unity or absolute simplicity.

This conception of internal unity or absolute simplicity was not derived by the Arabic-speaking Jews directly from Scripture, for the unity of God in Scripture meant only numerical unity. It was the Muʿtazilite stressing of internal unity or absolute simplicity that led them to interpret scriptural unity in that sense. Still, though directly they were led to this interpretation of the scriptural unity of God by the influence of the Muʿtazilites, ultimately they were following a principle which had originated in Judaism. For the conception of the unity of God in the sense of simplicity, an absolute simplicity implying the unknowability and ineffability of God and hence the rejection of real attributes, was introduced by Philo as an extension, by philosophic reasoning, of the scriptural principle of the unlikeness of God.[5] It was a conception new in philosophy; it is not to be found in Greek philosophy before him.[6] But

[5] Cf. *Philo*, II, pp. 94–126.

[6] Cf. my paper "The Knowability and Describability of God in Plato and Aristotle," *Harvard Studies in Classical Philology*, 66–67: 233–249 (1945–46).

once introduced by Philo, it penetrated into pagan Greek philosophy [7] and into Christian philosophy,[8] and from the latter it was adopted by the Muʿtazilites.[9] When the spokesmen of Judaism of that period chose to follow the Muʿtazilites rather than Muslim orthodoxy, ultimately, unbeknown to themselves, they were following Philo and, like Philo, they used the scriptural teaching of the unlikeness of God, aided by the various philosophical analyses of the meaning of one, as proof for the absolute unity of God. No literary opposition to this conception of the unity of God, as far as we know, appeared among Jewish philosophers of this period. It was not until later, when opposition to rationalist philosophy of religion, as represented by Maimonides, appeared in Judaism, that direct opposition to the Philonic conception of the unity of God, like that raised in Islam by Ghazālī, made its appearance in Judaism.[10]

Though the problem of attributes was introduced, or rather reintroduced into Judaism, during that period, from Islam, it is not treated as a foreign importation. It is treated as a general religious problem which, while it was raised in Islam, could have been raised also in Judaism. Every possible opinion is examined on its own merit and, while the doctrine of real attributes, which is rejected by them, happened to have become identified with Muslim orthodoxy, it is not identified by them with Islam, as is the Trinity identified by them with Christianity. Thus Maimonides, in wishing to refer to doctrines which are peculiarly characteristic of Christianity and Islam, mentions "the Trinity" as characteristic of the Christians and "the Word," that is, the uncreated Koran, as characteristic of "some sects" in Islam.[11] No mention is made by him in that

[7] Cf. my paper "Albinus and Plotinus on Divine Attributes," *HTR*, 45: 115–130 (1952).

[8] Cf. my paper "Negative Attributes in the Church Fathers and the Gnostic Basilides," *HTR*, 50: 145–156 (1957).

[9] Cf. *Kalam*, pp. 132–137.

[10] Cf. my paper "Crescas on Divine Attributes," *JQR*, n.s. 7.1: 1–44 and 7.2: 175–221.

[11] *Moreh* I, 71, p. 123, ll. 6–7.

place of the doctrine of real attributes as being characteristic of Islam or of some of its sects.

Chronologically the first among spokesmen of Judaism of that period to deal with attributes and the Trinity are contemporaries, al-Muḳammaṣ and Saadia, the two, according to an unsupported rumor reported by Judah ben Barzillai, having known each other personally and the latter having been instructed by the former.[12] We shall start our discussion with these two contemporaries.

I. AL-MUKAMMAS [1]

Al-Muḳammaṣ opens his discussion of attributes, as would anyone who was going to deny the existence of real attributes, with an explanation that the term "one," as applied to God, does not mean a mere external unity in the sense of a denial of polytheism; it means internal unity, that is, an affirmation of the absolute simplicity of God and a denial of any compositeness in Him. "We maintain," says al-Muḳammaṣ, "that God is one, not like one in genus nor like one in species nor like one in number nor like one [in virtue of continuity] by nature but one in absolute simplicity, in which there is no diversity and no composition; He is one in virtue of His essence and there is no other like Him." [2] Here then we have a definite rejection of the Christian view that the unity of God is only a relative kind of unity, like that described by Aristotle as unity in genus [3] or in species [4] or in virtue of being continuous, especially when it is "continuous by nature," [5] and here also we have a definite reassertion of the Philonic conception that the unity of God is unlike any other unity; it is absolute unity.

[12] *Perush Sefer Yeṣirah* (1885), p. 77; cf. Malter, *Life and Works of Saadia Gaon* (1921), p. 67.

[1] Citations here are from the excerpts in Hebrew translation of his Arabic work *'Ishrūn Maḳālāt* in Judah ben Barzillai's *Perush*, compared with the original Arabic copied many years ago by the late Professor A. S. Yahuda from a manuscript in the then Imperial Library in St. Petersburg.

[2] *Ibid.*, p. 78, ll. 1–3.

[3] *Metaph.* V, 6, 1016a, 24.

[4] *Ibid.*, 1016b, 23–24, 31–32.

[5] *Ibid.*, 1016a, 4.

Having thus rigorously explained the meaning of the scriptural conception of the unity of God, he proceeds to reject the various Muslim theories of real attributes as well as the Christian conception of the Trinity.

Using the term "living" in its predication of God as a model attribute, he constructs on it two model formulae, each of which is shown by him to be susceptible of two meanings, thus resulting in four formulae,[6] which would represent three theories of attributes, of which two are rejected by him and one accepted.

One theory of attributes he finds to be represented by the formula "God is living in virtue of life" when taken to mean that "God acquired (*ḳanah: istaḥdath*) life and thereby became living, even as one among us described as knowing acquires knowledge and thereby becomes knowing." [7] Muḳammas summarily dismisses this theory on the ground of its being contrary to the established belief that "God is eternally living," [8] adding the following remark: "And there is no need for us to dwell any longer on this theory, for we have not found any man (*lo maṣinu adam*) who professed it" or, as the original Arabic reads: "for we do not know anyone who (*lā na'rif man*) professed it." [9] This last remark lends itself to three interpretations. It may mean that Muḳammaṣ had no knowledge of anyone who believed in created attributes in general, in which case he was ignorant of the various reports about the existence of such belief in the Kalam.[10] Or it may mean that he had no knowledge of anyone whose belief in created attributes included the attribute "living," in which

[6] *Perush*, p. 78, l. 39–p. 79, l. 26. The four formulae on p. 78, l. 39–p. 79, l. 10, are not exactly the same as those on p. 79, ll. 10–26.

[7] *Ibid.*, p. 79, ll. 11–13. Cf. *Intiṣār* 74, p. 85, ll. 16–17: "Hishām [b. al-Ḥakam] maintained that God acquires (*yastafīd*) the knowledge of a thing, just as men acquire it, only at the moment of its coming into existence and its coming to pass, and that before He acquired that knowledge, God was ignorant of affairs, not knowing what will come into existence and what will come to pass."

[8] *Perush*, p. 79, l. 14.

[9] *Ibid.*, l. 15.

[10] Cf. *Kalam*, pp. 143–146.

case he was ignorant of two reports about one subsect of the Rāfiḍah, the Zurāriyyah,[11] and one report about another anonymous subsect of Rāfiḍah,[12] which explicitly include the attribute "living" among the attributes which they believed to be created. But probably what it means is that he had no knowledge of any orthodox Muslim who believed in any kind of created attributes.

Another theory of attributes would be represented by the formula "God is living in virtue of life" when taken to mean that, while life is coeternal with God both *a parte ante* and *a parte post*, it is "other (*ḥuṣ*: *ghayr*) than God and part (*miḳṣat*: [*ba'ḍ*]) of Him." [13] This theory of attributes is that of the orthodox Muslim Attributists, which is expressed by them in their description of the attributes as being "other (*ghayr*) than God" [14] and as being "superadded (*zā'idah*) to the essence of God." [15] Though the expression "part of God" is never used, as far as I know, by any Attributist,[16] it would seem to have been introduced here by Muḳammaṣ as a substitute for the expression "superadded to the essence of God," evidently justifying himself by the reasoning that if attributes are superadded to the essence of God, they are part of God. This theory of attributes is refuted by him on two grounds. First, he refutes it on the ground that "he who says that God's life is other than He lands in polytheism (*kafranut*), for he posits another [eternal] being by the side of God, which is exactly the error of the Christians, who say concerning God that He is living in virtue of life, which is the Holy Spirit, and He is knowing in virtue of knowledge, which is the Word or that which they call the Son. This is sheer polytheism (*kafranut*: *shirk*)." [17] Second, he refutes it on the ground that he who says that "God is living in virtue of a life which is

[11] Cf. *Kalam*, p. 144, nn. 9–10. [12] *Ibid.*

[13] *Perush*, p. 79, ll. 11 and 15–16 and 17–18.

[14] Cf. *Kalam*, p. 214. [15] *Ibid.*, pp. 214, 215.

[16] It is explicitly rejected by Hishām b. al-Ḥakam even as a description of his created attributes. *Ibid.*, p. 207.

[17] *Perush*, p. 79, ll. 18–21.

part (*miḳṣat: ba'ḍ*) of Him"[18] introduces composition into God, "and he thus makes God something composite (*merukkab*), but this is not the nature (*derek*) of the Creator"[19] or, as the Arabic original reads, "and this necessarily implies that God is something composite (*murakkab*) and has a composer (*murakkib*), but whoever is like this is not the Lord (*rabb*)."

The theory of attributes which is acceptable to him is that which would be represented by the following two formulae: (1) "God is living in virtue of life" when taken, as before, to mean that life is coeternal with God both *a parte ante* and *a parte post*, but to which is added the statement: "but His life is himself";[20] (2) "God is living not in virtue of life" when taken to mean that "God is living not in virtue of life but in virtue of himself."[21] Of these two formulae, the first is that used by Abū al-Hudhayl,[22] and the second is that used by Naẓẓām.[23] Now Shahrastānī, who lived after Muḳammaṣ, distinguishes between these two formulae, taking that of Abū al-Hudhayl to be an anticipation of Abū Hāshim's theory of modes and that of Naẓẓām to be an absolute denial of attributes.[24] Muḳammaṣ, however, here takes Abū al-Hudhayl's formula to mean, like Naẓẓām's formula, the absolute denial of attributes, asserting that, "while there is between these two formulae a difference in phrasing, there is no difference in meaning."[25] It may be remarked, however, that the fact that Muḳammaṣ took the trouble to point out that the two formulae, though different in phrasing, are the same in meaning would seem to show that he knew that someone did not consider them to have the same meaning. That someone, as I have suggested, is Ibn al-Rāwandī.[26]

2. SAADIA

A similar rejection of the reality of attributes as well as of the Christian Trinity on the ground of their incompatibility

[18] *Ibid.*, ll. 22–23.
[19] *Ibid.*, l. 24.
[20] *Ibid.*, ll. 11 and 15–16.
[21] *Ibid.*, ll. 7–9 and 21 and 25–26.
[22] Cf. *Kalam*, p. 225.
[23] *Ibid.*
[24] *Ibid.*, p. 229.
[25] *Perush*, p. 79, ll. 21–22.
[26] *Cf. Kalam*, pp. 230–233.

with the absolute unity of God is to be found in Saadia. His discussion of the unity of God as well as of attributes and the Trinity is, however, more elaborate than that of al-Muḳammaṣ.

Saadia starts his discussion of attributes by establishing, both by means of Scripture [1] and by means of what he terms "speculation" (*naẓar*: *'iyyun*), the numerical unity of God,[2] that is to say, the denial of polytheism. What kind of polytheism in particular Saadia had in mind in stressing the numerical unity of God he does not say. Certainly he could not have meant the old kinds of idolatry of Biblical times which had long been dead and gone and were no longer subjects of vital discussion at the time of Saadia. It must have been some polytheistic conception of God, or at least a conception of God considered by Saadia as polytheistic, which was still a vital subject of discussion in Saadia's time. What was that?

An answer to this question is to be found in the passage immediately following his discussion of the unity of God. In that passage, a suppositional opponent is made to argue that certain expressions in Scripture would seem to show that Scripture itself is not averse to a certain kind of polytheism. Two kinds of such expressions are quoted.

The first kind of expression quoted by the suppositional opponent is that contained in the verses where God is spoken of as "the Lord God" (Gen. 2:5) or "My Lord and my God" (Ps. 35:23) or "the Lord" and "the Most High" (2 Sam. 22:14).[3] Now it happens that the rabbis of old, in refutation of certain Dualists who thought they had found an excuse for believing that there are "two Powers" in the names "Lord" (Jehovah) and "God" (Elohim) used in Scripture, quote the verse "I am the Lord thy God" (Exod. 20:2) in order to show that the two names refer to one and the same God.[4] When, therefore, Saadia refers to an opponent who might argue from

[1] *Emunot* II, 1, p. 79, ll. 13, 15–18.
[2] *Ibid.*, l. 15; p. 80, l. 14–p. 81, l. 2.
[3] *Ibid.* II, 3, p. 83, ll. 4–13.
[4] *Mekilta, Baḥodesh* 5 (ed. Lauterbach, II, p. 231); *Exodus Rabbah* 29, 1.

the use of the names "Lord" and "God" or "Lord" and "Most High" that Scripture itself recognizes more than one God, the opponent referred to is one of the various followers of Zoroastrian Dualism, known to the Muslims at the time of Saadia, and even after his time, as Manichaeans, Mazdakites, Bardesanians, and Marcionites,[5] and are refuted by Saadia himself in another part of his work.[6]

The second kind of expression quoted by the suppositional opponent is that contained in the verse "And now the Lord God hath sent me, and His spirit" (Isa. 48:16), from which his opponent was evidently supposed to show that Scripture itself taught that there is more than one God.[7] Now, here again, it happens that this very verse is quoted in an Arabic work by the Christian Abucara as evidence of the mention of the Christian Trinity in the Hebrew Scripture.[8] When, therefore, Saadia refers to an opponent who might argue from this verse that Scripture itself recognizes more than one God, the opponent referred to is a Christian, who believed in the Trinity. So also in his Commentary on his own Arabic translation of Proverbs (9:13–18; 24:21–22) does he couple the Dualists and the Trinitarians as infringers upon the true principle of the unity of God.[9]

Saadia then goes on to establish the internal unity of God, His unity in the sense of His simplicity. He does not do so directly; he does it indirectly by discussing the meaning of the terms "life," "power," and "wisdom" as predicates of God — the three terms which, as we have seen,[10] were the original subject of controversy between the Attributists, who did not believe in the internal unity of God, and the Antiattributists, who did believe in His internal unity. In this indirect way of establishing the internal unity or simplicity of God, Saadia

[5] Shahrastānī, *Milal*, pp. 188, ll. 7 ff.
[6] *Emunot* I, 3, 5th Theory, pp. 48, ll. 12 ff.
[7] *Ibid*., II, 3, p. 84, ll. 5–7.
[8] Abucara, *Mimar* III, 10, p. 153; *Mimar* VII, 15, pp. 193–194.
[9] Edition J. Derenburg and Mayer Lambert, pp. 53, 138.
[10] *Kalam*, pp. 125–127.

begins with the statement that "by means of speculation" he has found that God, who "created all things," must be "living" and "powerful" and "knowing,"[11] that "these three attributes (*ma'ānī*: *'inyanim*) are grasped by our minds all at once,"[12] that they are not "varied attributes" but are all implied in the "attribute describing Him as Creator,"[13] that it is only due to the lack of any single term embracing the three connotations of these three attributes that we have to use three different terms,[14] and that to coin some new single term for the purpose would be useless, since it would be unintelligible to readers without lengthy explanations.[15] Summing up, he says: "Just as our application of the term 'Creator' to God does not signify any addition to His essence but only signifies that there is here something created by Him, so our application to Him of the terms 'living' and 'powerful' and 'knowing,' being as they are explanations of the term 'Creator' to the effect that only one who possesses these attributes all at once can be a Creator, does not signify any addition to His essence but only signifies that there is here something created by Him."[16] Thus Saadia tacitly aligned himself with the Muslim Antiattributists against the Muslim Attributists.

With this indirect proof "by means of speculation"[17] for the internal unity of God, Saadia goes on to show that such internal unity is implied also in the scriptural teaching of the unity of God, introducing the subject as follows: "After my contemplation on this [problem of the meaning of the terms

[11] *Emunot* II, 4, p. 84, ll. 14–15; cf. II, 1, p. 79, ll. 12–13, and p. 80, ll. 6–7.

[12] *Emunot* II, 1, p. 75, ll. 3–4. The term *ma'ānī*, which is used by Muslim Attributists in the sense of "things," that is, real attributes (cf. *Kalam*, pp. 115–117), is used here by Saadia in the sense of "concepts" of the mind. Elsewhere (*Emunot* I, 3, 2nd Theory, p. 42, ll. 13 and 17) Saadia uses the term *ma'ānī* (Hebrew: *debarim*) with reference to various accidents, of which he says that they are "attributes (*ṣifāt*: *to'arim*) of bodies" in contrast to the term *ashyā'*, "things," (Hebrew: *debarim*), which he uses with reference to atoms. There, again, *ma'ānī* and *ṣifāt* are used by him in contrast to real things. Cf. quotation from Ibn Kullāb, *Kalam*, p. 117.

[13] *Ibid.*, l. 7.

[14] *Ibid.*, ll. 8–10.

[15] *Ibid.*, ll. 10–11.

[16] *Ibid.*, ll. 16–17.

[17] *Emunot* II, 4, p. 84, ll. 14–15.

'living,' 'powerful,' and 'wise' predicated of God] and the conclusions which I have arrived at concerning it, I went back to the Holy Scriptures and I found in them statements implying the rejection of any otherness (*al-ghayriyyah*: *ha-zulat*) than God." [18] The denial of any "otherness" in God means the denial of any internal plurality in God, thus raising the conception of the unity of God to that of the simplicity of God.

The first of these texts is a quotation in Hebrew of a verse which in the Authorized Version reads: "There is none else beside Him" (Deut. 4:35). Now this verse has been previously quoted by him as a scriptural proof-text for numerical unity.[19] On what ground he now quotes it again as a scriptural proof-text for internal unity is not clear. But it happens that in his translation of the Pentateuch, this verse is translated by him to read: "There is no other than He and there is none except Him." [20] According to this translation then the verse contains two statements: (1) "There is no other than He"; (2) "There is none except Him." Accordingly, we may assume, Saadia takes the first statement to be an assertion of numerical unity and the second statement to be an assertion of internal unity.

Similarly, the second scriptural text quoted by him as proof for internal unity can be explained on the basis of his own Arabic translation of it. The text quoted by him in Hebrew is part of a verse in Job, here italicized, which in the Authorized Version reads as follows: "Lo, these are parts of His ways: *but how little a portion is heard of Him*?" (Job 26:14). In his Arabic translation of the Book of Job, however, this verse reads: "Lo, these are some of His descriptions (*auṣafuhu*), but what thing thereof (*shay min al-umūr*) is heard of Him?" Now the term *shay*, "thing," as well as the term *maʿnā*,

[18] *Ibid.*, p. 85, ll. 19–21. [19] *Ibid.*, 2, p. 82, ll. 15–16.

[20] It is to be noted that, in contrast to his splitting up the single Hebrew statement in Deut. 4:35 into two Arabic statements, a similarly constructed Hebrew statement in Isa. 45:21 is translated by Saadia into a single Arabic statement, which reads: "There is no God other than I."

"thing," as we have seen,[21] is used in the Kalam as the equivalent of the term *ṣifah*, "attribute," and Saadia himself speaks of the second and third persons of the Christian Trinity, which are regarded as analogous to the orthodox Muslim attributes, as *shay'ani*, "things." [22] Accordingly, in quoting the verse of Job as proof-text for the internal unity of God, Saadia takes that verse to mean that none of His "descriptions," that is, none of the terms which are predicated of God, is a "thing," that is, a real attribute existing in God as something other than He.

The third text quoted by him is the verse which reads in part: "the Lord shall be one and His name one" (Zech. 14:9). Here quite evidently the verse was taken by Saadia to contain affirmations of two kinds of unity. The first part of the verse, namely, "the Lord shall be one," was thus taken by him as an affirmation of numerical unity, and the second part, namely, "and His name one," was taken by him to mean that whatever names or terms are predicated of Him they all are but one name, being only various ways of describing Him as Creator, for, as he himself said, the terms "living," "powerful," and "knowing" are only explanations of the term "Creator." [23]

With this conception of the unity of God, Saadia takes up the refutation of the Christian doctrine of the Trinity, which indirectly contains a refutation of the orthodox Muslim doctrine of attributes. He opens his discussion by referring to two views on the Trinity current among Christians. He describes them as the view "of the common people (*'awāmm*: *'ame haareṣ*) among them" who "confess a Trinity which is conceived of only in corporeal terms" and "the elite (*ḫawāṣṣ*: *ḥakamim*) among them." [24] The expression "common people" in the description of one of the two contrasting views referred to by him does not give us an accurate idea of the view he had in mind. The exact meaning of the view which he had in mind here may be gathered from the work of his younger con-

[21] *Kalam*, p. 117.
[22] *Ibid.*
[23] Cf. above, p. 11.
[24] *Emunot* II, 5, p. 86, ll. 5–7.

temporary Yaḥyā Ibn ʿAdī, a Christian apologist writing in Arabic. In that book, Yaḥyā tries to answer a certain Muslim critic of Christianity who argued that the Trinitarian formula "one substance (*jauhar*), three hypostases (*aḳānīm*)," supplemented by the Christian belief that each hypostasis is God, must logically mean a belief in three substances and three Gods.[25] In answer, Yaḥyā draws a distinction between "what the ignorant (*juhhāl*) among Christians imagine concerning the hypostases" and "what the most learned (*ʿulamāʾ*) among the Christians and those versed in their doctrine say," ascribing to the former the view that "the hypostases are essences of three subjects, each of which differs from the others in virtue of its own self," and characterizing this view as being "only error and impiety and as one from which indeed it would have to follow that its exponents believed that the Creator is three substances and three Gods." [26] Now by "the ignorant among Christians," as I have shown above, Yaḥyā does not refer simply to the common people. He refers to that Christian sect known as the Tritheites, whose chief representatives are John Askusnages and John Philoponus; for the description of "the ignorant among Christians" as given by Yaḥyā corresponds exactly to the description of the Tritheites in Photius, which reads as follows: "Some of the more shameless, having taken nature (*φύσιν*) and hypostasis (*ὑπόστασιν*) and essence (*οὐσίαν*) to mean the same, did not shrink from affirming also that in the Holy Trinity there are three essences (*οὐσίας*), whence they teach, if not in word, yet at least in thought, that there are three Gods and three Divinities." [27] Like Yaḥyā's "ignorant among Christians," therefore, Saadia's "common people among them" is to be taken to refer to the Tritheites as represented by John Askusnages and John Philoponus.

As opposed to the view of "the common people among

[25] Cf. Périer, *Petits*, p. 44, l. 5–p. 45, l. 2.
[26] *Ibid.*, p. 45, ll. 2–8.
[27] Photius, *Biblioth.* 230 (PG 103, 1080 BC); cf. *Kalam*, p. 335.

them," Saadia mentions the view of those whom he calls "the elite among them." He describes them as follows: "They are those who maintain that they adopted their belief in the Trinity as a result of speculation and subtle reasoning. First, by reasoning that only a thing (*shay*: *dabar*) that is living and knowing can create, they arrived at these attributes (*ṣifāt: middot*) and adhered to them. Second, by coming to believe that the life and knowledge of that thing, namely, the Creator, are two things (*shay'ayni*: *shene debarim*) other than the essence of that thing, they came to regard these as three things." [28]

In this restatement of the view of "the elite among them," which is the orthodox Christian conception of the Trinity,[29] Christians are represented by Saadia as starting out quite rightly by showing that God as Creator must be living and knowing and hence that He has two "attributes" (*ṣifāt*: *middot*). As the term *ṣifah* throughout his work is used by Saadia not in the narrow sense of "real attribute" but rather in the general sense of any term predicated of a subject, irrespective of what the relation of the predicate to the subject may be,[30] quite evidently it is in this general sense that the term is used by him here. But then, Saadia goes on to say, instead of taking "living" and "knowing" as *ma'ānī*, a term which besides its use in the sense of things is also used in the sense of concepts of the mind,[31] in which sense it is used here also by Saadia — Christians take them as *shay'ani*, that is, as two real things or hypostases, and they thus speak of "three." The term "three" here is to be taken to mean "three things" or "three hypostases" and not "three Gods," for in his criticism he does not charge this conception of the Trinity with Tritheism. It is to be noted that no mention is made by Saadia

[28] *Emunot* II, 5, p. 86, ll. 7–10.

[29] For the phrasing of the Trinitarian formula by Saadia, *Kalam*, p. 121.

[30] Cf. the term *ṣifah* or *ṣifāt* as used by Saadia in *Emunot* II, 3, p. 83, l. 21 (Hebrew: *sippur*); II, 5, p. 86, l. 16 (Hebrew: *to'ar*); II, 8, p. 92, l. 11 (Hebrew: *to'arim*), l. 14 (Hebrew: *to'ar*), l. 19 (Hebrew: *to'arim*); cf. also *auṣāf* (Hebrew: *to'arim*) in l. 21.

[31] Cf. above, p. 11, n. 12.

of a third conception of the Trinity, that of the heretical Sabellianism, which is analogous to the Muʿtazilites' and his own conception of attributes.[32]

Having thus restated the orthodox Christian conception of the Trinity, Saadia undertakes to refute it. But unlike his refutation of "the common people among them," which was based upon scriptural verses denying the numerical plurality of God,[33] his refutation of "the elite among them," he says, is to be "based on reason," with the help of "Him who is one in the true sense of unity." [34] Not all those who were opposed to Tritheism are taken up by Saadia. No mention is made by him of such extreme opponents of Tritheism as the Sabellians and Arians. The "elite" of whom he speaks are those who represent the orthodox conception of the Trinity as approved of by the Ecumenical Church Councils. The corresponding "most learned among Christians" of Yaḥyā ibn ʿAdī are more precisely described by the latter as "the learned Imams, such as Dionysius [the Areopagite], Gregory [of Nazianzus or of Nyssa], Basil the Great, John Chrysostomos," [35] on whose Trinitarian view "all the sects of Christians agree," [36] by which he means the Malkites, the Nestorians, and the Jacobites. It is this orthodox conception of the Trinity that Saadia undertakes to discuss.

The arguments raised by Saadia against the orthodox Christian conception of the Trinity are two.

First, he argues in effect that the belief in the Trinity involves a violation of the Law of Contradiction, for, on the one hand, the Christians profess that God is not material, but, on the other hand, they insist that in God there is a numerical distinction between the three persons. Evidently having in mind Aristotle's statement that "all things that are many in number have matter," [37] Saadia concludes that the Christian assertion of a numerical distinction between the persons implies that God is material. The doctrine of the Trinity thus implies

[32] Cf. *Kalam*, pp. 134–136.
[33] Cf. above, p. 9.
[34] *Emunot* II, 5, p. 86, ll. 3–4.
[35] Cf. Périer, *Petits*, p. 53, ll. 4–6.
[36] *Ibid*., p. 54, l. 8–p. 55, l. 1.
[37] *Metaph*. XII, 8, 1074a, 33–34.

at once two contradictory statements, one that God is not material and the other that God is material. To quote: "If [as they openly profess] they do not believe that God is a body, then their allegation that there exists in Him an otherness (*ghayriyyah*: *shinnuy* = *zulatiyyut*) to the extent that one attribute of His is not identical with any other attribute of His is equivalent to an allegation on their part that He is really corporeal, to which they only give expression by another term, for anything in which there is otherness is inevitably a body." [38] This argument could also be used against those Muslim Attributists who maintain that God is not corporeal.

Second, he argues again in effect that if the Christians believe that the existence of the second and third persons in the sense of the attributes of life and knowledge is compatible with the unity of God, why did they limit the persons to these two and not add other persons to correspond to the attributes of power and hearing and seeing and the like? [39] A similar criticism of the doctrine of the Trinity is reported by Ibn Ḥazm in the name of the Ashʿarites, who, as he was told by one of them, found fault with the Christians "because they assume that there coexist with God only two things (*shay'ayni*) and do not assume that there coexist with Him a greater number of things," [40] of which he mentions the number "fifteen." [41]

After this refutation, Saadia undertakes to refute Christian interpretations of certain verses in the Hebrew Bible as referring to the Trinity.[42] The number of such verses quoted by him is six. Of these six verses, the four middle ones, namely, Job 33:4, Psalms 33/32:6, Proverbs 8:22, Genesis 1:26, are, again, to be found so interpreted in Abucara's work.[43] As for

[38] *Emunot* II, 5, p. 86, ll. 13–16.

For the Hebrew *shinnuy*, "alteration," the context requires *zulatiyyut*, "otherness." The underlying Arabic term *ghayriyyah* stands for the Greek ἑτερότης, "otherness." Cf. Neumark, *Geschichte*, II, p. 210, n. 4.

[39] *Emunot* II, 5, p. 87, ll. 11–19.

[40] *Fiṣal* IV, p. 207, ll. 22–23.

[41] *Ibid.*, l. 21. For an answer to this objection by Elias of Nisibis, see *Kalam*, p. 315.

[42] *Emunot* II, 5–6, p. 88, l. 2–p. 90, l. 16.

[43] Cited above, n. 8. The verses occur in Abucara as follows: (2) Job

the other two verses, the sixth, "And the Lord appeared unto him . . . and, lo, three men" (Gen. 18:1–2), is taken by some Church Fathers to refer to the persons of the Trinity; [44] but I could not find any work where the first verse, "The spirit of the Lord spoke by me and His word was upon my tongue" (2 Sam. 23:2), was similarly used as a proof-text for the Trinity. It is to be noted how careful Saadia is in his choice of words. The four verses which he himself must have seen used by Abucara as proof-texts for the Trinity he introduces by such expressions as "I find some of them cite as proof" [45] . . . "And they say"; [46] "I also found one of them who interpreted"; [47] "I have seen others who rely on . . . and say." [48] The sixth verse, which he has not found in Abucara but he must have heard had been used by the Church Fathers, is introduced by the words "Others conjecture . . . and say," [49] whereas the first, for which he evidently had no source at all, is introduced by the words "If they derive their proof from Scripture, as, for example, someone of them might assert." [50] In other words, he himself supplied the Christians with a proof-text only to refute it.

3. KIRKISĀNĪ

A series of arguments against the Christian doctrine of the Trinity, which, by implication, are arguments against the Muslim doctrine of the eternity of the Koran, is to be found in the work of a contemporary of Saadia, the Karaite Ya'ḳub al-Ḳirḳisānī.[1]

Ḳirḳisānī begins with a restatement of the Christian doctrine that God is "one substance (*jauhar*) [=essence], three hypos-

33:4 in III, 10, p. 143; (3) Ps. 33/32:6 in VII, 16, p. 196; (4) Prov. 8:22 in III, 20, p. 153; VII, 14, p. 193; (5) Gen. 1:26 in III, 20, p. 153, VII, 16, pp. 195–196.

[44] Cf., e.g., Justin Martyr, *Dial.* 56 and 126; Irenaeus, *Adv. Haer.* IV, 10, 1; Eusebius, *Hist. Eccl.* I, 2, 7.

[45] *Emunot* II, 5, p. 88, l. 9.

[46] *Ibid.*, l. 11.

[47] *Ibid.* III, 6, p. 89, ll. 9–10.

[48] *Ibid.*, ll. 16–17.

[49] *Ibid.* II, 6, p. 90, l. 2.

[50] *Ibid.*, 5, p. 87, l. 20–p. 88, l. 1.

[1] *Anwār* III, 2, p. 186, l. 17–p. 190, l. 9.

tases (*akānīm*)." [2] Then, in the course of his discussion he brings out the additional information that the one substance is what the Christians call the first hypostasis, the Father, and that the other two hypostases are "knowledge" (*'ilm*), which is what they call Son, and "life" (*al-ḥayāh*), which is what they call Spirit,[3] and also that the three hypostases are "three in number (*al-'adad*) and one in essence or nature or meaning (*ma'nā*)." [4] Against this doctrine of the Trinity he raises three objections, two of which we shall reproduce here.

First, the only reason, he says, why Christians attribute to the Creator knowledge and life as something distinct from each other as well as distinct from His essence is the analogy of corporeal agents in the world of our observation.[5] Still, he argues, despite this analogy with corporeal agents, the Christians maintain that, unlike corporeal agents, the Creator is not corporeal and possesses no corporeal organs and no corporeal dimensions and is immovable. Why then, he asks, should they not be consistent and say also that the Creator, unlike corporeal agents, is knowing and living "according to His essence" (*bi-dhātihi*) and not by a knowledge and a life which are each "other than himself" (*ghayruhu*)? [6] This argument, as will be noticed, though directly aimed at the Trinity, is also applicable as an argument against the Muslim reality of attributes.

Second, he argues, just as it is impossible to say that "that which is eternal and that which is created are two in number and one in essence or nature or meaning," so it should also be impossible to say that "the Father and the Son and the Spirit are three in number and one in essence or nature or meaning." [7]

[2] *Ibid.* III, 2, 1, p. 186, ll. 1–2.

[3] *Ibid.* III, 2, 4. On this formulation of the doctrine, see *Kalam*, pp. 121–125.

[4] *Ibid.* III, 2, 6, p. 189, l. 21–p. 190, l. 1. Cf. use of the term *ma'na* in III, 2, 2, p. 187, ll. 12–13. Usually the contrast to "three in number," which is approved of, is "one in formula" or "one in subject ." The expression "one in *ma'na*," contrasted here with "three in number," is evidently used here with reference to "one in formula," and hence I take it to be used here in the sense of "essence" or "nature" or "meaning."

[5] *Ibid.* III, 2, 4.

[6] *Ibid.* III, 2, 5, p. 189, ll. 4 and 8.

[7] *Ibid.* III, 2, 6, p. 189, l. 20–p. 190, l. 1.

What he means to say is that the Christian assertion that Father and Son and Spirit are both three and one is, like the assertion that that which is eternal and that which is created are both two and one, a violation of the Law of Contradiction; for, according to Aristotle, the Law of Contradiction applies not only to "contradictories" (ἀντιφάσεις) but also to "contraries" (ταναντία),[8] that is to say, not only to such an assertion as "the Father and Son and Spirit are both three and not three" but also to such an assertion as "the Father and Son and Spirit are both three and one." This is a common criticism in Islam against the Trinity, which, as we have seen, Yaḥyā Ibn 'Adī answered by showing that the qualification of the term "three" by the phrase "in number" and the qualification of the term "one" by the phrase "in essence" frees the formula of the charge of being a violation of the Law of Contradiction.[9] The same type of argument, as we shall see, is raised by Ḳirḳisānī against both the Christian and the Muslim doctrines of the eternity of the Word.

4. JOSEPH AL-BASĪR

Joseph al-Baṣīr's discussion of the problem of attributes and of the Trinity is to be found in two works.

In *Maḥkimat Peti*, he starts his discussion of the unity of God with a general statement as follows: "The true meaning of the term one is indivisible, for that which is divisible is not one, and this is what we wish to express when we say that God is one, namely, that He does not consist of parts nor is He capable of being divided into parts."[1] This reflects the Aristotelian statement that "in general those things that do not admit of division are one in so far as they do not admit it."[2]

He then goes on to say that in ordinary speech the term "one" is applied to things which are not what he calls "one in the true sense of the term"[3] but one only "in a metaphorical

[8] *Metaph.* IV, 6, 1011b, 15–22.
[9] Cf. *Kalam*, pp. 325–327.
[1] *Maḥkimat Peti* 21, p. 117a, ll. 18–20.
[2] *Metaph.* XII, 8.
[3] *Maḥkimat Peti* 21, p. 117a, l. 17.

sense."[4] The true oneness of God, he says, means not only that there is no other God but also that there is no likeness between God and any other being that we can think of.[5] By this he wishes to say that the unity of God does not mean only external unity and a denial of polytheism but also internal unity, or simplicity, and a denial of divisibility and compositeness, for the scriptural principle of the unlikeness of God to other beings implies the internal unity and simplicity of God. This is also how Philo has arrived at the principle of the internal unity and simplicity of God.[6]

Then, like Saadia, he proceeds to contrast this conception of God as one with the conception of God of adherents of other religions, mentioning (1) the Manichaeans (*al-mānawiyyah*), (2) the Daiṣanites (*al-dayṣaniyyah*), (3) the Magians (*al-majūs*), (4) the Christians (*al-naṣāra*), and (5) the Attributists (*al-ṣifātiyyah*). Of the last two he says: "The view of the Christians is analogous to the view of the Attributists. The Attributists assert that we do not describe the knowledge of God either as existent or as nonexistent, either as created or as eternal, either as the same as God or as other than God. The Christians likewise assert that, with regard to the three hypostases (*al-aḳānīm*),[7] we do not say that they differ from each other and we do not say that they are each the same as the other, so that, with regard to the hypostasis of the Son, they do not say either that it is the same as the hypostasis of the Father or that it is other than it, and in a similar way they say: Three hypostases, one substance, one God. Thus they are contradictory both in expression and in meaning."[8]

[4] *Ibid.*

[5] *Ne'imot*, Arabic, p. 262; Hebrew, p. 20b, ll. 9–10.

[6] Cf. *Philo*, II, pp. 94–126.

[7] The Hebrew translator of al-Baṣīr, who was a Greek-speaking Jew (cf. M. Steinschneider, *Hebr. Uebers.*, p. 453; Z. Ankori, *Karaites in Byzantium*, p. 80, n. 58; p. 190, n. 78), added in explanation of the Arabic *aḳānīm*, "hypostases," here the Greek φύσεις in Hebrew transliteration. This is not the proper Greek equivalent of the Arabic *aḳānīm*.

[8] *Ne'imot*, p. 22b, ll. 16–23; Arabic, p. 44b, l. 14 - p. 45a, l. 3.

In this passage, the formula which al-Baṣīr ascribes to the Attributists is not the common formula used by the Attributists; it is one of the formulae used by some of them, especially the early ones.[9] Subsequently, in the course of his discussion, "the Attributists," to whom al-Baṣīr ascribes here this formula, are identified with followers of Ibn Kullāb, who, as we have seen, is one of those who used this particular formula.[10] Similarly the Christians quoted by him here are, as I have shown,[11] that "splinter group of Nestorians" who, while orthodox in their belief in the reality of the three hypostases of the Trinity, adopted a new Trinitarian formula modeled after what we refer to as the Kullabite formula for attributes. It is to be noted that, in the Hebrew translation of the passage quoted in the preceding paragraph, after the words "the Attributists," for which the word used is the Arabic *al-ṣifātiyyah* written in Hebrew characters, the Hebrew translator adds: "and they are those who say that God has no attributes (*sippurim*)."[12] On the assumpton that the Hebrew word for "no" here is not a scribal error, what the translator probably meant to say by this remark of his is that "the Attributists" referred to here by the author are not those who use such formulae as that the attributes "subsist in God" and are "superadded to God" and are "other than God"[13] but rather those whom he goes on to quote as saying that the attributes are neither existent nor nonexistent, neither God nor other than God.

To the Christians, it will be noticed, al-Baṣīr ascribes two statements. The second statement, namely, "three hypostases, one substance, one God," quite evidently reflects the Cappadocian formula "one *ousia*, three hypostases," in which the *one ousia* implies one God. As for the first statement, which says in effect that neither are the three hypostases different from each other nor are they each the same as the other, it

[9] Cf. *Kalam*, pp. 207–209. [10] *Ibid.*, p. 208. [11] *Ibid.*, pp. 345–347.
[12] *Ne'imot*, p. 22b, l. 18; Arabic, p. 44b, l. 16.
[13] Cf. *Kalam*, pp. 214–215.

has, as I have tried to show,[14] a double meaning. What the Christians referred to really meant by it was to express the orthodox Christian view that while the hypostases were all the same in essence, they differed from each other, as explained by Basil, after the analogy of "Peter, Andrew, John, and James," who are one in *ousia*, "man," but are different as individuals.[15] But what they meant by phrasing their statement the way they did was to accommodate, verbally, the Christian conception of the Trinity to the orthodox Muslim conception of attributes as expressed by the formula that the attributes were neither God nor other than God.

Al-Baṣīr's concluding remark, "thus they are contradictory both in expression and in meaning," was meant to refer both to the two statements quoted in the name of the Christians and to the formula quoted in the name of the Attributists, to which the Christian statements were said by him to be analogous. The fault he finds in the first Christian statement is that it infringes upon the Law of Excluded Middle, and he also finds the same fault in the formula he ascribes to the Attributists. This, as we have seen, is the stock argument against the same formula as used by the Modalists.[16] The fault he finds in the second Christian statement is that it infringes upon the Law of Contradiction, which, as we have seen,[17] is the argument raised by Kindī against the Cappadocian formula "one *ousia*, three hypostases."

Though the belief in real attributes as conceived by the Attributists is rejected by al-Baṣīr, he did adopt the theory of modes as taught by Abū Hāshim. This we gather from a passage in which he refers to certain people who argued, as he says, that "our own view is like the view of the Kullabites . . . for [they contend] the objectionable consequence which we have shown to follow from their view would also follow from our own belief in modes (*al-aḥwāl*), saying to us, you

[14] Cf. *Kalam*, pp. 343–347.

[15] *Epist.* 38, 2 (PG 32, 325 B); cf. 38, 3 (328 A); cf. *The Philosophy of the Church Fathers*, I, p. 337.

[16] *Kalam*, pp. 199–200.

[17] *Kalam*, pp. 325–327.

have only changed the term, but what you mean by our term is the same as what they mean by their term: they speak of *ṣifah*, attribute, and you speak of *ḥāl*, mode."[18] Underlying this argument is the fact, as we have shown above, that the same formula which al-Baṣīr quotes here in the name of the Attributists and criticizes is used by Abū Hāshim for his theory of modes.[19] As for the assurance with which those certain people mentioned above referred to al-Baṣīr as a follower of the theory of modes, it is probably based upon his nonextant work known by its title *Kitāb Aḥwāl al-Fā'il*, "Book of the Modes of the Maker [of the World]." In neither of his two extant works does he explicitly declare himself in favor of the theory of modes. However, his formulae for attributes in both his works[20] indicate, as we shall see, a modalistic conception of attributes.

The argument quoted by al-Baṣīr from those anonymous certain people afforded him the opportunity to define what he thought was the difference between modes and attributes or, as he says, "between us and them." Evidently having in mind the Kullabite statement that by "God is knowing" is meant that "God possesses knowledge,"[21] he infers that, in the bipartite formula of the Kullabites, the first part, which states in effect that attributes are "not God," means that God possesses attributes, so that the attributes possessed by God are "something knowable and distinguishable" apart from Him, whereas the second part, which states in effect that attributes are "not other than God," means that God does not possess attributes as "something knowable and distinguishable" apart from Him. The formula of the Kullabite Attributists, he concludes, is thus contradictory to the Law of Excluded Middle. The Modalists, however, he goes on to argue, have never said anything that would imply that modes are "something know-

[18] *Ne'imot*, Arabic, p. 45b, l. 8; Hebrew, p. 23a, ll. 20–21.

[19] Cf. *Kalam*, p. 211.

[20] *Maḥkimat* 16, Hebrew, p. 112a, Arabic, p. 9b; 17, Hebrew, p. 112b, Arabic, p. 10b. *Ne'imot*, Hebrew, p. 14b ff., Arabic, p. 25b ff.

[21] Cf. *Kalam*, p. 208.

able and distinguishable" apart from God. They have only said that the modes are "not known and not unknown," in which the two negations are not of the same predicate, for, when in the first part the modes are said to be "not known," it means that they are not known by themselves apart from the essence of God; but when in the second part the modes are said to be "not unknown," it means that they are known together with the essence of God, for, according to the Modalists, "God is known together with His modes." [22] Accordingly, the same formula, when used by the Modalists, is not in violation of the Law of Excluded Middle.[23] It is to be noted that the same distinction between modes and attributes is made later by Rāzī in his statement that "Abū Hāshim is of the opinion . . . that the mode is not known by itself but that the divine Essence is known together with it, whereas, according to us, the Attributists, the attributes are known by themselves." [24]

5. JOSEPH IBN SADDIK

In his discussion of the problem of divine attributes, Joseph Ibn Ṣaddiḳ deals with three topics: (1) a criticism of a particular view with regard to the attribute of will,[1] which will be dealt with later in the section entitled "Pre-existent Throne, Will, and Angel"; (2) a criticism of what we shall show to be a certain formula used by certain Antiattributists in expressing their denial of attributes,[2] which will be dealt with later in the section entitled "The Semantic Aspect of the Problem of Attributes"; (3) an exposition of his own view of both (a) the ontological and (b) the semantic aspect of the problem of attributes,[3] of which the semantic aspect will, again, be dealt with later in the section entitled "The Semantic

[22] *Ne'imot*, Arabic, p. 46b, l. 2; Hebrew, p. 23b, ll. 8–9 (passage quoted by Frankl, *Ein Mu'tazilitischen*, pp. 53–54, Note VI).

[23] Cf. *Kalam*, pp. 203–204.

[24] *Muḥaṣṣal*, p. 131, ll. 4–5.

[1] *'Olam Ḳaṭan* III, p. 44, l. 29 – p. 46, l. 2.

[2] *Ibid.*, p. 46, l. 3 – p. 47, l. 9.

[3] *Ibid.*, p. 48, l. 1 – p. 59, l. 2.

Aspect of the Problem of Attributes." Here we shall deal with his treatment of the ontological aspect of the problem.

Like all his predecessors, Ibn Ṣaddiḳ starts the discussion of his own view on attributes with an analysis of the meaning of the unity of God. As in the case of Saadia, his discussion of the unity of God falls into two parts, external unity and internal unity. By the principle of the external unity of God,[4] he denies any form of polytheism, mentioning especially the dualism of the belief held by "Daiṣan"[5] (Bardaiṣān, Bardesanes), who, as we have seen, is mentioned among others by Joseph al-Baṣīr.[6] By the principle of the internal unity of God, he denies any kind of composition in God, of which he mentions the composition of substance and accident,[7] and of the latter he mentions the accidents of quality and quantity.[8] Thus the unity of God is described by Ibn Ṣaddiḳ as "true unity,"[9] and the confession of the belief that God is one is described by him as meaning "one in every respect,"[10] that is to say, God is one not only in the sense of a denial of polytheism but also in the sense of an affirmation of His absolute simplicity.

6. JUDAH HADASSI

This denial of real attributes, which we have found in the five representative Jewish philosophers, Rabbanites as well as Karaites, is common to all other Jewish philosophers of the Arabic period, though not all of them openly discuss either the Trinity or attributes. Solomon ibn Gabirol, Baḥya ibn Paḳuda, Abraham ibn Ezra, Judah Halevi, and Abraham ibn Daud make their denial of real attributes clear by their conception of the unity of God as meaning His simplicity and by their statements, in various ways, as to what they mean by terms attributed to God. Judah Halevi, indeed, makes the Christian in his speech before the King of the Khazars explain

[4] *Ibid.*, p. 49, l. 29–p. 51, l. 6.
[5] *Ibid.*, p. 50, l. 31.
[6] Cf. above, p. 21.
[7] *'Olam Ḳaṭan* III, p. 51, ll. 30–31.
[8] *Ibid.*, ll. 6–7.
[9] *Ibid.*, l. 8.
[10] *Ibid.*, l. 11.

the Christian doctrine of the Trinity,[1] and he makes the rabbi in his exposition of the Kalam restate what is the Muʿtazilite theory of attributes,[2] but his work contains no open argument either against the Christian Trinity or the orthodox Muslim attributes. Two philosophers, however, the Karaite Judah Hadassi and the Rabbanite Moses Maimonides, deserve special mention.

In Judah Hadassi there is the usual analogy between the Christian Trinity and the Muslim attributes, but his restatement of these two doctrines contains certain peculiarities. He begins with a restatement of the Christian Trinity as follows: "They say that He is Father and Son and Holy Spirit. The Father contains the principle of Godhood, His Word is the Son, who became clothed with flesh in the fashion of men, and the Holy Spirit is His Wisdom and the prophecy of His prophets. All the three of them are equal and they are one." [3] The statement in this passage, "the Father contains the principle of Godhood," is an exact restatement of the Nicene Creed, which was shared by all the Fathers but Augustine and the author of the Quicumque of the so-called Athanasian Creed, who considered the Godhood as the common substratum of all the three persons.[4] Whether his mention of this point indicates a knowledge of the two views about it in Christianity is doubtful. Later, in the same chapter, he reproduces a Hebrew version of the Cappadocian formula, which reads as follows: "The Holy One, blessed be He, is three *iḳyonin* (or *iḳyunin*) and one *ḥatikah*." [5] This Hebrew reproduction of the formula calls for a discussion of two points.

First, a question may be raised with regard to the term *iḳyonin* (or *iḳyunin*) as to whether it is a corrupt translitera-

[1] *Cuzari* I, 4. [2] *Ibid.* V, 18.

[3] Omitted portion of *Eshkol ha-Kofer* published by W. Bacher, in *JQR*, 8: 432 (1896).

[4] Cf. *The Philosophy of the Church Fathers*, I, pp. 352–354. Cf *Kalam*, p. 129 n. 89.

[5] *Eshkol ha-Kofer*, p. 439.

tion in Hebrew characters of the Arabic *aḳānīm* properly understood to mean "hypostases" or whether it is a scribal error of *iḳunin*, which is the plural of the Aramaic *iḳuna* (Greek εἰκών), and is thus a translation of the Arabic *aḳānīm* erroneously taken to mean "images." [6] It is, however, to be noted that, while the term εἰκών, "image," is applied in the New Testament (2 Cor. 4:4; Col. 1:15) to the second person and while the Greek Fathers commonly maintain that the term "image" applies also to the third person,[7] it is never used as a description of all three persons.

Second, a question may be raised as to Hadassi's use of the term *ḥatikah*, ordinarily meaning "atom," [8] in a context where one should expect the use of a term meaning "essence" or "substance." The answer which I should like to suggest is that the term *ḥatikah* — literally, "piece," "portion" — which in the sense of "atom" is a literal translation of the Arabic term *juz'*,[9] "portion," "piece," "atom," [10] occurs also as a translation of the Arabic term *jauhar* in a passage where that Arabic term has the meaning of "atom." [11] But inasmuch as the term *jauhar*, being a translation of the Greek οὐσία, primarily means "substance" or "essence," it would seem that the term *ḥatikah* through its being a translation of *jauhar*'s secondary meaning of "atom" has acquired *jauhar*'s primary meaning of "substance" or "essence," and it is in this secondary meaning of it that Hadassi uses the term *ḥatikah* in his Trinitarian formula. Whether Hadassi himself has translated this formula from the Arabic into Hebrew or whether he has taken it from some other work, I am at the present writing not in a position to say.

His description of attributes reads as follows: "The fol-

[6] Cf. discussion of the same term by Bacher (*loc. cit.*, 437, n. 3).

[7] Cf. Thomas Aquinas, *Sum. Theol.* I, 35, 2 c.

[8] So used by Hadassi himself (*Eshkol ha-Kofer* 65).

[9] Cf. Schreiner, *Studien*, p. 27, n. 1.

[10] Cf. *Moreh* I, 51, Arabic p. 76, l. 4; *al-juz'*; Hebrew: *ha-ḥeleḳ she-eino mitḥaleḳ*.

[11] Cf. *Ne'imot*, Arabic p. 39b, l. 17: *al-jauhar*; Hebrew: *ha-ḥatikah*.

lowers of the Attributists (*bene al-ṣifātiyyah*) have also joined and concurred with the Christians by their assertion that God has no attributes (*sippurim*) in the sense of eternal properties (*ishshurim*),[12] for they maintain that His knowledge and His power and His existence and His life belong to Him not in virtue of His self but are the result of an act of creation, even as thou art."[13] As a theory of attributes, this statement reflects the belief in created attributes as held by the Zurāriyyah and the Karrāmiyyah.[14] The Christian conception of the Trinity, with which he compares this belief in created attributes, reflects the view of the Arians, according to which the second and third persons were created.[15] But why he should select these sectarian views as representing the Muslim doctrine of attributes and the Christian doctrine of the Trinity is rather strange. That he had knowledge of the orthodox Christian belief in the coeternity of the three persons is quite evident from his description of the persons as being "equal" and as being "one atom," which, as we have seen, means "one substance."

7. MAIMONIDES *

INCLUDING HIS VIEW ON MODES AND UNIVERSALS

In Maimonides, criticisms of the belief in real attributes occur frequently. Of these, two characteristic ones may be reproduced here.

In one place he says: "As for him who believes that God is one but possesses many attributes, he says by his spoken word that God is one but believes Him in his thought to be many,

[12] This statement reflects the following passage in *Ne'imot* (Hebrew p. 14a, l. 30 – p. 14b, l. 1; Arabic p. 24b, ll. 14–16): "Of attributes which refer to the self those which necessarily apply to God are four, namely, powerful, knowing, living, existing." It then goes on to show that they are eternal.

[13] Bacher's fragment of *Eshkol ha-Kofer*, p. 433.

[14] Cf. *Kalam*, pp. 143–146.

[15] Cf. *The Philosophy of the Church Fathers*, I, pp. 585–587.

* Reprinted, with a few revisions and the addition of four paragraphs at the beginning, from *Studies in Rationalism, Judaism, and Universalism, in Memory of Leon Roth* (Humanities Press and Routledge and Kegan Paul, 1966), where it appeared under the title "Maimonides on Modes and Universals."

and this is like the saying of the Christians: God is one but also three and the three are one." [1] The criticism here of both the belief in attributes and the belief in the Trinity, as I have tried to explain elsewhere,[2] is not that these beliefs are polytheistic but rather that they introduce into God a distinction which is logically contradictory to the conception of His unity as meaning absolute simplicity.

In another place, trying to define exactly what is wrong with the belief in attributes, he says that he who affirms real attributes of God is not an "associator" (*mushrik*: *meshattef*), that is, a polytheist, for an associator, he says, is one who takes what is true of one essence and affirms it also of another essence, "but the attributes, according to those who believe in them, are not the essence of God but things superadded to His essence," [3] that is to say, the attributes are not regarded by them as gods. What is really wrong with the belief in attributes, he then says, is that "he who affirms that God has real attributes . . . has unwittingly denied his belief in the existence of God." [4] What he means by this, as may be gathered from his subsequent statements, is that to affirm of God that He has real attributes is a violation of the Law of Contradiction, for it is contradictory to His unity in the sense of absolute simplicity [5] and hence for a believer in the unity of God to affirm that God has real attributes is tantamount to the affirmation that God is both one and not one. Now, according to a view expressed by Maimonides elsewhere,[6] the conception of anything that is in violation of the Law of Contradiction is the conception of an impossibility which has no existence. Consequently, to conceive of God as having attributes is to conceive of an impossibility which has no existence.

In Maimonides, there are also several passages which contain, or may contain, references to the theory of modes. But as to

[1] *Moreh* I, 50, p. 75, ll. 7–9.

[2] Cf. my paper "Maimonides on the Unity and Incorporeality of God," *JQR*, n. s., 56: 112–136 (1965).

[3] *Moreh* I, 60, p. 99, ll. 15–18.

[4] *Ibid*., ll. 11–12.

[5] *Ibid*., p. 100, ll. 8–14.

[6] *Ibid*. III, 15, p. 332, l. 2.

what these passages convey as to Maimonides' view on modes is a question which calls for discussion.

In one passage, he says: "You must know that God has no essential attributes in any manner (*wajh*: *panim*) and in any mode (*ḥāl*: *'inyan*) whatsoever." [7]

The term *ḥāl*, at the time of Maimonides, when used in the discussion of the problem of attributes, was generally used in its acquired technical sense of mode which it had acquired from Abū Hāshim's theory of modes,[8] but it still retained its many nontechnical meanings, such as "condition," "circumstance," "case," and the like. Similarly, the term *wajh* was used in many nontechnical senses, such as "aspect," "manner," "way," and the like, but it was sometimes used as the equivalent of *ḥāl* in its technical sense of "mode." [9] And with regard to the theory of modes, we have shown [10] that originally it appeared as a theory of predication and universals, which, on its application to terms predicated of God, assumed the form of a theory at once opposed to both the orthodox affirmation of attributes and the Mu'tazilite denial of them. In the course of time, however, certain orthodox Attributists harmonized modes in the sense of divine predicates with their own affirmation of attributes.

In view of the fact, then, that by the time of Maimonides modes had already been harmonized by some orthodox with the affirmation of their belief in attributes, when Maimonides says here that "God has no essential attributes in any *wajh* and in any *ḥāl* whatsoever," the following question arises: Does his rejection of attributes here include also a rejection of modes or does it not include a rejection of modes? In the former case, the phrase "in any *wajh* and in any *ḥāl*" was used by him significantly in order to emphasize the inclusion of modes among the attributes rejected by him; in the latter case, the phrase was used by him only to emphasize that attributes are

[7] *Ibid.* I, 50, p. 75, ll. 5–6.
[8] Cf. *Kalam*, pp. 167–182.
[9] *Ibid.*, pp. 180, 202.
[10] *Ibid.*, pp. 168–171.

to be rejected no matter how their real meaning may be disguised by the use of some evasive formula.

The same question with regard to Maimonides' attitude toward modes arises also in connection with another passage, which reads as follows: "Some people of speculation got to the point where they said that the attributes of God are neither His essence nor anything extraneous to His essence." [11]

This type of formula, though usually associated with the name of Abū Hāshim [12] and the theory of modes of which he is the founder, was used long before him in the sense of the affirmation of attributes first by Sulaymān b. Jarīr and his followers [13] and then by Ibn Kullāb and his followers.[14] Subsequently, among the Ashʿarites it was used by some in the sense of the affirmation of attributes [15] and by others in the sense of the affirmation of modes.[16] Accordingly, in Maimonides' ascription here of this type of formula to "some people of speculation," the following question arises: Does he use this type of formula only in the sense of an expression of a belief in attributes or does he use it in the sense of an expression of a belief in modes?

In his refutation of this formula, Maimonides goes on to say the following: "But this is similar to the saying of some others that the modes (*al-aḥwāl*: *ha-ʿinyanim*), that is, the universal concepts (*al-maʿānī al-kulliyyah*: *ha-ʿinyanim ha-kelaliyyim*), are neither existent nor nonexistent and similar to the saying of still others that the atom is not in a place (*makān*: *maḳom*) but it occupies space (*yashghul al-ḥayyiz: yaṭrid ha-gebul*) and that man has no action at all but he has acquisition (*al-iktisāb*: *ha-ḳeniyyah*). All these are sentences (*aḳāwil*: *debarim*) which are only said, so that they exist in words (*alfāẓ*: *millot*) and not in rational judgments (*adhhān*: *deʿot*), and all the more, they have no existence outside the mind (*dhihn*: *sekel*)." [17]

[11] *Moreh* I, 51, p. 76, ll. 24–26.
[12] *Kalam*, p. 211.
[13] *Ibid.*, p. 207.
[14] *Ibid.*, pp. 208–209.
[15] *Ibid.*, pp. 214–215.
[16] *Ibid.*, pp. 215–216.
[17] *Moreh* I, 51, p. 76, l. 26 – p. 77, l. 2.

At first sight, his statement that the formula which he has previously ascribed to "some people of speculation" is similar "to the saying of some others" about "modes" would seem to indicate that the "some people of speculation" were not those who believed in modes. But when right after mentioning the term "modes" he explains that he means by it "the universal concepts," he clearly indicates that he was aware of the distinction between modes as a theory of predication and universals and modes as a theory of divine attributes, and hence the "some people of speculation" may very well be those who harmonized attributes with modes.

But then there is another question in connection with this refutation. Why should Maimonides object to the formula that modes in the sense of universals are neither existent nor nonexistent? Those who considered universals as modes held, as we have seen,[18] that universals have a conceptual existence, and that a conceptual existence is a kind of existence which is intermediate between the existence of things and the nonexistence of words, and that, because universals are intermediate between existence and nonexistence, to say of them that they are neither existent nor nonexistent is not a violation of the Law of Excluded Middle. Now Maimonides himself admits that universals, while they are not extramental things, are "mental things (*maʿānī dhihniyyah*: *debarim sikliyyim*)."[19] Moreover, from his contention that a definition implies that the definiendum is composed of genus and specific difference which are causes of the definiendum,[20] it is to be inferred that universals, described by him as "mental things," have some kind of existence. The kind of existence which, according to him, universals could have would be, we may assume, like that ascribed to them by Avicenna in his triple stage theory of the existence of universals, namely, before multiplicity (*ḳabl al-kathrah*), in multiplicity (*fī al-kathrah*), and after multiplicity (*baʿd al-kathrah*), which, as I have shown, is traceable

[18] Cf. *Kalam*, pp. 201–204.

[19] *Moreh* III, 18, p. 343, ll. 9–10.

[20] *Ibid.* I, 52, p. 77, ll. 19–25.

to Ammonius Hermiae.[21] Now, according to this theory, universals in their after-multiplicity stage, that is, the stage during which they exist in the human mind, may be said to have a conceptual existence [22] analogous to that ascribed to them by the Muslim Modalists and may thus be described as being neither existent like extramental things nor nonexistent like mere words. In view of this, why should Maimonides object to the formula that universals are neither existent nor nonexistent when that formula can be interpreted as not being an infringement upon the Law of Excluded Middle?

Let us see how Maimonides would answer this question as to why he objects to the modalistic formula about universals, and from his answer to this question, we shall try to find out what his answer would be to the questions we have raised with regard to his view on modes in the sense of divine predicates.

In his answer to this question, Maimonides, I imagine, would say that though he was willing to admit that the formula could be interpreted so as not to infringe upon the Law of Excluded Middle, he still objected to it on the ground that in its form, in its phrasing, it does infringe upon that Law. To him, he would argue, for a formula to be right it must be one which both in form and in substance is logically sound. By such a logically sound formula, he would go on to explain, he meant a formula which conforms to what Aristotle calls an "enunciative sentence" (*λόγος ἀποφαντικός* : *al-ḳaul al-jāzim*), by which Aristotle means a logical proposition which is sub-

[21] Cf. my paper "Avicenna, Algazali, and Averroes on Divine Attributes," *Homenaje a Millás-Vallicrosa*, 2: 547–550 (1956).

[22] Cf. my interpretation of Maimonides' theory of universals in terms of Avicenna's triple-stage theory of universals in my paper "Crescas on the Problem of Divine Attributes," *JQR*, n. s., 7:11–13 (1916). At that time I thought of Maimonides' triple-stage theory of universals as a sort of moderate realism and hence I described his criticism of the modalistic formula for universals in *Moreh* I, 51, as a criticism of conceptualism. According to my present way of thinking, however, all theories of universals between extreme realism and extreme nominalism are to be considered as various shades of conceptualism. Maimonides' theory of universals is, therefore, one of the various shades of conceptualism.

ject to the description of being either true or false,[23] and the test as to whether it is true or false is, according to him, its correspondence or noncorrespondence to something outside the mind.[24]

It is in accordance with this conception of his as to what constitutes the right kind of formula that Maimonides goes on to reject the four formulae under consideration as unsound. The formula that "the atom is not in a place (*makān*) but occupies space (*yashghul al-ḥayyiz*)" may indeed in its external form be a well constructed logical proposition, for externally it appears that the predicate that is negated in the first part of the proposition is not the same as the predicate affirmed in the second part. Still, in meaning, the proposition infringes upon the Law of Contradiction, for, inasmuch as by definition "place" (*makān*) is that which is occupied only by an extended body,[25] the statement in the first part of the proposition, namely, that "the atom is not in a place," implies that the atom is not an extended body, but, inasmuch as only those who believe that the atom is an extended body say that the atom occupies space,[26] the statement in the second part of the proposition, namely, that the atom "occupies space," implies that the atom is an extended body. Similarly, the formula that "man has no action at all but he has acquisition" may, again, be a well constructed logical proposition in its external form. Still, in meaning, it is an infringement upon the Law of Contradiction, for the "acquisition" affirmed in its second part is itself an "action" and thus is contradictory to the denial of "action" in the first part. As for the formula quoted by Maimonides from certain Attributists, we may assume that he knew that Ibn Kullāb and the others after him had used it in such a way that by their denying that attributes are "His

[23] *De Interpr.* 4, 17a, 1–3.

[24] *Metaph.* IV, 7, 1011b, 27.

[25] Jurjānī, *Kitāb al-Ta'rifāt*, ed. Flügel, p. 244, l. 20–p. 245, l. 1; cf. Munk, *Guide des Égarés*, I, 51, p. 186n.

[26] *Masā'il*, ed. p. 38, l. 15, and p. 41, l. 18–p. 42, l. 2 (pp. 46 and 49); *Irshād*, p. 10, l. 7 (p. 28).

essence," they meant to deny the Muʿtazilite view that the attributes of God are "His essence" and that by their denying that the attributes are "extraneous to His essence," they meant to deny the view of the Zurāriyyah and Karrāmiyyah that the attributes are created and hence are "extraneous to His essence,"[27] so that, in meaning, the formula does not infringe upon the Law of Excluded Middle. Still, in its external form, it is an infringement upon that Law, since it denies both that the attributes are "His essence" and that they are "extraneous to His essence," that is to say, they are neither the same as His essence nor other than His essence. Similarly, we may assume that he knew that the Modalists by their denying that universals are "existent" meant to deny that they are existent like extramental real things and that by their denying that universals are "nonexistent" meant to deny that they are nonexistent like mere words, so that the formula is no infringement upon the Law of Excluded Middle.[28] Still, in its external form, it is an infringement upon that Law. What, according to Maimonides, would be the right formula for conceptual universals is suggested by him in the statement that "no species exist outside the mind, but species and other universals are mental things."[29] The right formula would thus be that "universals are nonexistent outside the mind but they are existent in the mind."

That Maimonides' criticism here is aimed only at the formulae used in the four theories he mentions and not at the theories themselves is evidenced by his use of the term *aḳāwīl* in his opening statement, namely, "these are all *aḳāwīl* (Hebrew: *debarim*)."[30] The term *aḳāwīl* is the plural of *ḳaul*, which in the Arabic translation of *De Interpretatione*[31] translates the Greek term λόγος in the passage quoted above, where Aristotle, starting with an explanation of the general meaning of the term λόγος, "sentence," of which he subsequently says

[27] *Kalam*, pp. 210–211.

[28] *Ibid.*, pp. 203–204.

[29] *Moreh* III, 18, p. 343, ll. 9–10.

[30] *Ibid.* I, 51, p. 76, l. 29.

[31] Cf. I. Pollak's edition of the Arabic translation of the *De Interpretatione*, and Badawi's edition of the *Organon*.

that it may be either enunciative, which conveys judgment as to truth and falsehood, or verbal, which does not convey judgment as to truth and falsehood, he goes on to say that "a word" (*φάσις*, *lafẓah*), such as the word "man," which is part of a sentence, never conveys "affirmation or negation," [32] that is, it never conveys judgment as to truth and falsehood. Thus Maimonides' opening statement means to say that all these formulae are only what Aristotle would consider mere verbal sentences, for, as he goes on to explain, "they are only said and consequently they exist only in words (*alfāẓ*: *millot*) and not in rational judgments (*adhhān*: *deʿot*)." [33] By this he means to say that they are combinations of words which form only verbal sentences that convey no judgments as to truth and falsehood. He then adds: "and all the more, they have no existence outside the mind (*dhihn*: *sekel*)." [34] By this he means to say that, more than merely being sentences which *do not* convey judgments as to truth and falsehood, these formulae are like words which, according to Aristotle, *never* convey judgments as to truth and falsehood,[35] seeing that there can never exist outside the mind anything to correspond to any of these formulae.

Finally, in trying to explain in concrete terms what his objections really are to the four formulae he mentioned, he makes two statements. First, anyone who uses these formulae, he says, "endeavors to make exist something that does not exist." [36] By this he refers to two of the four formulae quoted by him, namely, those used by some Atomists and the Acquisitionists, both of which, as I have tried to explain, are in meaning infringements upon the Law of Contradiction, which, as quoted by Aristotle in the name of Heraclitus, reads: "It is impossible for anyone to suppose that the same thing exists

[32] *De Interpr.* 4, 16b, 27–28.

[33] *Moreh* I, 51, p. 77, l. 1. For my translation of *adhhān* by "rational judgments," see Avicenna's descriptions of *dhihn* quoted by Goichon in *Lexique*, § 263, pp. 132–134. This explains also why Ibn Tibbon translated it by *deʿot*.

[34] *Ibid.*, ll. 1–2.

[35] *De Interpr.*, 4, 16b, 26–30.

[36] *Moreh* I, 51, p. 77, l. 6.

and does not exist." [37] Second, anyone who uses these formulae, he says again, "endeavors . . . to create an intermediate between two contraries (*ḍiddāni*: *shene hafakim*) between which there is no intermediate," [38] that is, they infringe upon the Law of Excluded Middle. Here, it will be noticed, Maimonides himself indicates that this criticism is aimed at the other two of the four formulae quoted by him, namely, those used by some of the Attributists and by the Modalists in their conception of universals, for immediately after this criticism, he goes on to say that there is no intermediate between the contraries "existent" and "nonexistent" and between the contraries "same" and "other," [39] that is, the two pairs of contraries denied respectively in the formula of the Modalists in their conception of universals and in the formula of some of the Attributists. Maimonides' carefully phrased statement that the contraries between which the users of these formulae endeavor to create intermediates are those "between which there is no intermediate" reflects Aristotle's statement that with respect to opposites which are "by way of contraries (ὡς τὰ ἐναντία: *'alā ṭarīḳ al-muḍāddah*)," some have intermediates and some have no intermediates, and those which have no intermediates are "such that the subject in which they naturally exist, or of which they are predicated, must necessarily contain either the one or the other of them," [40] the implication being that the subject cannot be said to contain neither the one nor the other.

The upshot of our discussion is that with respect to modes in the sense of universals, Maimonides agrees with the Modalists that they have a conceptual existence which is neither existent like things nor nonexistent like words, but he disagrees with them as to the logical propriety of the use of their formula. With regard to the use of modes as an interpretation of divine predicates, inasmuch as in his discussion of divine attributes Maimonides has made it clear that no term predi-

[37] *Metaph.* IV, 3, 1005b, 23–24.
[38] *Moreh* I, 51, p. 77, l. 6.
[39] *Ibid.*, ll. 7–8.
[40] *Categ.*, 10, 11b, 33–12a, 3.

cated of God can be a universal,[41] it follows that no term predicated of God can be a mode. Consequently, with regard to divine predicates, he not only disagrees with the Modalists in the use of their formula, he disagrees with them also in their interpretation of divine predicates as modes.

By this we are now able to answer the other questions we have raised. The terms *ḥāl* and *wajh* in the first passage are quite definitely used by him in the technical sense of "mode," and similarly the "some men of speculation," to whom he ascribes the formula that "the attributes of God are neither His essence nor anything extraneous to His essence," include both those who use this formula in the sense of attributes and those who use it in the sense of modes, for to him modes as an interpretation of divine predicates are not to be distinguished from attributes; the former no less than the latter are to him incompatible with the conception of the absolute simplicity of God.

The conclusion we have arrived at in our interpretation of two vague passages also throws light on a third vague passage in the *Moreh Nebukim*. In that passage, dealing with those who believe in attributes, Maimonides says: "Some of them express themselves clearly on the existence of attributes, enumerating them as things superadded to the essence." [42] This quite evidently refers to those Ash'arites whose formulation of the doctrine of attributes contains the expression "superadded to the essence." [43]

Maimonides then goes on to say: "Others among them do not state this clearly, but that this is their belief is quite clear, even though they do not express themselves in clear-cut language, as is the case of some of them who say that God is powerful in virtue of His essence, He is knowing in virtue of His essence, He is living in virtue of His essence, He is willing in virtue of His essence." [44] Now the expression "in virtue of

[41] *Moreh* I, 52, p. 77, l. 19–p. 78, l. 1.
[42] *Ibid.* I, 53, p. 82, ll. 1–2.
[43] *Nihāyat*, p. 181, ll. 1–4; *Kashf*, p. 56, ll. 3 and 7; cf. *Kalam*, p. 214.
[44] *Moreh* I, 53, p. 82, ll. 2–4.

His essence" as a description of terms predicated of God has been used in various senses. According to Ash'arī, the formula that "the names and attributes of God are in virtue of His essence" was used by Ibn Kullāb together with his formula that "they are not God and they are not other than God" as an expression of his belief that "they subsist in God,"[45] by which he means, as he makes it even more clear elsewhere,[46] that God possesses real attributes. According to Shahrastānī, the expression "in virtue of His essence" was used by Jubbā'ī in the sense of the denial of attributes, and by Abū Hāshim in the sense of the affirmation of modes.[47] From the context of the passage, which deals directly with Attributists, it is not clear whether "the others among them" who use the expression "in virtue of His essence" include Attributists only or also Modalists. In the light, however, of our conclusion that Maimonides was opposed to modes no less than to attributes, it is quite certain that "the others among them" include also Modalists. But, though in this passage the use of the expression "in virtue of His essence" is rejected by Maimonides only with reference to its use as an affirmation of either attributes or modes, from other passages it may be inferred, as I have shown elsewhere,[48] that Maimonides would not use it even in the sense of the absolute denial of attributes, and one of the reasons for his not using it is the fact of its being used by others in the sense of the affirmation of either attributes or modes. To him, any formula describing the meaning of terms predicated of God must be free of any vagueness and ambiguity.

II. The Semantic Aspect of the Problem of Attributes

To Jewish philosophers during the Kalam period, as we have seen, there was no problem of attributes in its ontological

[45] *Maḳālāt*, p. 169, ll. 12–13; cf. *Kalam*, p. 208.
[46] *Ibid.*, ll. 10–12; *Kalam*, p. 209.
[47] *Milal*, p. 55, l. 19–p. 56, l. 3; cf. *Kalam*, p. 229.
[48] Cf. my paper "Maimonides on Negative Attributes," *Louis Ginzberg Jubilee Volume* (1945), pp. 415–418.

aspect. They all rejected real attributes and, with the exception of Joseph al-Baṣīr, none of them followed the theory of modes. If they did discuss the problem of attributes in its ontological aspect, it was only to express their opposition to the belief in the existence of real attributes as it was upheld by certain sects in Islam or to prevent Arabic-speaking Jews, in their excessive piety or in their ignorance, from coming under the influence of such a view.

But, while they had no problem of attributes in the ontological aspect, they had a problem of attributes in what we have called the semantic aspect. For though they denied that terms predicated of God implied the existence in God of real attributes, they still felt called upon, as did indeed all religious thinkers, such as the Palestinian rabbis,[1] the Alexandrian Philo,[2] the Church Fathers[3] before them, and the Muslim Mutakallimūn[4] of their own time, to explain the anthropomorphisms of the terms predicated of God in Scripture.

The need of explaining scriptural anthropomorphisms became all the greater to spokesmen of Judaism under Muslim rule during that period in view of the fact that in Muslim literature Jews were represented as anthropomorphists. This kind of representation of Judaism must have been introduced into Islam by Christians, among whom the charge that the Jews were literalists and anthropomorphists must have been a repercussion of a view current among the Church Fathers.[5] Barring the tradition of Muhammad's charging Jews with anthropomorphism,[5a] historically the first to acquaint Muslims with this charge against Jews was a Christian in a debate before the Egyptian ruler Aḥmad ibn Ṭūlūn (868–884). As reported by Mas'ūdī (1112–1182), during that debate an Egyptian Christian, pointing to a Jewish physician who was present, addressed Ibn Ṭūlūn as follows: "O prince, these people be-

[1] Cf. *Philo*, I, p. 135.
[2] *Ibid.*, p. 116.
[3] Cf. *The Philosophy of the Church Fathers*, I, pp. 74–77.
[4] Cf. *Kalam*, pp. 8–17.
[5] Cf. *The Philosophy of the Church Fathers*, I, p. 75.
[5a] *Milal*, p. 9, l. 11.

lieve that God created Adam in His image [Gen. 1:26, 27]. One of their prophets has it in his book, that one day he saw God, who had white hair and a white beard [Dan. 7:9]. Moreover, God said: I am a consuming fire, and a devouring fever" [cf. Deut. 4:24].[6] It will be noticed that the charge, as reproduced by Masʿūdī, is not only that the Jews take the anthropomorphic expressions in Scripture literally but that Scripture itself conceives of God anthropomorphically. This, we may assume, is how the Jews came to be regarded by Muslim writers as anthropomorphists. Consequently, when in Islam an extreme anthropomorphic sect appeared, those who were against them grouped the Jews together with the anthropomorphists in their own religion. Thus Ibn Ḥazm, in his criticism of the Pentateuch,[7] dwells at length upon its anthropomorphisms, and, when a Jew referred him to an anthropomorphic expression in the Koran similar to one he had quoted from the Pentateuch, he answered that the Koranic expression is to be interpreted figuratively,[8] quite oblivious, or perhaps ignorant, of the traditional Jewish view that the anthropomorphic expressions in Scripture are not to be taken literally. It is interesting to note that among the examples of anthropomorphism quoted by Ibn Ḥazm from the Pentateuch are also those of Genesis 1:26 and 27 [9] and of Deuteronomy 4:24,[10] which had been quoted by the Egyptian Christian in his address to Ibn Ṭūlūn. Shahrastānī, in one place, says: "The Jews liken the creator to a creature, and the Christians liken a creature to the Creator." [11] In another place, he first ascribes to Jews, to all of them without any distinction, a belief in "likeness," because, he says, the Torah is full of many instances of "likeness," such as the expression "image of God" and the description of God as speaking mouth to mouth, as talking

[6] Masʿūdī, *Murūj XXXI*, p. 389. Cf. Schreiner, "Zur Geschichte der Polemik zwischen Juden und Muhammedanern," *ZDMG*, 42: 597 (1888).

[7] *Fiṣal* I, p. 116, l. 11–p. 224. Cf. Sweetman, *Islam and Christian Theology*, II, 1, pp. 178–231.

[8] *Ibid.* I, p. 160, ll. 5 ff.

[9] *Ibid.*, p. 117, ll. 21 ff.

[10] *Ibid.*, p. 160, ll. 2–5.

[11] *Milal*, p. 132, ll. 7–8.

aloud, as descending upon Mount Sinai, as sitting on the throne, and as seeing from above,[12] but then, contrasting the Rabbanites with the Karaites, he says of the latter that they correspond to the Likeners (*al-mushabbihah*), that is, the anthropomorphists, in Islam.[13] Then, again, in one place he says that the Muslim "Likeners" borrowed most of their anthropomorphisms from the Jews,[14] without any qualification, but in another place he says that "anthropomorphism in its sheer and utter form is already found among Jews, not among all of them, but among the Karaites." [15] With regard to the Karaites, however, Masʿūdī says quite the opposite, that "the Ananites (that is, the Karaites) are those who believe in justice and unity," [16] that is to say, they are like the Muʿtazilites, who, under unity, deny attributes, which also means a denial of anthropomorphism.

In view of all this misinformation, the spokesmen of Judaism of that time, both Rabbanites and Karaites, start their discussion of the semantic aspect of the problem of attributes with a reassertion of the traditional Jewish view that the anthropomorphic expressions in Scripture are not to be taken literally.[17] In support of this traditional Jewish view, they quote from Scripture itself such verses as "To whom then will ye liken God? or what likeness will ye compare unto Him?" (Isa. 40:18) [18] and similar other verses. The Rabbanites adduce additional support from what they call "tradition" (*al-manḳūl*: *ha-meḳubbal*) or "the sages (*ʿulamāʾ*: *ḥakamim*) of our people," [19] such as Onkelos, who in his Aramaic version of the Pentateuch avoids translating anthropomorphic expressions literally,[20] or the Talmudic rabbis, from whom they quote such statements as "Great is the boldness of the prophets who

[12] *Ibid.*, p. 164, ll. 14–16.

[13] *Ibid.*, l. 18. Cf. *Liḳḳuṭe Ḳadmoniyyot*, p. 9.

[14] *Milal*, p. 77, ll. 19 ff.

[15] *Ibid.*, p. 65, l. 1.

[16] Masʿūdī, *Tanbīh*, p. 112, l. 18 – p. 113, l. 1 (159).

[17] On the question of the corporeality of God among Arabic-speaking Jews during the Kalam period, see *Kalam*, pp. 97–111.

[18] *Emunot* II, 9, p. 94, ll. 2–3; *Anwār* I, 4, 1, p. 31, l. 14.

[19] *Emunot* I, 9, p. 95, l. 11.

[20] *Ibid.*, ll. 17–21; cf. *Moreh* I, 27.

describe God by the likeness of the creature"[21] and "the Torah speaks according to the language of men."[22] Aware of what scriptural verses were quoted in Muslim literature as outstanding examples of Jewish anthropomorphism, these early spokesmen of Judaism in the Muslim world include these verses among the verses discussed by them. Thus both Saadia and Ḳirḳisānī explain the expression that God created man in His own image (Gen. 1:26, 27) figuratively as being used only "by way of conferring honor."[23] The "Ancient of days" whom Daniel saw and described as having garments white as snow and hair like pure wool (Dan. 7:9) is said by Saadia not to refer to God but rather to some form created by God, which the rabbis call Shekinah.[24] The statement that God is a consuming fire (Deut. 4:24) is explained by Saadia figuratively, as meaning that God's punishment is like a consuming fire.[25] And so from the very beginning both Rabbanite and Karaite writers try to explain in great detail the figurative meanings of the various anthropomorphic terms and expressions in Scripture.[26]

While both Rabbanites and Karaites joined hands in trying to show that anthropomorphisms in Scripture are not taken by Jews, or are not to be taken by them, literally, Karaitic writers were snapping at some of the anthropomorphic expressions found in post-scriptural rabbinic writings. The Karaite Salmon ben Yeruḥim, a contemporary of Saadia, in a work written in Hebrew, quoted passages from Talmudic and post-Talmudic literature to show that the rabbis had an

[21] *Genesis Rabbah* 27, 1.

[22] *Berakot* 31b. Both these statements are quoted by Maimonides (*Moreh* I, 46) as rabbinic proof-texts for the nonliteral interpretation of anthropomorphic expressions in Scripture.

[23] *Emunot* II, 9, p. 94, l. 14; *Anwār* II, 28, 12, p. 176, ll. 7–8; *Cuzari* IV, 3, p. 240, l. 27–p. 242, l. 8; p. 243, ll. 4–14; cf. *Moreh* I, 1, and Philo, *Opif*. 23, 69.

[24] *Emunot* II, 10, p. 99, ll. 18–20; cf. *Cuzari* IV, 3, p. 242, ll. 8–10; p. 243, ll. 14–15.

[25] *Emunot* II, 9, p. 94, ll. 18–20; VII, 2, p. 212, ll. 12–15. Cf. also *Moreh* I, 30.

[26] *Emunot* II, 10, p. 95, ll. 21ff.; *Anwār* II, 28, pp. 171–178.

anthropomorphic conception of God.[27] Of post-Talmudic literature he explicitly mentions the mystical works *Sefer Shem ben Noah*,[28] *Otiyyot de-Rabbi Akiba*,[29] and *Shiʿur Ḳomah*,[30] and quotes from other works of the same type without mentioning them by title.[31] Judah ben Barzillai mentions a nonextant book by Saadia written against "a certain heretic," who had accused "the sages of the Talmud," and also the post-Talmudic *Shiʿur Ḳomah*, of attributing to the Creator of the world likeness and figure.[32] Jewish scholarship has long been debating the question whether this nonextant book of Saadia referred to by Judah ben Barzillai is not the same as Saadia's nonextant book known by its Arabic title *Kitāb al-Radd ʿalā Ibn Sāḳawaihi*, "Refutation of Ibn Sāḳawaihi," and also whether that Ibn Sāḳawaihi is not the Arabic name of the aforementioned Salmon ben Yeruḥim.[33] But, whether one contemporary or two contemporaries of Saadia began an attack upon the anthropomorphisms of the Talmud and of the mystical post-Talmudic works, from that time on this kind of attack was continued in Karaite writings. It is from these Karaite writings, most of them in Arabic, or perhaps directly from Karaite informants, that Ibn Ḥazm must have derived his tirades against the rabbis (*aḥbār*),[34] the mention of which word is sometimes followed by the expression "God curse them" (*laʿanahum Allah*),[35] referring especially to the anthropomorphisms of the post-Talmudic *Shiʿur Ḳomah*, to which he erroneously refers as a part of the Talmud,[36] and

[27] *Milḥamot Adonai* XIV–XVII (ed. Israel Davidson), pp. 108–132.
[28] *Ibid.* XIV, v. 46.
[29] *Ibid.*, v. 76.
[30] *Ibid.*, v. 85.
[31] *Ibid.*, vv. 37–38, and Davidson's n. 22 *ad. loc.*
[32] *Perush*, pp. 20, 21.
[33] Cf. latest discussions of this problem in Malter, *Saadia Gaon*, pp. 265, 383 d, and Davidson's introduction to his edition of Salmon ben Yeruḥim's *Milḥamot Adonai* (1934), pp. 21–28.
[34] *Fiṣal* I, p. 217, ll. 14 ff.
[35] *Ibid.*, p. 221, l. 10. The same malediction is used by him five lines later (l. 15) after mentioning the name of "Paul, of the tribe of Benjamin" (cf. Rom. 11:1).
[36] *Ibid.*, ll. 2–3.

also to the anthropomorphism of *Seder Nashim*, to which excusably enough he refers as "another book of the Talmud," but erroneously describes it as "a commentary on the ritual laws of menstruation," and inaccurately attributes to it a statement which occurs in another part of the Talmud,[37] namely, *Ḥagigah* 13b. It is with reference to the Muslim charges of anthropomorphisms in Scripture and the Karaitic charges of anthropomorphisms in the Talmud that Moses Ibn Ezra complains that the "heretics" have joined the "gentiles" in the reproach of anthropomorphism.[38]

How Saadia answered the charge of anthropomorphism against the Talmud in his nonextant "Refutation of Ibn Sāḳawaihi" or in his nonextant book against that unnamed "heretic" referred to by Judah ben Barzillai is not known. But from his answer to the charge of anthropomorphism against the Talmud and the *Shi'ur Ḳomah*, as quoted by Judah ben Barzillai,[39] it may be gathered that he applied to the Talmudic anthropomorphism the same method of figurative interpretation that the Talmud itself applies to the scriptural anthropomorphisms.

The denial of the literalness of anthropomorphic terms and expressions was the first step in the discussion of the semantic aspect of the problem of attributes by Jewish religious philosophers of that period. The next step in their discussion of this aspect of the problem was to determine the proper meaning of the terms predicated of God not only as a denial of the likeness of God to other beings but also as a denial of the existence in God of real attributes assumed to be unlike corresponding attributes existing in created beings. Having aligned themselves with the Mu'tazilites in denying the existence of real attributes in God, they were now going to examine the various formulae framed by the Mu'tazilites in expressing this denial

[37] *Ibid.*, ll. 6–9.

[38] *'Arugat ha-Bosem* in *Zion*, 2: 137 (1842–43). Cf. Steinschneider, *Jewish Literature*, p. 313, n. 28; Goldziher, "Mélanges Judéo-Arabes," *REJ*, 47: 183 (1903).

[39] *Perush*, pp. 20–21, 34.

of real attributes, with a view to determining which of them could most appropriately be used as an expression of such a denial. The examination of these formulae started with al-Muḳammaṣ and Saadia and continued throughout the history of medieval Jewish philosophy. We shall discuss here the philosophers of the Kalam period and also statements in the works of later Jewish philosophers of the Arabic period which deal directly with the Kalam formulae.

1. AL-MUKAMMAS

Like all those who denied the reality of attributes, al-Muḳammaṣ was troubled by the question as to how one can speak of God so as not to imply a belief in attributes. Two opinions are quoted by him on this question. According to the opinion of some, it is impossible at all to predicate of God any kind of terms.[1] By this he undoubtedly refers to the author of *Liber de Causis*[2] and to the pseudo-Socrates and the pseudo-Xenophanes of the Arabic doxographies.[3] According to the opinion of others, however, it is possible to predicate of God certain terms, provided those terms are taken to be the same as His essence and hence unlike corresponding similar terms predicated of other beings.[4] By this he undoubtedly refers to the Muʿtazilites. Following the opinion of the latter, he consequently begins to investigate as to what formula should be used in predications of God so as not to imply a belief in the existence of attributes.

In our discussion above of al-Muḳammaṣ' treatment of the ontological aspect of the problem of attributes, we have seen how only the following two types of formulae are acceptable to him: (1) Abū al-Hudhayl's formula, which reads: "God is living in virtue of life, and His life is himself"; (2) Naẓẓām's formula, which reads: "God is living not in virtue of life, but in virtue of himself." Unlike the view later expressed by

[1] *Perush*, p. 78, ll. 6–7.
[2] *Liber de Causis* 5, pp. 69, 168.
[3] *Milal*, p. 279, ll. 5 ff.; p. 291, l. 12. Cf. Kaufmann, *Attributenlehre*, p. 324, n. 186.
[4] *Perush*, p. 78, ll. 7–10.

Shahrastānī, he takes Abū al-Hudhayl's formula to mean the same as Naẓẓām's formula, namely, a complete denial of attributes, including also a denial of what later came to be known as modes.[5]

In addition to his acceptance of these two formulae, al-Muḳammaṣ goes on to show that one may predicate of God any laudatory term with the understanding that it is not used as an affirmation of any attribute in God but only as a negation of its opposite derogatory term. To quote: "When we affirm of God the term 'living,' we negate of Him 'death' and, when we affirm of Him the term 'knowing,' we negate of Him 'ignorance' or 'folly' and, when we affirm of Him the term 'hearing' and 'seeing,' we negate of Him 'deafness' and 'blindness.' "[6] In other words, one can affirm of God any laudatory term provided the proposition, which is affirmative in form, is taken to be negative in meaning. In support of this allowable use of divine predications, al-Muḳammaṣ quotes in the name of "Aristotle the philosopher" the following statement: "Negative attributes are more truly and more appropriately predicable of God than affirmative attributes."[7] Two comments are called for here. First, Aristotle did not make that statement; but such a statement is ascribed by Shahrastānī to Plato.[8] Second, the statement is not altogether the same as his own statement, for which he quotes it in confirmation, for his own statement is not about direct negative predications of God but rather about negative interpretations of terms affirmatively predicated of God. As I have shown elsewhere, it was Albinus who first used negative interpretations of affirmative predications of God,[9] and it was Najjār and Ḍirār who first made use of this device in Islam.[10]

Thus, according to al-Muḳammaṣ, there are three types of

[5] Cf. above, p. 8.

[6] *Perush*, p. 80, ll. 25–26.

[7] *Ibid.*, ll. 26–28.

[8] *Milal*, p. 288, l. 16. Cf. Kaufmann, *Attributenlehre*, p. 330, n. 198.

[9] Cf. my paper "Albinus and Plotinus on Divine Attributes," *HTR*, 45: pp. 115–130 (1952).

[10] Cf. *Kalam*, pp. 223–224.

formula which one may use in divine predications: (1) Abū al-Hudhayl's formula: God is living in virtue of life, but His life is himself; (2) Naẓẓām's formula: God is living not in virtue of life, but in virtue of himself; (3) Najjār's and Ḍirār's formula: God is living, taken to mean God is not dead.

2. SAADIA *

Saadia, unlike al-Muḳammaṣ, does not discuss the semantic aspect of the problem of attributes directly in the form of comments upon certain formulae used by the Mutakallimūn, but throughout his discussion of the unity of God are scattered statements in which he touches upon some of the guiding principles used by all those who before him have dealt with the meaning of terms predicated of God.

In the first of these statements, like all those who before him discussed the meaning of terms predicated of God, he lays down the principle of the unlikeness of God to other beings,[1] in support of which he quotes a representative scriptural verse.[2] Subsequently he tries to explain in philosophic terms what this denial of likeness means by alluding to Aristotle's explanation of what is meant by the affirmation that things are "like." [3]

Then, having in mind the commonly accepted view that to predicate actions of God does not imply any plurality in God, he offers two explanations why the predication of action does not imply a likeness between God and man, especially if one believes that man has the power to act. First, alluding to Aristotle's demonstration that God, unlike all other movers, is an immovable mover, he shows that God, unlike all other agents, is not affected by His actions.[4] Second,

* This is an abridgment of part of my paper entitled "Saadia on the Semantic Aspect of the Problem of Attributes" in *Salo W. Baron Jubilee Volume* (1974); it appears here by permission of The American Academy for Jewish Research.

[1] *Emunot* II, 1, p. 79, ll. 13–14.

[2] *Ibid*., p. 80, ll. 5–6, quoting Ps. 86:8.

[3] *Metaph*. X, 3, 1054b, 5–6 and 9–11.

[4] *Emunot* II, 12, p. 104, ll. 16–18.

alluding to his own arguments in proof of creation *ex nihilo*, he shows how God's action, unlike the action of any other agent, is in no need of anything for its performance.[5]

Then, again, having in mind the rabbinic teaching that inappropriate descriptions of God in Scripture should be interpreted non-literally, and using for this rabbinic non-literal interpretation the philosophic term metaphor, he says that any inappropriate description of God should be interpreted metaphorically.[6] Drawing, therefore, upon two commonly used methods of the non-literal interpretation of inappropriate terms predicated of God, namely, to interpret them as actions or to interpret them as negations, he makes his own use of these two methods. Thus referring to the terms "living" and "powerful" and "knowing," which in their predication of God are taken by the Attributists as real attributes in God, he interprets them as "explanations of the term Maker." [7] By this he tries to show that such a proposition as "God is living and powerful and knowing" really means that "God, the Maker, is living and powerful and knowing" and is thus analogous to the proposition "the becoming is beautiful," in which, according to Aristotle, one term is explained by another term.[8] Similarly, referring to the term "one," which in various senses, according to Aristotle, is applicable to all kinds of things,[9] he tries to show that in its application to God it is to be taken negatively as a denial not only of a plurality of gods but also of that kind of plurality within the one God which would be implied by a belief in the reality of attributes.[10]

Finally, besides the interpretation of inappropriate terms predicated of God as explanations of the term Maker or as negations, there are certain inappropriate terms of which he says that they are to be interpreted as being "merely a means

[5] *Ibid.*, p. 104, l. 18 – p. 105, l. 1.

[6] *Ibid.* II, 1, p. 83, l. 20 – p. 84, l. 2.

[7] *Ibid.* II, 4, p. 85, ll. 17–18.

[8] *Top.* I, 5, 102a, 2–6.

[9] *Metaph.* V, 6.

[10] *Emunot* II, 4, p. 85, l. 20–p. 86, l. 2. Cf. above pp. 10–11.

of expressing esteem and reverence," [11] that is to say, man's subjective glorification of God. As an example of such terms, he mentions the term "king," [12] which he assumes, would be what Aristotle describes as "relative," and as such would be dependent upon its "correlative," [13] which in this case would be the term "subjects." [14]

3. JOSEPH AL-BASĪR

In the ontological aspect of the problem of attributes, Joseph al-Baṣīr, as we have seen, denies the reality of attributes but aligns himself with those who believe in modes.[1] In the semantic aspect of the problem, he uses two formulae to express his belief in modes. First, he uses the formula: "God is powerful, knowing, living, and existing in virtue of His self" [2] or, as he also phrases it, "God is powerful, knowing, living, and existing, and these four [predicates] refer to the self." [3] Second, he uses the formula: "God is powerful not in virtue of power; He is knowing not in virtue of knowledge; He is living not in virtue of life." [4]

Of these two formulae, the first, or rather its equivalent where the phrase "in virtue of His essence" is used instead of "in virtue of His self," was a subject of controversy. Jubbā'ī used it as a denial of attributes altogether, whereas Abū Hāshim used it as an affirmation of modes.[5] Saadia, as we have shown, used it as a denial of attributes.[6] Al-Baṣīr, as a Modalist, quite evidently uses it in the sense of an affirmation of modes. As for the second formula, 'Abbād b. Sulaymān, who was a denier of attributes and used the formula "God is knowing not in virtue of knowledge," was explicitly opposed to the use of "in virtue of His self" or "in virtue of His essence," [7]

[11] *Ibid.* II, 11, p. 101, l. 16.

[12] *Ibid.*, l. 13.

[13] *Categ.* 7, 6a, 36; 6b, 28; 7b, 15–22.

[14] *Emunot* II, 11, p. 101, l. 15.

[1] Cf. above, pp. 23–25.

[2] *Maḥkimat* 15, Hebrew, 112a, l. 18; Arabic, p. 9b, ll. 10–11.

[3] *Ne'imot*, Hebrew p. 14b, ll. 26–27; Arabic p. 25b, l. 14.

[4] *Maḥkimat* 17, Hebrew, p. 112b, ll. 11–12; Arabic, p. 10b, l. 1.

[5] *Milal*, p. 55, l. 19 – p. 56, l. 3.

[6] Cf. above, p. 11.

[7] Cf. *Kalam*, p. 230.

whereas Naẓẓām, also a denier of attributes, used the combined formula "God is . . . knowing . . . in virtue of His self, but not in virtue of knowledge." [8] What al-Baṣīr does is to use both these formulae, separately, and each of them as an affirmation of modes.

4. JOSEPH IBN SADDIK *

With his denial of the existence of real attributes,[1] Ibn Ṣaddiḳ would be expected to reject any formula used by Attributists in affirming their belief in the reality of attributes. He does not do so directly, but he does so indirectly. Having in mind the Ashʿarite formula affirming that the attributes are "other than God," [2] he says: "No one should say that God's laudatory attributes are other than He or that He is other than they." [3]

The unfolding of his view as to what would be the proper formula to be used in expressing the denial of attributes, as it must have been logically formed in his mind, began with a formal restatement of the problem, which he did from two viewpoints: first, from the viewpoint of the principle of the unlikeness of God with other beings; second, from the viewpoint of the unknowability of God.

As for the principle of the unlikeness of God, it is to be found in Scripture, and scriptural philosophers ever since Philo [4] usually quote such verses in the discussion of the semantic aspect of the problem. Ibn Ṣaddiḳ, however, does not quote any scriptural proof-text in support of it, probably assuming that his readers were already acquainted with whatever proof-text he could quote. He prefers to treat the matter as something which can be demonstrated by reason. Thus start-

[8] Cf. *Kalam*, p. 225.

* Reprinted by permission, with some revisions, from *JQR*, n.s., 55:277–298 (1965), where it appeared as the greater part of an article entitled "Joseph Ibn Ṣaddiḳ on Divine Attributes."

[1] Cf. above, p. 26.

[2] *Fisal* II, p. 126, l. 23; IV, p. 207, ll. 8 and 13; cf. *Kalam*, pp. 212–214.

[3] *ʿOlam Ḳaṭan* III, p. 57, ll. 13–14.

[4] Cf. *Philo* II, pp. 96–98, 151–152.

ing with the principle that God is an uncreated creator or uncaused cause, which to him follows from his proof of the creation of the world,[5] he builds upon it two arguments for the unlikeness of God.

One argument reflects Aristotle's statement that "things are like (ὅμοια) if, while not being the same absolutely . . . the respects in which they are the same are more than those in which they differ," [6] the implication being that things which are like are the same in one respect and different in another. With this Aristotelian statement in the back of his mind, Ibn Ṣaddiḳ argues as follows: "If God were like anything else, then in that respect in which they are alike they would be agreeing and equal, whereas in other respects they would be different. Now . . . since in God and in that something else the likeness must have a cause, God would have a cause . . . But we have already shown that God is the cause of everything and himself has no cause. Therefore, nothing is like unto Him." [7]

The other argument reflects Aristotle's statement that "likeness and unlikeness can be predicated with reference to quality only . . . so that it is peculiar to quality that the like and the unlike are predicated with reference to it." [8] With this Aristotelian statement in the back of his mind, Ibn Ṣaddiḳ argues that "if God be like any other thing, then He would possess quality, inasmuch as it is peculiar to quality that it is with reference to it that one thing is said to be like another." [9] But "quality," he continues, "is borne in a substance," and hence is an accident, but that which is composed of substance and accident has already been shown by him to be created, but God, unlike other things, is uncreated." [10]

As for the principle of the unknowability of God, the first to establish it was Philo, wherein he was followed by both pagan and Christian philosophers, whence also by Muslim

[5] *'Olam Ḳaṭan*, p. 49, ll. 21–25. Cf. Saadia above pp. 11–13.

[6] *Metaph*. X, 3, 1054b, 3–4, 11–12.

[7] *'Olam Ḳaṭan*, p. 51, ll. 20–25.

[8] *Categ*., 8, 11a, 15–18.

[9] *'Olam Ḳaṭan* II, p. 21, ll. 17–19.

[10] *Ibid*., ll. 19–20.

philosophers.[11] Ibn Ṣaddiḳ undertakes to prove it. Evidently first having in mind Aristotle's statement that "we do not think that we know a thing unless we are acquainted with its primary causes and first principles," [12] he sets out by saying that "things are known by their causes" [13] and then, having in mind his own proof that God is an uncaused cause,[14] he concludes that, "when it has been established concerning anything that it has no cause, it has thereby been established that in no wise can be it known." [15]

By the same principle by which he has established the unlikeness and unknowability of God he then tries to establish the indescribability of God. Having in mind the Aristotelian classification of all terms into substance and accidents, he says in effect that, on the basis of the principle that God is an uncreated creator or uncaused cause, it must necessarily follow that God is neither a substance nor an accident, inasmuch as those created by Him are each either a substance or an accident.[16] In the course of his discussion, he mentions as examples four of the nine accidents in Aristotle's list of ten categories, namely, quality,[17] quantity,[18] place,[19] and time,[20] showing how these accidents, when predicated of a subject, imply that the subject is a body [21] and hence dependent upon a cause.[22] In the course of his discussion, again, he shows, how on the basis of the same principle that God is an uncaused cause, it is also impossible to predicate of Him terms implying

[11] Cf. *Philo*, II, pp. 101–126, 153–160, and my papers "The Knowability and Describability of God in Plato and Aristotle," *Harvard Studies in Classical Philology*, 56–57: 233–249 (1947); "Albinus and Plotinus on Divine Attributes," *HTR*, 45: 115–130 (1952).

[12] *Phys.* I, 1, 184a, 12–13; cf. *Anal. Post.* I, 2, 71b, 9–12.

[13] *'Olam Ḳaṭan*, p. 48, l. 10.

[14] *Ibid.*, p. 49, ll. 21–25.

[15] *Ibid.*, p. 48, ll. 10–11.

[16] *Ibid.*, p. 51, ll. 30–31.

[17] *Ibid.*, p. 48, l. 19.

[18] *Ibid.*, p. 54, ll. 18 ff.

[19] *Ibid.*, p. 48, ll. 19–20; cf. p. 55, ll. 17–21; p. 53, l. 30.

[20] *Ibid.*, p. 48, l. 20; cf. p. 55, ll. 21–24; p. 53, l. 30.

[21] *Ibid.*, p. 55, ll. 24–26.

[22] *Ibid.*, p. 48, ll. 20–21.

a "definition" which consists of genus and differences [23] or a "description" which consists of properties and accidents [24] or a final cause [25] or a species.[26] This additional statement as to what divine predicates of God would have to consist of, including as it does definition, genus, species, difference, property, and accidents, reflects the terms definition, genus, property, and accident, in Aristotle's four-fold list of predicables [27] and the terms genus, species, difference, property, and accident in Porphyry's fivefold list of predicables.[28]

Since there is no predicate which does not signify either a substance or an accident or a property or a genus or a species or a difference, is it possible to describe God at all? "Most of the ancients," says Ibn Ṣaddiḳ, "refrained from applying to God any description for fear that this would make Him the subject of predicates and would thus make Him consist of a real attribute and a subject of the attribute." [29] The reference

[23] *Ibid.*, p. 48, l. 19, and p. 55, ll. 3–6. The Hebrew term *min* (p. 55, l. 4), which usually means "species," is used here by the Hebrew translator of the work as a translation of the Arabic term *jins*, "genus," for on p. 40, ll. 9–10, using the Arabic term *nau'*, "species," he says that "there is not a *min* but it has under it a *nau'* and there is not a *nau'* but it has above it a *min*."

[24] *Ibid.*, p. 55, ll. 6–9; cf. Kaufmann, *Attributenlehre*, p. 314, n. 165.

[25] *Ibid.*, p. 48, ll. 19–20; cf. p. 55, ll. 10–13.

[26] *Ibid.*, p. 48, l. 19; cf. p. 55, ll. 13–16.

[27] *Top.* I, 4, 101b, 25; cf. 38.

[28] *Isagoge* (ed. A. Bousse), p. 1, ll. 4–5.

[29] *'Olam Ḳaṭan*, p. 57, ll. 9–10. The Hebrew terms *mesapper u-mesuppar* undoubtedly stand here for the Arabic terms *ṣifah wa-mauṣūf*, for which Kaufmann (*Attributenlehre*, p. 267, n. 44) gives reference to Averroes' *Kitāb Faṣl al-Maḳal* (ed. M. J. Müller), p. 56, l. 9, and which he translates: "Qualification und Qualificirbar." But the combination of the same two terms occurs before the time of Ibn Ṣaddiḳ in Ghazālī's *Tahāfut al-Falāsifah* VI, § 5, p. 166, ll. 3–4 (ed. M. Bouyges), and there it is used in the orthodox technical sense of "attribute and the subject of the attribute." We may, therefore, assume that the two terms here mean "attribute and the subject of the attribute" in the technical sense as used by the orthodox Attributists. Since the Hebrew *mesapper* stands for the Arabic *ṣifah*, one would be inclined to think that the Hebrew *middah* here stands for some other Arabic term, which has the same various shades of meaning as the term *ṣifah*, perhaps the term *na't* as in *Çuzari* II, 2, p. 70, l. 2, and p. 71, l. 1: *nu'ūt-middot*. Similarly one would be inclined to think that the Hebrew *sippur*, also used in this work (cf. p. 51, l. 27; p. 65, l. 12), stands for the Arabic *waṣf*, as in *Moreh Nebukim* I, 53, p. 81, l. 27: *waṣf-sippur*. However, in

to "most of the ancients," it may be remarked, is to the pseudo-Aristotelian *Liber de Causis* [30] and to the pseudo-Socrates and the pseudo-Xenophanes of the Arabic doxographies.[31]

Ibn Ṣaddiḳ disagrees with this view, for Scripture and religious people in general do describe God by certain terms. "Seest thou not how every people that professes a religion predicates of God some kinds of epithet and applies to Him some kinds of name, each according to the manner in which it conceives of God." [32] Still reason has shown that God is unknowable and indescribable. How, then, could one reconcile the finding of reason with what one finds in Scripture and in the common usage of religious people?

By the time of Ibn Ṣaddiḳ there were the following answers to this difficulty.

First, beginning with Philo,[33] a distinction was made between the essence and the existence of God, and, while the former was unknowable, the latter could be known from the manifestation of God in the world through His actions. Accordingly, it was held that God could be described both by negating of Him terms implying imperfections and by affirming of Him terms implying perfections, but in the latter case, though in form the terms were adjectival, in meaning they were taken to signify actions by which God manifested himself in the world and by which His existence could become known to us. Second, beginning with Albinus,[34] all terms implying perfections, which in form were affirmed of God, in meaning were taken to emphasize a negation — not a negation of the mere respective opposites of the terms affirmed of God but a

one place in *'Olam Ḳaṭan*, the Hebrew translator himself indicates that he uses the Hebrew *middah* as a translation of the Arabic *ṣifah* (cf. 47, ll. 5–7). Probably the same term as *ṣifah* with its various shades of meaning, was translated by all these three Hebrew terms, according to the particular shade of meaning the translator wanted to convey.

[30] *Liber de Causis* 5, pp. 69, 168.

[31] Shahrastānī, *Milal*, p. 279, ll. 5 ff.; p. 291, l. 12; cf. Kaufmann, *Attributenlehre*, p. 324, n. 186.

[32] *'Olam Ḳaṭan*, p. 58, ll. 19–20.

[33] Cf. *Philo*, II, pp. 73, 126–149, 155–157.

[34] Cf. my paper "Albinus and Plotinus on Divine Attributes," pp. 115–130.

negation of any likeness between the perfections implied in the terms affirmed of God and the perfections implied in the same terms when affirmed of created beings.

Ibn Ṣaddiḳ makes use of these solutions.

First, he shows how all the terms predicated of God are descriptions of His actions and how all that these descriptions of His actions tell us about God that He exists and is the author of these actions, but they tell us nothing about His essence. To quote: "The attainment of a knowledge of the Prime Substance in any respect is, on the one hand, not possible and, on the other, not absolutely impossible. What is possible of such a knowledge is that which comes through a description of His attributes as manifest by the actions proceeding from Him. What is impossible of it is a knowledge of the [Prime] Substance stripped from the actions proceeding from Him. Hence it is clear that concerning God one may not inquire as to what He is . . . but only as to whether He is . . . and the road and means to this kind of knowledge about Him is by way of His actions in the universe, for the existence of an act necessarily shows the existence of its agent." [35]

Second, he shows how through these actions of God we come to negate of Him all the imperfections which may mar human actions and hence to predicate of Him all the terms by which we ordinarily describe the various perfections of human actions. To quote: "The manner in which men came to apply attributes to God may be described as follows: They looked at the work of God, and therefrom they inferred the fact of His existence. Then they reflected on this Existent Being and found that He is not weak [as we have explained above], wherefore they described Him as mighty, using this word of ordinary human speech only to convey the idea that He is not weak. Then upon further examination they found that His work is arranged in the most orderly manner, and so they described Him as knowing, inasmuch as ignorance could not

[35] *'Olam Ḳaṭan*, p. 48, ll. 16–25; cf. 57, ll. 20–21.

possibly be conceived of Him, for if ignorance could be applied to Him, His work would not be orderly arranged." [36] And in the same way, by a study of the work of God, men learned to describe Him by all the other terms which are found in the various scriptures and traditional literatures, mentioning the terms "rich" (*ghanī*, Surah 10:69, cf. *ma'ashir*, 1 Sam. 2:7), "just" (*ṣaddiḳ*, Deut. 32:4), "beneficent" (*meṭib*, Ps. 119:68), and "merciful" (*raḥman*, Surah 2:158: *raḥman*, *Tos. Baba Ḳamma* IX, 30 = *raḥum*, Exod. 34:3).[37]

Third, he shows how terms describing perfections of human actions affirmed of God are to be taken to mean a twofold negation: (1) a negation of the opposites of those perfections; (2) a negation of any likeness between those perfections when affirmed of God and when affirmed of human beings. He quotes with approval an apocryphal saying attributed to "the Philosopher," that is, Aristotle, stating that "it is more truly appropriate to predicate something of God in negative form than to predicate of Him anything in the affirmative form." [38] On the basis of this statement, Ibn Ṣaddiḳ goes on to say that the affirmation of "wise" and "mighty" could be more appropriately expressed by the negation of their opposites, namely, "He is not ignorant," "He is not weak." But while he agrees with "the Philosopher" in the greater appropriateness of the negation of terms of imperfections than in the affirmation of terms of perfection, he does not think that there is really need of using direct negations, for one can use propositions which are affirmative in form and interpret them as negative in meaning, in accordance with the aforementioned

[36] *Ibid.*, p. 57, ll. 20–25. The bracketed addition in my translation is required by the context. The reference is to his proof that God is not weak which occurs previously on p. 52, ll. 17–19. Such a cross reference to a proof occurring earlier in his work is given by him explicitly later (ll. 25–26) in connection with the attribute *'ashir*, "rich," that is, self-sufficient.

[37] *Ibid.*, p. 57, l. 25–p. 58, l. 10.

[38] *Ibid.*, p. 58, ll. 11–12. The view is attributed by Shahrastānī (*Milal*, p. 288, l. 16) to Plato. Cf. Kaufmann (*Attributenlehre*, p. 330, n. 198), though by "the Philosopher," Ibn Ṣaddiḳ usually means Aristotle. Cf. Max Doctor, *Die Philosophie des Josef (Ibn) Zaddik*, pp. 11–12.

twofold use of negation. He illustrates his point by the term "living," which is so often predicated of God in Scripture. Expecting us to assume that the proposition "God is living," after the analogy of the propositions "God is mighty" and "God is knowing," referred to by him before, really means "God is not dead," he says: "And let no ignorant person think that, in affirming of God life, we believe that life subsists in Him," [39] that is to say, that life subsists in God as an attribute like the life of created living beings which subsists in them as an attribute. He then goes on to explain that the life which is affirmed of God means "eternal duration," [40] so that its affirmation of God implies the negation of its likeness to the temporary duration that is meant by life when affirmed of created living beings. He thus concludes: "In truth, the terms

[39] I follow here the reading in the Hamburg manuscript as emended by Jellinek in his edition in preference to the reading in the four manuscripts adopted by Horovitz in his edition, for the following reason.

In the passages on p. 57, l. 20 – p. 58, l. 8, preceding this quotation, Ibn Ṣaddiḳ emphatically argues that God is to be described by certain terms, but that these terms are to be taken to have the following two meanings: (1) a negative meaning, so that "mighty" means "not weak," "knowing" means "not ignorant," and by implication "living" means "not dead"; (2) a positive meaning, so that the affirmation of God of such terms as "mighty" and "knowing" and "living" means that God has the attributes of "mightiness" and "knowledge" and "life," but that these attributes are identical with the essence of God, for "neither are His attributes external to His essence nor is His essence external to His attributes." After such a twofold emphasis, namely, that any term affirmed of God, such, for instance, as the term "living," means (1) the negation of its opposite "death" and (2) the affirmation of "life" as an attribute which is identical with the essence of God, it is more likely that Ibn Ṣaddiḳ should say "and let no ignorant person think that, if we affirm of Him the term life, it must mean that we believe that life exists in Him as an attribute" rather than that he should say "and let no ignorant person think that, if we do not affirm the existence of life in Him as an attribute, it must mean that death exists in Him as an attribute." Then, also, Ibn Ṣaddiḳ's answer to what supposedly an ignorant person might think, whether we translate it by "but that which we predicate of Him means eternal existence" or by "but that which we describe in that term means eternal existence," the expression "but that which we predicate of Him" or "but that which we describe by that term" refers to a statement reading, as in the Jellinek edition, "that, if we affirm of Him the term life, etc." rather than the reading, as in the Horovitz edition, "that, if we do not affirm the existence of life as an attribute in Him, etc."

[40] *'Olam Ḳaṭan*, p. 58, l. 9.

predicated of God cannot be appropriately predicated of anything else and the perfection which they each signify and in which He stands alone belongs to Him alone, inasmuch as [He alone has true existence, for] the existence of anything else is not existence in the true sense of the term but only existence by way of relation to something [which is its cause]."[41] The inference he expects us to draw from this is that, though in meaning terms predicated of God are actions and negations, in their adjectival affirmative form they express perfections identical with the essence of God. The question whether those terms which express perfection identical with God should be taken in an equivocal sense, as later insisted by Maimonides,[42] or in an ambiguous sense, as held by Arabic philosophers,[43] Ibn Ṣaddiḳ does not discuss.

What formula should be used in expressing the denial of attributes, Ibn Ṣaddiḳ does not directly say. But from his discussion it may be inferred that he would approve of two types of formula.

(1) A negative proposition such as "God is not ignorant."

(2) A simple affirmative proposition such as "God is knowing," which in meaning should be taken as (a) an action and as (b) a twofold negation.

With this view of his that attributes have no real existence and that the proper way of expressing this denial of the reality of attributes is by the use of a unipartite formula consisting either of a negative proposition or an affirmative proposition to be interpreted either as expressing an action or as emphasizing the two kinds of negation, Ibn Ṣaddiḳ undertakes to criticize the formula "God is living not in virtue of life; He is powerful not in virtue of power; He is knowing not in virtue of

[41] *Ibid.*, p. 58, ll. 24–26.

[42] Cf. my paper "Maimonides and Gersonides on Divine Attributes as Ambiguous Terms," *Mordecai M. Kaplan Jubilee Volume* (1953), pp. 513–530.

[43] Cf. my paper "Avicenna, Algazali, and Averroes on Divine Attributes," *Homenaje a Millás-Vallicrosa*, II (1956), pp. 545–571.

knowledge." [44] Though this formula is ascribed by him to "the opinion of those who say," previously he has quoted it from a work by Joseph al-Baṣīr, where, too, he introduces it by the words "and thus in their assertion." [45] So the formula quoted here is that used by al-Baṣīr which is taken by Ibn Ṣaddiḳ to represent the view of a certain group of people.

Now al-Baṣīr, in addition to the formula of the type of "God is living not in virtue of life," [46] uses also the formula of the type of "God is living in virtue of His self (*le-nafsho*)," [47] that is, in virtue of His essence. Prior to al-Baṣīr, however, ʿAbbād b. Sulaymān used the formula of the type of "God is living not in virtue of life" as a denial of attributes,[48] but he rejected the use of the formula of the type of "God is living in virtue of His essence (*li-dhātihi*)," [49] whereas Naẓẓām, as an expression of the denial of attributes, used a combination of both these two types of formula, namely, "God is living in virtue of His self (*li-nafsihi*), not in virtue of life." [50] There arises, therefore, the following question: Is al-Baṣīr's deviation from both ʿAbbād b. Sulaymān and Naẓẓām in his use of these formulae of any significance or not? and, if it is, what is it?

The answer to this question is to be found in a passage in his work *Al-Muḥtawī* (Hebrew: *Neʿimot*), where al-Baṣīr is referred to by others and is described by himself as a follower of the theory of *aḥwāl*,[51] that is, Abū Hāshim's theory of modes. Accordingly, the two types of formula used by him here are both used by him in the sense of an affirmation of modes, for so also is the formula of the type of "God is living

[44] *ʿOlam Ḳaṭan* III, p. 46, ll. 3–4.

[45] *Ibid.*, p. 44, ll. 20–25. Al-Baṣīr's work is referred to there by the title of *Manṣūrī*, which is the same as his work known by the title of *Kitāb al-Tamyīz* (Hebrew title: *Maḥkimat Peti*). Cf. Frankl, *Ein Muʿtazilitischen*, p. 9.

[46] *Maḥkimat Peti* 17, p. 112b, ll. 11–12; Arabic, p. 10b, l. 1.

[47] *Ibid.*, 15, p. 112a, l. 18; Arabic, p. 96, ll. 10–11.

[48] *Maḳālāt*, p. 166, ll. 1–2, 6–8.

[49] *Ibid.*, l. 4.

[50] *Ibid.*, p. 169, ll. 10–13.

[51] *Neʿimot*, Arabic, p. 1. Hebrew, p. 23b, ll. 6–7. Hebrew quoted by Frankl, *Ein Muʿtazilitischen*, p. 54.

in virtue of His essence" used by Abū Hāshim in the sense of modes.[52] Now the affirmation of modes differs from both the affirmation of attributes and the denial of attributes. It differs from the former in that the affirmation of attributes means that attributes are "other (*ghayr*) than God" [53] and are "subsisting (*ḳā'imah*) in His essence," [54] which essence is described by Ghazālī as the "subject" (*mauṣūf*) of the attribute,[55] whereas modes are not other than God and do not subsist in the essence of God as in a subject. It differs from the latter in that the denial of attributes means that predications of God are identical with God and are mere names,[56] whereas predications of God regarded as modes are not identical with God and are not mere names. The usual description of modes is that they are not existent and they are not nonexistent; [57] they are not identical with God and they are not other than God,[58] so that with reference to such predicates as "living," "knowing," "powerful," God would be described as "not living and not non-living," "not knowing and not not-knowing," "not powerful and not not-powerful." Al-Baṣīr, however, preferred to express his conception of modes by the formula "God is living not in virtue of life; He is powerful not in virtue of power; He is knowing not in virtue of knowledge." Moreover, in the course of his discussion, al-Baṣīr draws a distinction between the predicates "powerful," "knowing," and "living," which are to be affirmed of God, and the predicate "bodily," which must be negated of Him. The reason given by him for the affirmation of the first three predicates is that God is a creator and doer of things and "among us he who does things must be powerful" [59] and "knowing" [60] and "living." [61]

[52] *Milal*, p. 56, ll. 1–2.

[53] *Fiṣal* IV, p. 207, ll. 7–9.

[54] *Nihāyat*, p. 181, ll. 3–4.

[55] *Tahāfut al-Falāsifah* VI, 5, p. 166, ll. 3–4; cf. n. 29.

[56] Ash'arī, *Maḳālāt*, p. 166, ll. 6–8; Shahrastānī, *Milal* (ed. Cureton), p. 56, ll. 13–14, and *Nihāyat*, p. 133, ll. 6–10.

[57] Baghdādī, *Farḳ* (ed. Badr), p. 182, l. 5; Shahrastānī, *Nihāyat*, p. 198, ll. 4–5.

[58] Baghdādī, *Farḳ*, p. 182, l. 14.

[59] *Maḥkimat Peti* 9, p. 109b, ll. 21–22; Arabic, p. 3b, l. 14.

[60] *Ibid.*, 10, p. 110a, l. 19; Arabic, p. 5a, l. 1.

[61] *Ibid.*, 11, p. 110a, l. 25; Arabic, p. 56, l. 1.

The reason given by him for the negation of the predicate "bodily" is that a body, being composed of parts, must be created,[62] whereas God is an uncreated creator, and for the same reason he opposes those orthodox in Islam who maintained that "God is a body unlike other bodies." [63]

That Ibn Ṣaddiḳ knew that the formula was used by al-Baṣīr not in the sense of a denial of attributes but rather in the sense of the affirmation of modes may be gathered from his earlier quotation of the same formula from a work of al-Baṣīr which he mentions by title. That earlier quotation reads as follows: "He is living not in virtue of life in a subject; He is powerful not in virtue of power, and so on," [64] which later, in his third argument, he explains to mean that "these descriptive predicates," according to their users' opinion, "are not in a subject." [65] Now the phrase "in a subject" is not used here by al-Baṣīr.[66] It was added by Ibn Ṣaddiḳ himself, and it was added by him, we may assume, for the purpose of showing that, unlike its usage by 'Abbād b. Sulaymān and Naẓẓām, the formula is used by al-Baṣīr not as a denial of attributes altogether but rather as a denial of attributes conceived, according to the expression used by Ghazālī, as existing in God as in a subject (*mauṣūf*); they are, however, to be conceived as modes, which have some sort of existence but not an existence in God as in a subject.[67]

[62] *Ibid.*, 18, p. 113b, ll. 14 ff.; Arabic, p. 126, ll. 3 ff.

[63] *Ibid.*, 10, 114b, ll. 8–9; Arabic, p. 14a, l. 14 - p. 146, l. 1.

[64] *'Olam Ḳaṭan*, p. 44, ll. 24–25.

[65] Cf. below at n. 85.

[66] The phrase "not in a subject" is, however, used by al-Baṣīr in his discussion of "will," where, following certain Mu'tazilites (*Milal*, p. 34, l. 20 – p. 35, l. 2, p. 54, ll. 8–9; cf. *Kalam*, pp. 140–141) who, despite their denial of attributes or their affirmation of modes, believed that "wills" are created by God "not in a subject (*maḥall*)," he says (*Maḥkimat Peti*, fol. 122b) that "God is willing in virtue of a created will which does not abide in a subject," the Hebrew for "subject" or rather *maḥall* here, being in *Maḥkimat Peti ḥanayah*, whereas in Ibn Ṣaddiḳ's restatement of it in *'Olam Ḳaṭan* (p. 45, l. 16) it is *munaḥ*. In connection with "will," it may be remarked, the phrase "not in a subject" means that "will" is created by God as an incorporeal being which is neither an attribute nor a mode.

[67] In *Attributenlehre*, p. 266, Kaufmann (1) takes the expression "not in a subject" here to describe the Mu'tazilite view of the absolute denial of attributes; (2) he thus also takes al-Baṣīr to be an absolute denier of attri-

His criticism[68] consists of three arguments, of which the first two, we shall try to show, are aimed neither at the theory of modes itself nor at the original modalistic formula that "modes are not existent and they are not non-existent," on the analogy of which, with reference to such a predicate as "living," the formula would be "God is not living and not not-living." Ibn Ṣaddik undoubtedly knew of the stock argument against the modalistic formula, namely, that it was in violation of the Law of Excluded Middle,[69] and undoubtedly he also knew of the various attempts to answer that argument.[70] None of this is of his concern here. Here he is concerned only with the formula of the type of "God is living not in virtue of life" as used by al-Baṣīr for modes, and it is concerning this type of formula that he is going to show that it is in violation not of the Law of Excluded Middle, which can be answered, but rather of the Law of Contradiction, which cannot be answered. His first argument against al-Baṣīr's formula "God is living not in virtue of life" may be restated as follows: Taking the first part of the formula to imply that those who use it agree with the Attributists and assume that God consists, as says Ghazālī, "of an attribute (*mesapper* = *ṣifah*) and a subject (*mesuppar* = *mauṣūf*), so that, on the one hand, "God is comprehensible as to [His] essence," and taking the wording of the

---

butes; (3) he consequently takes Ibn Ṣaddiḳ's arguments to be aimed at the absolute denial of attributes. However, (1) those who absolutely deny attributes never use the expression "not in a subject." Only with reference to certain attributes, such as "will" and "word," do some absolute deniers of attributes use that expression, but, in these cases, they mean by it that "will" and "word" exist outside of God as incorporeal created beings (cf. *Kalam*, p. 141, and the preceding note). (2) Al-Baṣīr, as we have seen (cf. above at n. 51), explicitly declared himself to be a Modalist. (3) Ibn Ṣaddiḳ's third argument is definitely not aimed at the absolute denial of attributes and cannot be interpreted as an argument against the absolute denial of attributes.

[68] With what follows, compare the interpretation of Ibn Ṣaddiḳ's criticism of al-Baṣīr in Kaufmann (*Attributenlehre*, pp. 266–272) and Vajda (*op. cit.*, pp. 147–149).

[69] Shahrastānī, *Milal*, p. 57, ll. 5–6; p. 67, ll. 2–3; *Nihāyat*, p. 134, ll. 12–14; Baghdādī, *Farḳ*, p. 182, ll. 1–7.

[70] Cf. *Kalam*, pp. 203–204.

second part to imply that they agree with the Muʿtazilites and "reduce the descriptive predicates of God to absolute nullity, [so that, on the other hand, God is incomprehensible as to His essence,]" he concludes in his mind that the formula logically becomes bipartite and means, as he says later in his second argument, that "God is living and He is not living." But this, he argues, is in violation of the Law of Contradiction, for it both affirms and denies of God one and the same predicate.[71] Undoubtedly he knew that the same argument could be raised also against ʿAbbād b. Sulaymān who used this type of formula in the sense of a denial of attributes. But, again, his concern here was only al-Baṣīr. Moreover, he argues, the very same reason that al-Baṣīr has given for the use of the predicates "living," "powerful," and "knowing," namely, that "among us" those who do things possess life, power, and knowledge, applies also to the predicate "bodily," for among us those who do things have a body. As for the reason given by al-Baṣīr for rejecting the predicate "bodily," namely, that bodies as we have them are composed of parts, it applies also to life, power, and knowledge, for those who have life and power and knowledge as we know them have also bodies. Of course, al-Baṣīr will say that the life and power and knowledge predicated of God are unlike our life and power and knowledge, but so is also the body predicated of God by some orthodox in Islam said by them to be unlike other bodies, and still this explanation is rejected by al-Baṣīr himself.[72]

This is the first of three arguments raised by Ibn Ṣaddiḳ against al-Baṣīr.

The second argument against the formula "God is living not in virtue of life" reads as follows: "If 'God is living not in virtue of life,' then it must inevitably follow that either the first part of their statement, namely, 'God is living,' is true and the second part of their statement, namely, 'not in virtue of life,' is false, unreal, and unfounded, or their latter statement, namely, 'not in virtue of life,' is true, and their former

[71] *ʿOlam Ḳaṭan*, p. 46, ll. 6–8. [72] *Ibid.*, ll. 8–17.

statement, namely, 'God is living,' is false. Should they say: Our affirmation that He is living is only meant to negate of Him the predicate of death, for how can a creator be conceived as not having life? To this we answer and say," [73] and here follows his answer.

The plea which Ibn Ṣaddiḳ has put in the mouth of those who used al-Baṣīr's formula does not say clearly and fully all they could have said in their own defense. Let us then say for them all that they could have said and would have said if they were given a chance. They would start by declaring that they were going to prove that their bipartite formula is not self-contradictory. To do this they would begin, I imagine, by arguing that one should not judge their formula by its phrasing; one should rather consider its meaning. In its phrasing, the first part of the formula indeed reads "God is living," but it is so phrased, they would maintain, only out of a sense of piety and the decorum of language, for how could any scripturally religious person, when speaking of God, avoid saying that "He is living," when Scripture constantly speaks of God as living? What the first part of the formula really means is that "God is not dead." As for its second part, namely, "not in virtue of life," they would accept Ibn Ṣaddiḳ's interpretation that it means "He is not living," and so the bipartite formula really means "God is not dead and He is not living." The formula so understood, they would continue to argue, does not violate the Law of Contradiction, for by the Law of Contradiction only the affirmation and negation of the same predicate is impossible. But here in the proposition "God is not dead and He is not living" there is only the negation of two contrary predicates. But if one should ask, is not the negation of two contrary predicates a violation of the Law of Excluded Middle? — the answer they would give, I imagine, would be as follows: The Law of Excluded Middle, according to certain statements by Aristotle, applies only to cases where the predicates are contraries between which there is no inter-

[73] *Ibid.*, ll. 18–21.

mediate, as, for instance, odd and even, for, as he says, "it is necessary that the one or the other be present in numbers," [74] but it does not apply to cases where the predicates are contraries between which there are intermediates, as, for instance, blackness and whiteness, for, again, as he says, "it is not necessary that either the one or the other should be present in the body, inasmuch as it is not true to say that everybody must be white or black." [75] Still less does it apply to cases where the predicates are opposites of the type which Aristotle describes as "privation" (στέρησις) and "habit" (ἕξις),[76] of which the examples mentioned by him are "blindness" and "sight," [77] "toothless" and "having teeth," [78] "bald-headed" and "long-haired" (κομήτης).[79] In connection with such opposites, he says that "it is a universal rule that the pair of opposites of this type has reference to that to which the particular habit is natural." [80] Accordingly, it is only of a subject which by nature has sight that by the Law of Excluded Middle one cannot say that it is neither seeing nor blind, but of a subject which by nature is excluded from the universe of discourse of both sight and blindness one can say that it is both not seeing and not blind. So also here, they would argue, God is excluded from the universe of temporary life and its privation death. One can, therefore, say of Him that He is neither dead nor living. As for the term "living," which out of a sense of piety is used as a predication of God, they would explain, it refers to a life which is unlike the temporary life of created living beings.

We can anticipate what Ibn Ṣaddiḳ's refutation of this answer would be. He would argue as follows: If by the expression "God is living" you mean "God is not dead," then what need is there for adding the phrase "not in virtue of life," which, we agree, means "and He is not living?" You are indeed quite right in saying that of a subject which by nature is excluded from the universe of the opposites of habit and priva-

[74] *Categ.*, 10, 12a, 6–8.
[75] *Ibid.*, 12–13.
[76] *Ibid.*, 26.
[77] *Ibid.*, 27.
[78] *Ibid.*, 31–32.
[79] *Ibid.*, 13a, 35.
[80] *Ibid.*, 12a, 27–29.

tion one may negate both the habit and the privation. But while one may do so, it is really not always necessary to do so. In the case of a subject which is known to be excluded from the universe of a certain habit and its privation, one can negate of it either only the habit or only the privation, without having to negate also its respective opposite. Thus Alexander Aphrodisiensis in his commentary on Aristotle's *Metaphysics* says with regard to the opposites "blindness" and "sight" that in the case of a "wall," being as it is excluded from the universe of both these opposites, one cannot use the affirmative proposition "the wall is blind," but, inasmuch as one can logically say "the wall does not see," [81] one can use the negative proposition "the wall is not seeing," and presumably one can also use the negative proposition "the wall is not blind" and presumably also, since the negation of neither of these predicates implies the affirmation of its opposite, in neither of these two negative propositions is it necessary to add the negation of the respective opposites of their predicates. And so here, what need is there for adding to the statement "God is not dead" the unseemly sounding statement "and He is not living?"

With all this in the back of his mind, Ibn Ṣaddiḳ says: "When a subject is not susceptible of a certain predicate, it does not necessarily follow that it is susceptible of its opposite, for the subject may be of the kind that [by its very nature] is not susceptible of either the one or the other, that is, of either one of what in Arabic is called *al-ṣifatāni*, the-pair-of-predicates, in which case we cannot reasonably argue that, inasmuch as [we say that] the subject is not susceptible of the predication of death, we should say that it is susceptible of

[81] Alexander in *Metaphysica*, ed. M. Hayduck, p. 327, ll. 18–20, on *Metaph.* IV, 6, 1011b, 15 ff. τὸ γὰρ οὐχ ὁρᾷ καὶ ἐπὶ τοῦ τυφλοῦ ἀληθὲς καὶ ἐπὶ τοῦ τοίχου, ὅς οὐδὲ ὅλως ὄψεως δεκτικός . . . οὐχ οὕτω καὶ ἡ τυφλότης. This passage is the source of Maimonides' statement "as, for instance, we say of a wall that it is not seeing" (*Moreh Nebukim* I, 58), which is used by him for the purpose of showing that to negate of God any such predicate as "life" means His exclusion from the universe of discourse of both "life" and its opposite "death." (Cf. my paper "Maimonides on Negative Attributes," pp. 425 ff.)

the predication of life. Thus, for instance, in the case of a stone, when we say of it that it is not long-bearded (*alḥā*), it does not mean that it is as yet only covered with down (*amrad*),[82] for by its very nature it is not susceptible of either of these predicates: so also, when we say of a stone that it is not having teeth, [it does not mean that sometime it may have teeth], for by its very nature it is not disposed to be the recipient of that predicate [of having teeth]; so also, when we say of the rational soul that it is not triangular, it does not imply that it is a square or any of the other figures, for by its very nature it has no figure at all; so also, when we say of it

[82] Of the two Arabic words in this passage, which appear in corrupted Hebrew transliteration in the various manuscripts, the first was emended by Horovitz to read *multaḥan,* "bearded." I prefer to emend it to read *alḥa,* "*long-bearded.*" Cf. Horovitz, "Introduction," p. XIV, and Vajda, p. 148.

In connection with this passage, Horovitz (*ibid.*) quotes from Themistius' paraphrase of the *Physics*, ed. Spengel, p. 145 [ed. Schenkl, p. 27, ll. 2–4] the following ἐφ' ὧν γοῦν ἀληθὴς ἀπόφασις, ἡ στέρησις οὐ συνέπεται. οὐ γὰρ ἐφ' ὧν τὸ μὴ δίκαιον, καὶ τὸ ἄδικον, οὐδὲ ἐφ' ὧν τὸ μὴ κομῶν, καὶ τὸ φαλακεόν.

In this quotation, Themistius, like Alexander, quoted in the preceding note, makes the point that of a subject which is excluded from the universe of discourse of a certain "habit" and its "privation" one can negate the habit but not affirm the privation. His illustrative examples, however, call for some comment. Translated, Themistius' statement reads as follows: "With reference to [certain] things of which negation is true, privation is inapplicable to them. For, concerning that of which one may say that it is not just, one cannot [always] say that it is unjust and, concerning that of which one may say that it is not wearing long hair, one cannot [always] say that it is bald." In my translation of this statement I have added within brackets the qualifying terms "certain" before "things" and "always" after "cannot" for the following reason: According to Aristotle, as we have seen, of the inanimate wall one may use only the negative proposition "the wall does not see" but not the privative proposition "the wall is blind," whereas of a man one may use both the negative proposition "the man is not seeing" and the privative proposition "the man is blind" (cf. quotation from Alexander in n. 81 above). Thus also, according to Aristotle, one may use of rational human beings both the negative proposition "they are not just" and the privative proposition "they are unjust," for they may be something intermediate between the two extremes (cf. *Categ.* 10, 12a, 10–25). It is only in such cases as irrational animals, being as they are excluded from the universe of discourse of both justice and injustice, that one can say only that they are not just but one cannot say that they are unjust. Similarly, it is only in the case of creatures which by nature can have no hair, but not of creatures which have not yet reached the stage when having hair is natural to them, that one can say that they are not wearing long hair but one cannot say that they are bald.

that it is not red, it does not imply that it is black or white or any of the other colors, for by its very nature it has no color at all. So also God is by His very nature not susceptible of the predication of either death or life." [83] The conclusion he wants us to draw is that the simple negative formula "God is not dead" or the simple positive formula "God is living" interpreted either as an action or as implying the two kinds of negation is the proper way for one to express himself in praise of the divine perfections.

While the first two arguments were aimed merely at the formula used by al-Baṣīr in expressing his belief in modes, the third argument is aimed at the theory of modes itself. The argument, however, is not the commonly used stock argument that the theory of modes is an infringement upon the Law of Excluded Middle. It is an entirely new argument. Ibn Ṣaddiḳ, in his restatement of al-Baṣīr's formula, as we have seen, took al-Baṣīr's conception of modes to mean that, though the modes do not exist in God as in a subject, they have some kind of existence. Now Ibn Ṣaddiḳ himself, early in his work, restated what was a common philosophic view that everything that exists must either exist in itself, in which case it is a substance, or exist in something else, in which case it is an accident.[84] Consequently, since modes have some kind of existence, that kind of existence of theirs must be either in themselves or in something else, neither of which, he tries to show, is possible. To quote: "Those descriptive predicates of God, concerning which their opinion is that they are [of some kind of existence, but of an existence which is] not [in God as] in a subject must inevitably either exist in themselves or in something else. Now if they existed in themselves, then [they would be substances and thus] God would acquire His knowledge and life from eternal substances, which eternal substances would be entitled more than God to be considered as necessary with regard to perfection. And if those descriptive predicates existed in something else, then they would be accidents

[83] *'Olam Ḳaṭan*, p. 46, l. 21–p. 47, l. 4.

[84] *Ibid.*, p. 8, l. 17–p. 9, l. 6.

in substances, so that it would be those substances together with their accidents which would cause God to acquire [the perfections described by] those predicates."[85]

In my interpretation of Ibn Ṣaddiḳ's three arguments against the formula "God is living not in virtue of life; He is powerful not in virtue of power; He is knowing not in virtue of knowledge," I tried to show that in his first two arguments he aimed only at the phrasing of the formula, contending that its phrasing would lead to certain logical difficulties. As such, these two arguments could have been urged by him equally against those who used this formula in the sense of a denial of attributes as against those who used it in the sense of the affirmation of modes. He chose, however, to urge them against al-Baṣīr, who used the formula in the sense of the affirmation of modes. And since he chose to use these two arguments as arguments against the mere phrasing of the formula as used by al-Baṣīr as an expression of his belief in the theory of modes, he added a third argument directed against the theory of modes itself. The third argument, it is to be noted, could not apply to those who used this formula in the sense of the absolute denial of attributes.

5. JUDAH HALEVI

In his restatement of the view of the Antiattributists among the Mutakallimūn, Judah Halevi reproduces two formulae about divine attributes. The first formula, which is approved of by them, reads as follows: "God is living in virtue of the life of His essence, which is not acquired, and similarly He is powerful in virtue of His own power and willing in virtue of His own will,"[1] wherein evidently the expressions "in virtue

[85] *Ibid.*, p. 47, ll. 5–7.

[1] *Cuzari* V, 18 (10), p. 336, ll. 8–9; p. 337, ll. 5–6. On the basis of the reading in the Hebrew version, which is supported by the context, I have emended the Arabic on p. 336, l. 9, to read *bi-ḳudratihi* and *bi-irādatihi*. Schreiner (*Polemik*, p. 625), on the basis of a passage in Ghazālī's *Iḥyā'*, emended these two terms to read *bi-ḳudratin* and *bi-irādatin*. But this seems to me to be wrong, for the formula used by Ghazālī in that passage of the

of His own power" and "in virtue of His own will" are used by him in the sense of "in virtue of the power of His essence, which is not acquired" and "in virtue of the will of His essence, which is not acquired." The second formula is contained in a passage which, in the printed Arabic text, reads as follows: "For it is impossible for a thing and its contradictory to exist at the same time, and therefore one cannot simply say: 'He is powerful not in virtue of power.' "[2]

Of the two formulae mentioned here by Halevi, the first, and approved one, reflects the formula "God is knowing in virtue of himself (*li-nafsihi*)," which is used by the Antiattributists Najjār[3] and Ḍirār,[4] and the formula "God is knowing in virtue of His essence (*li-dhātihi*)," which is used by the Antiattributist Jubbā'ī.[5] The second formula, which Halevi quotes with disapproval on the ground that "it is impossible for a thing and its contrary to exist at the same time" is exactly the formula which, as we have seen, was used by 'Abbād b. Sulaymān as a denial of attributes and by Joseph al-Baṣīr as an affirmation of modes.[6] Its use by al-Baṣīr as an affirmation of modes has been rejected by Joseph Ibn Ṣaddiḳ, as we have seen, on the ground that in its phrasing the formula is self-contradictory, but, as we have remarked,[7] on the mere ground of its phrasing, it would be rejected by him even if used in the sense of an absolute denial of attributes. Halevi's rejection of it here on the ground of its being self-contradictory similarly means that on the mere ground of its phrasing it is to be rejected even when used in the sense of an absolute denial of attributes.[8]

Iḥyā' is meant to affirm the reality of attributes, whereas the formula reproduced here by Halevi is meant to deny the reality of attributes.

[2] *Cuzari* V, 18 (10), p. 336, ll. 9–10; p. 337, ll. 6–7.

[3] Cf. *Kalam*, p. 223.

[4] *Ibid.*

[5] Cf. *Ibid.*, p. 229.

[6] Cf. above, p. 61.

[7] Cf. above, p. 71.

[8] Cf. discussion of this second formula in *Ḳol Yehudah* and *Oṣar Neḥmad, ad loc.*; David Cassel, *Das Buch Kuzari* (1869), p. 413, n. 4; Hartwig Hirschfeld, *Das Buch Al-Chazarī* (1885), p. 269, n. 2; David Kaufmann, *Attributenlehre* (1877), p. 270, n. 50; S. Horovitz, *Psychologie* (1906), p. 155, n. 23.

6. MAIMONIDES *

Maimonides mentions various types of formulae for divine attributes which are rejected by him.

First, referring to those who believe in attributes, he says that some of them enumerate them "as things superadded to the essence." [1] This is the formula used by some Ash'arites.[2]

Second, referring, again, to those who believe in attributes, he quotes in their name the Ash'arite formula that "God is knowing in virtue of knowledge." [3] He rejects it even though those who use it take the term "knowledge" in the sense of a knowledge which is one, unchangeable, and eternal.[4]

Third, referring to "some people of speculation," he ascribes to them the formula that "the attributes of God are neither His essence nor anything extraneous to His essence." [5] Maimonides rejects it not only when used in the sense of the affirmation of attributes but also when used in the sense of the affirmation of modes.[6]

Fourth, referring to certain people of whom he says that, though it is clear that they believe in attributes, "they do not express themselves in clear-cut language," he ascribes to them the formula that "God is powerful in virtue of His essence, knowing in virtue of His essence, living in virtue of His essence, and willing in virtue of His essence." [7] The people whom Maimonides criticizes here are, as I have shown, not only Attributists but also Modalists, and the reason why he describes them as those who "do not express themselves in

* See also my papers "The Aristotelian Predicables and Maimonides' Division of Attributes," *Essays and Studies in Memory of Linda R. Miller* (1938), pp. 201–234; "Maimonides on Negative Attributes," *Louis Ginzberg Jubilee Volume* (1945), pp. 411–446; "Maimonides and Gersonides on Divine Attributes as Ambiguous Terms," *Mordecai M. Kaplan Jubilee Volume* (1953), pp. 515–530.

[1] *Moreh* I, 53, p. 82, ll. 1–2.

[2] *Nihāyat*, p. 181, ll. 1–4; *Kashf*, p. 56, ll. 5 and 7.

[3] *Moreh* I, 60, p. 98, ll. 22–24; *Milal*, p. 67, l. 8; cf. *Kalam*, p. 212.

[4] *Moreh* I, 60, p. 98, l. 24–p. 99, l. 1; cf. my paper "Maimonides on Negative Attributes," pp. 440–441.

[5] *Moreh* I, 51, p. 76, ll. 25–26.

[6] Cf. above, p. 32.

[7] *Moreh* I, 53, p. 82, ll. 2–4.

clear-cut language" is that the same formula is also used by Antiattributists. But though this formula is also used by Antiattributists, Maimonides, as I have suggested, would disapprove of it on the ground that it is equally used by Attributists and Modalists.[8]

The formulae used by Maimonides himself as an expression of his denial of attributes are two: (1) "God's essence is His knowledge and His knowledge is His essence," which he quotes with approval in the name of "the philosophers," [9] and (2) "He is existing not in virtue of existence, and similarly living not in virtue of life, powerful not in virtue of power, knowing not in virtue of knowledge," [10] of which type of formula he says elsewhere that it has been demonstrated "in the divine science, that is, metaphysics." [11] Of these two types of formulae, the first reflects the formula ascribed to the Muʿtazilites as well as to the philosophers, namely, that "the knowledge of the Creator is the Creator" [12] or that "the meaning of knowledge [predicated of God] is an affirmation of the essence of the Creator." [13] Similarly, the second formula has been used in the sense of the denial of attributes by the Muʿtazilite ʿAbbād b. Sulaymān.[14] Though Joseph al-Baṣīr has used the same formula in the sense of the affirmation of modes [15] and though both Joseph Ibn Ṣaddiḳ [16] and Judah Halevi [17] have rejected it, Maimonides makes no reference or allusion to them.

III. Christology

As in the case of the Trinity so also in the case of Christology the original sources of Judaism could not furnish the Jews of Muslim countries with an adequate knowledge of

[8] Cf. above, pp. 39–40.
[9] *Moreh* III, 20, p. 348, l. 28.
[10] *Ibid.* I, 57, p. 90, l. 10; *Mishneh Torah: Yesode ha-Torah* II, 10.
[11] *Shemonah Peraḳim* 8, p. 37, ll. 8–10.
[12] *Maḳālāt*, p. 173, l. 15.
[13] *Ibid.*, p. 174, l. 9; cf. *Kalam*, p. 217.
[14] *Ibid.*, p. 166, ll. 1–2, 6–8.
[15] Cf. above, p. 61.
[16] Cf. above, p. 63.
[17] Cf. above, p. 72.

that doctrine. From their own original sources they could get only such possible allusions to some semblance of Christology as the statement that God says "I have no father . . . I have no brother . . . I have no son," which occurs in a comment on the verse "I am Jehovah, thy God" (Exod. 20:2),[1] or that "if a man says 'I am God,' he lies," which occurs in a comment on the verse "God is not a man, that He should lie" (Num. 23:19),[2] or that an angel came down and smote Nebuchadnezzar on the face, saying, "Hath God a Son?" which occurs in a comment on the verse quoting Nebuchadnezzar as saying, "and the form of the fourth is like the son of God" (Dan. 3:25).[3] The Arabic-speaking Muslims, however, through their contact with the Christian population among them, had become acquainted with some of the fine points about this doctrine, and they also knew of the division of opinion about it among the Christians themselves, though their descriptions of this variety of views may sometimes puzzle the student of Christian doctrine. Out of such works the Jews in Muslim countries learned something of the various views on Christology current among Christians. Let us then see how this knowledge is reflected in Jewish writings of the time.

Isolated references to the Christian doctrine of the Incarnation are to be found in the works of some Karaite authors. Thus Ḳirḳisānī, after restating the Christian doctrine of the Trinity and mentioning the three hypostases, the Father, the Son, and the Spirit, adds: "And the Son is Jesus and he is divine-human, for the Creator, who is the substance, was united with him."[4] Then Joseph al-Baṣīr, referring to the Incarnation, writes of the Christians: "They say that God and the Nazarene Jesus became one after the analogy of the mixture of wine and water or of fire and coals."[5] Such analogies are common in the literature of the Church Fathers.[6] But they

[1] *Exodus Rabbah* 29, 5.

[2] *Jer. Ta'aniyot* II, 1, 65b.

[3] *Jer. Shabbat* VI, 10, 8d.

[4] *Anwār* I, 8, 3, p. 43, l. 14. Cf. *Kalam*, p. 312 n. 6.

[5] *Ne'imot* 18, fol. 24a.

[6] *The Philosophy of the Church Fathers*, I, pp. 378, 381, 398, 399, 405.

occur also in Arabic literature. Thus Ibn Ḥazm reports that "the Jacobites say that it is like the union of water with wine . . . and the Malkites say it is like the union of fire with a heated iron." [7] Shahrastānī, speaking of the Jacobites, says that "in the same way it is said the coal became fire." [8] Finally, Judah Hadassi, after mentioning the Trinity of the Father and the Son and the Holy Spirit, says: "And His is the Son, who became clothed with flesh in the fashion of men." [9]

The fullest discussion of the views of the various Christian sects on Christology is to be found in the Rabbinite Saadia.[10] He enumerates four sects, three of whom he describes as older and one as that which had appeared only recently. It would be futile to identify these four sects with any of the sects known to us from modern works on the history of Christian doctrine; attempts made by students of Saadia to identify these sects by that method have proved only confusing.[11] We must go to descriptions of Christian sects in Arabic sources for the identification of these four sects enumerated by Saadia. Though the sources which we shall quote come from a time after Saadia, they undoubtedly reproduce Christological views as understood by Muslim writers at the time of Saadia.

The first sect is described by Saadia as that which believes that "both the body and the spirit of their Messiah are from the Creator." [12] Before we try to identify this sect, let us com-

[7] *Fiṣal*, I, p. 53, ll. 16–17, 18–19.

[8] *Milal*, p. 177, ll. 10–11.

[9] Portion omitted in the printed *Eshkol ha-Kofer*, *JQR*, 8: 432 (1896).

[10] *Emunot* II, 7, p. 90, l. 17–p. 91, l. 16.

[11] Here are attempts to identify these four sects by the following authors: Kaufmann, *Attributenlehre*, pp. 50–51; Guttmann, *Saadia*, pp. 108–113; Neumark, *Geschichte*, Zweiter Band 2, pp. 191–192; Ventura, *Saadia*, p. 184.

Kaufmann: (1) No identification; (2) Apollinaris; (3) Theodore of Mopsuestia; (4) Ebionites and Monarchians.

Guttmann: (1) Monarchianism and Sabellius; (2) Arianism; (3) Paul of Samosata; (4) [Spanish] Adoptianism.

Neumark: (1) Monophysites; (2) Dyophysites; (3) and (4) No identification.

Ventura: (1) Docetism of various Gnostic leaders; (2) Chalcedonian Creed; (3) Roman Adoptianism; (4) Spanish Adoptianism.

[12] *Emunot* II, 7, p. 90, l. 18.

ment on the terms "body" and "spirit" which are used by Saadia in his description of the various views of these sects on Christology. These two terms, we take it, stand for what in Christological controversies is known as the contrast between the "humanity" (*al-nāsūt*, ἀνθρωπότης) and "divinity" (*al-lāhūt*, θεότης) in Jesus, for it is the question of the "humanity" and "divinity" in Jesus, and in the case of Apollinaris also the question of "soul" or of "rational soul" in Jesus and not of "body" and "spirit" in him, that was the main point at issue in the Christological controversies. A similar use of the term "spirit," in the sense of "divinity," in contrast to "body," in the sense of "humanity," is implied in a passage in Shahrastānī, where, comparing two ways in which Christians explain the union of the Word with the body in Jesus, he reports that they either say that "it appears in it like the appearance of the spiritual in the corporeal" or they say that "the divinity puts on the humanity as a breastplate." [13] Taken in this sense, the statement that "both the body and the spirit of their Messiah are from God" means a denial of humanity or of a human nature in Jesus, and the sect thus described here by Saadia is to be identified with the Monophysites or, as they are known to the Muslims, the Jacobites. The Jacobites are described by the Muslims as believing that "the Word was transformed into flesh and blood, so that God became the Messiah and was manifest in his body, or rather He was himself the Messiah." [14] This is exactly what Saadia meant to say about the first sect, for from his subsequent criticism of this sect, it is clear that his statement that "both the body and the spirit . . . are from God" means that "some part of God became body and spirit." [15]

The second sect is described by him as that which believes that "his body was created but his spirit is from the Creator." [16]

[13] *Milal*, p. 172, ll. 6–7.
[14] *Ibid.*, p. 179, ll. 19–20; cf. Ibn Ḥazm, *Fiṣal* I, p. 49, l. 9.
[15] *Emunot* II, 7, p. 91, ll. 5–6.
[16] *Ibid.*, p. 90, l. 19.

This reflects exactly the following Muslim conception of the Nestorians: "They maintain that Mary did not give birth to God; she gave birth only to the man; and that God did not beget the man; He begot only the God."[17] What Saadia therefore means to say of the second sect is that they believed that the humanity in Jesus was created, that is to say, was given birth by Mary, but that the divinity in him was "from the Creator," that is to say, was begotten by God.

The third sect is described by him as that which believes that "both his body and his spirit were created, but that there was in him another spirit from the Creator."[18] This formula, I take it, is made up of two formulations of the Christology ascribed by Muslim writers to the Malkites, that is, to those who followed the Decree of Chalcedon (451). The first part of Saadia's formula, namely, "both his body and his spirit were created," reflects exactly that formulation of the Malkites' view which reads: "Mary bore the God and the man."[19] The second part of Saadia's formula, namely, "but there was in him another spirit from the Creator," reflects that formulation of the Malkites' view which, after stating that the Malkites believe that in Jesus there are two natures, a human and a divine, adds that they believe also "that the Messiah is a hypostasis (*aḳnūm*) of the nature of God only, and it is a nature uncompounded, [not] derived from the two aforementioned natures, and has union with man universal."[20] This formulation of the Malkite view thus emphasizes that the one "person" or "hypostasis" in the Chalcedonian formula "two natures . . . in one person and one hypostasis"[21] is derived from a source other than the two natures. It is a formu-

[17] *Fiṣal* I, 7, p. 49, ll. 6–7.

[18] *Emunot* II, 7, p. 90, ll. 19–20.

[19] *Fiṣal* I, p. 49, l. 4.

[20] *Al Ghazālī: Réfutation Excellente de la Divinité de Jésus Christ d'après les Évangiles*, Texte établi, traduit et commenté par Robert Chidiac (1939), p. 32, ll. 12–15 of the text and cf. correction of reading on p. 87 of the introductory material.

[21] See Denzinger et Bannwart, *Enchiridion Symbolorum* 14–15 (1922), p. 148.

lation like this of the Malkite view that we have reason to assume to be the basis of Saadia's statement that "there was in him another spirit from the Creator," the term "spirit" thus referring here to the one "hypostasis." It is to be noted, however, that what the Chalcedonian formula really means is that of the two natures in Jesus, the divine and the human, the divine nature, that is, the Word, is both a person and a nature, whereas the human nature is only a nature; and, therefore, it is the divine nature in Jesus, the Word, that constitutes the one person or one hypostasis that he is.[22]

That the conception of the Incarnation held by this third sect represents the orthodox view of the Malkites may be shown by a statement which occurs in Saadia's criticism of this sect. It reads as follows: "The adherents of this sect cite as an analogy to their conception of the Incarnation the descent of the glory of God on Mount Sinai and its appearance in the Bush and the Tent of Meeting." [23] This analogy is used by Abucara, in his Arabic work to which we have referred before, in defense of the orthodox conception of the Incarnation. He says: "It is to be astonished at those who deny the descent of God in this human body, which, as we have truly said, is the noblest of His creatures, that they do not deny his descent in the Bush, out of the midst of which He talked with Moses, and His descent in the pillar of a cloud, in which He came down into the tent of Moses and out of which He talked with Moses and in the presence of which every one of the people of Israel worshiped at the tent door in which he happened to be." [24]

Thus the first three sects mentioned by Saadia are the Jacobites, the Nestorians, and the Malkites, those whom Muslim historiographers describe as "their fundamental sects (*'umdatuhum*)" [25] or "their main (*kibār*) sects." [26] These three

[22] On the meaning of this, see the chapter on "The Mystery of the Incarnation," in my *Philosophy of the Church Fathers*, I, pp. 364–433.

[23] *Emunot* II, 7, p. 91, ll. 9–10.

[24] Abucara, *Mimar* VI, 6, 7, p. 183; cf. Exod. 33: 9–10.

[25] *Fiṣal* I, p. 48, l. 22.

[26] *Milal*, p. 173, l. 11.

sects, while differing in their Christological views, were all orthodox in their view on the Trinity, as is testified by Yaḥyā Ibn ʿAdi, who says that, with regard to the orthodox conception of the Trinity, "the three sects" are fully in agreement.[27] Ordinarily, in Muslim works dealing with Christianity, the Malkites are mentioned first, then come the Nestorians and the Jacobites,[28] and the Malkites are described by Masʿūdī as "the pillar (*ʿimād*) and the pivot (*ḳuṭb*) of the Christians,"[29] and by Ibn Ḥazm as "the most important of the three sects (*aʿẓamuhā*)."[30] Saadia, however, as will have been noticed, reverses the order, putting the Jacobites first and then the Nestorians and Malkites. The explanation, it seems to me, is that Saadia has arranged these sects in the order of his direct acquaintance with them. Born in Egypt, where he lived up to the age of twenty-three or thirty-three, he first became acquainted with the Jacobite view, for in Egypt the Jacobites were the dominant Christian sect. Then when he settled down in Iraq he became acquainted with the Nestorian Christology, for in Iraq the Nestorians were the dominant Christian sect. The Malkites who flourished mainly in Christian countries and in Muslim Spain always remained to him a far-off sect, which he knew only by hearsay. He therefore puts them last. So also, it may be added, the work on the refutation of the divinity of Jesus, attributed to Ghazālī,[31] which was written in Egypt,[32] in its dealing with the Christologies of these three sects, similarly puts the Jacobites first.

The fourth sect is described by Saadia as those who "assign to him the position of prophet only, interpreting the sonship of which they make mention when they speak of him just as we interpret the Biblical expression 'Israel is my first-born son' (Exod. 4:2), which is merely an expression of esteem and

[27] Périer, *Petits,* p. 55, ll. 1 ff.

[28] Masʿūdī, *Murūj* I, p. 200; *Tanbīh,* p. 154, l. 4 (French, p. 212), but on p. 142, l. 11 (French, p. 196), the order is: Malkites, Jacobites, Nestorians; *Fiṣal* I, pp. 48, l. 49; *Milal,* pp. 173, 175, 176.

[29] *Murūj* I, p. 200.

[30] *Fiṣal* I, p. 48, l. 3.

[31] Cited above, note 20.

[32] *Ibid.*, pp. 25–34.

high regard, or as others (Muslims) interpret the description of Abraham as the 'friend' of God (Surah 4:124)." [33] On the face of it, this description reflects the various heretical Christologies which shared in common the denial of the divinity of Jesus, such as the Christology of the followers of Paul of Samosata, which was known to the Muslims as the view that "Jesus was the servant of God and His apostle like all the other prophets" [34] or that "he was an upright created servant"; [35] and as the Christology of the Arians, which was known to the Muslims as the view that "Jesus was a created servant"; [36] and as the Christology of the Macedonians, which was known to the Muslims as the view that "Jesus was a created servant, a man, a prophet, an apostle of God like the rest of the prophets." [37] All these heretical Christologies may be described as reflecting the Ebionitic type of Christology, which was one of the three types of Christology that had existed in Christianity from the earliest time.[38] Ebionites as a sect or as a group of sects, it may be remarked, had disappeared before the rise of Islam and no longer existed at the time of Saadia. It is the common Christology of these three heretical sects that would thus seem to be reflected in Saadia's fourth sect. But there is the following question. Inasmuch as this type of Christology was known to the Muslims to have been shared by three sects and these sects were known to them to antedate the Nestorians and the Jacobites, why does Saadia designate those who follow this type of Christology as a single sect [39] and why does he describe them as a sect which appeared only recently?

The explanation which I should like to suggest is that, though the Christological view ascribed by Saadia to this fourth sect is exactly like that of the Samosatenians, Arians,

[33] *Emunot* II, 7, p. 90, l. 21–p. 91, l. 2.

[34] *Fiṣal* I, p. 48, ll. 13–14.

[35] *Milal*, p. 176, l. 12.

[36] *Fiṣal* I, p. 48, l. 9.

[37] *Ibid.*, ll. 19–20.

[38] Cf. section on "Heresies with Regard to the Born Christ" in *The Philosophy of the Church Fathers*, I, pp. 587–606.

[39] *Emunot* II, 7, p. 91, l. 3.

and Macedonians, it is not any of these sects that he has reference to here. His reference here is rather to an entirely new sect which we have reason to believe arose among Christians shortly before Saadia's birth in the same part of the Muslim world in which Saadia wrote his book. It happens that the Koran, while rejecting the orthodox Christian type of Christology, upholds the Ebionitic type of Christology in such verses as "And they say, God hath a son. No!" (2:110); "The Messiah, Jesus, son of Mary, is only an apostle of God" (4:169); "The Messiah, son of Mary, is only an apostle" (5:79). We know that debates between Christians and Muslims on this Christological view had been going on ever since their first encounter. We know that Christians as a minority group in Muslim countries were not entirely impervious to Muslim influence. We know also that the Christian Arabic literature, through its discussions of all sides of the Christological problems, had kept alive among Christians in Muslim countries a knowledge of the Ebionitic type of Christology of the heretical Samosatenians, Arians, and Macedonians and also a knowledge of all the arguments in favor of it. What with all this, is it not possible that a certain group of Christians in Muslim countries, shortly before the time of Saadia, succumbed to Muslim influence and adopted a type of Christology that was more agreeable to their Muslim masters? That the Christology of this fourth sect was advanced in an effort to accommodate itself to the Muslim environment is indicated by the fact that one of the ways, mentioned by Saadia, whereby this sect tried to explain why, with their denial of the divinity of Jesus, they still continued to call him son of God, was by referring to the Muslim explanation of the expression "Abraham, the friend of God," which had come into use on the basis of the Koranic verse "And God took Abraham for His friend" (4:124).[40]

Evidence that such a Christological view was held by a certain group of Nestorians in Iraq at the time of Saadia is

[40] *Ibid.*, p. 91, l. 2.

found in Shahrastānī's account of Nestorianism. On the basis of that account, I have shown how at about the beginning of the ninth century, under the impact of Islam, a modified formula for the Trinity appeared among certain Nestorians in Iraq.[41] Now in that same account of Nestorianism, Shahrastānī ascribes to one group of Nestorians a conception of Christology which reads as follows: "The Messiah took his origin from Mary; he is a righteous servant and created, except that God has honored him because of his obedience and called him 'son' by adoption and not by begetting and union."[42] This is exactly the Christological view ascribed here by Saadia to the fourth sect of which he says that it "appeared only recently." What we have here, then, is that a certain group of Nestorians — of whom Saadia knew that as a sect it "appeared only recently," that is, about seventy years before he was born (882) — during the reign of Caliph Ma'mūn (813–833) in an attempt to accommodate their belief about Jesus with that held by the Muslims, rephrased their original Nestorian Christological formula into an Ebionitic form of Christology. That they should have done so is not surprising. From its very beginning Nestorianism was variously represented. Already during the lifetime of its founder, two Latin Church Fathers represented it as an Ebionitic Christology, like that we have quoted from Shahrastānī, even, like Shahrastānī, comparing it to the Christology of Photinus and Paul of Samosata. Thus Cassian compares the Nestorian heresy to the Ebionitic and Photinian heresies and describes it as believing that Christ is a mere man (*homo solitarius*),[43] and Marius Mercator finds that Nestorius, like Paul of Samosata, believed that Christ is the son of God only as a reward of good actions and by adoption, not by nature (*pro meritis, et ex adoptione, non ex natura*).[44]

In criticism of all these conceptions of the Incarnation and

[41] *Kalam*, pp. 337–349.

[42] *Milal*, p. 176, ll. 10–13; cf. *Ibid* p. 348.

[43] *De Incarnatione Christi, Adversus Nestorium* I, 2 (PL 50, 18–19), and V, 2 (98 f.).

[44] *Epistola de Discrimine, etc.* 2 (PL 48, 773 B).

the Messiahship of Jesus, with its concomitant belief in the abrogation of the Law, Saadia refers to his arguments elsewhere in his book that the Messiah is yet to come [45] and that the Law was not to pass away.[46] In special criticism of the Monophysite view, he refers to his argument against the theory that the corporeal world was derived from God's own essence.[47] In special criticism of the Malkite view, he argues that it implies that a created body could become God through the association with it of something divine. In special criticism of the Nestorian view, he says that it is subject to his two special arguments against the Monophysites and the Malkites.

A precise description of the Christian doctrine of Christology, according to one of its interpretations, is to be found also in the *Cuzari*. It reads as follows: "The Godhead (*al-lāhūtiyyah*: *ha-'elohut*) was incarnated and became an embryo in the womb of the virgin from the noblest ranks of the Israelitish women. She gave birth to him, a being visibly human but invisibly divine, visibly a prophet sent forth but invisibly a God come down. He is the Messiah, who is called the Son of God." [48] In this presentation of the Christian doctrine of the Logos, the following two things are to be noticed:

First, the contrast between "visibly human" and "invisibly divine." This reflects the interpretation of the New Testament verse "Who is the image of the invisible God" (Col. 1:15), as given by Theodore of Mopsuestia. According to his interpretation, it means that the born Christ is the "image," that is, the visible man, of the "invisible God," that is, of the pre-existent Christ. Nearly all the orthodox patristic writers interpret the verse to mean that the pre-existent Christ is the "image," that is, an invisible image, of the "invisible God." [49]

Second, the statement that Mary gave birth to a man insofar as visible, and to a God only insofar as invisible. This reflects the view of both Theodore of Mopsuestia and Nestorius,

[45] *Emunot* VIII, 7–9.

[46] *Ibid.* III, 7–10.

[47] *Ibid.* I, 2, 3rd Theory.

[48] *Cuzari* I, 4, p. 10, ll. 3–6; p. 11, ll. 3–6.

[49] Cf. H. B. Swete, *Theodori Episcopi Mopsuesteni in Epistolas B. Pauli Commentarii*, I, 261, l. 18, n., and *ibid.*, p. 264, ll. 6–7.

according to which the proper designation of Mary is ανθρωποτόκος, "man-bearing," because it was a man whom she gave birth to, and if she is also to be called θεοτόκος, "God-bearing," it is only because God was incarnate in the man she brought forth.[50]

IV. The Pre-existent Koran and the Pre-existent Law

When the Jews in Arabic-speaking countries learned of the Muslim belief in a pre-existent uncreated Koran called the Word of God and when from Christian literature they also learned of the Christian belief in a pre-existent Christ called also the Word of God, they must have reminded themselves of their own Word of God which was the Torah. According to the rabbinic lore, they must have further reminded themselves, the Word of God in the sense of the Torah, like the Muslim Word of God and the Christian Word of God, was also pre-existent, but, unlike the Muslim Word and the Christian Word, this Word in the sense of the Torah, though pre-existent, was not uncreated; it was created prior to the creation of the world.[1] It is therefore interesting to know what repercussion these new Muslim and Christian views about the Word of God had in Judaism.

1. Minor Midrashim

A tacit allusion to the Muslim belief in a pre-existent uncreated Koran may possibly be discerned in a passage dealing with the tradition of a pre-existent created Torah in one of the Minor Midrashim entitled *Midrash Konen*. The passage reads as follows: "Should you say it was written down on a book, the answer is: no animal and beast were as yet created from whose skin a parchment could be made upon which to write. Should you say it was written on silver or

[50] Theodore, *De Incarnatione*, XV (PG 66, 991); F. Loofs, *Nestoriana*, Register C, p. 402, under "Maria."

[1] Cf. *Pesaḥim* 54a, *et al.*

gold or any other metals, the answer is: none of these was as yet created or smelted or mined. Should you say it was written on wood, the answer is: no trees were yet created in the world. On what then, was it written? It was written with black fire upon white fire and it was tied to the arm of God, for it is said, 'At His right hand was a fiery law unto them [Deut. 32:2]'." [1] An abridgment of this passage is quoted in *Midrash 'Aseret ha-Dibrot*,[2] another one of the Minor Midrashim, which was composed in the tenth century, presumably in Palestine.

Quite evidently the passage in *Midrash Konen* is an elaboration of a brief statement quoted in the name of the Palestinian Amora Resh Laḳish (c. 200 – c. 275), which reads as follows: "The Torah which the Holy One, blessed be He, gave to Moses, was given to him [in the form of] white fire engraved with black fire . . . for it is written, 'At His right hand was a fiery law unto them'." [3] Now if we assume that *Midrash Konen* was composed in Palestine when it was already under Muslim rule, then its elaboration on what the pre-existent Torah could not be may be taken to be aimed at a conception of the pre-existent Koran which as held by a certain Muslim sect is described as follows: "And the Ḥashwiyyah al-Mujassimah held that the separate letters, and the bodies written upon, and the colors in which the writing is executed, and everything between the two covers, are pre-existently eternal." [4] It is to be remarked that the statement "and it was tied to the arm of God" in the *Midrash Konen* may be taken to be an interpretation of the words "at His right hand" in the proof-text, for the expression "God's arm" is used in the Hebrew Scripture as the equivalent of the expression "God's right hand." [5]

[1] *Midrash Konen* (Jellinek, *Bet ha-Midrash* II, p. 23, ll. 10–15).
[2] Midrash *'Aseret ha-Dibrot* (*ibid.* I, p. 62, ll. 11–14).
[3] *Jer. Sheḳalim* VI, 1, 49d; cf. *Jer. Soṭah* VIII, 3, 22d.
[4] Ibn 'Asākir, *Tabyīn*, p. 150, ll. 15–16.
[5] Cf. Isa. 62:8; Ps. 98:1; cf. also Isa. 52:10. As for the anthropomorphism of this concluding statement in *Midrash Konen*, see discussion above, pp. 41–46.

While these two popular anonymous Midrashim accept the Talmudic lore of the pre-existence of a created Torah in its literal sense,[6] the outstanding spokesmen of Judaism of that time, we shall now see, refuse to take literally this Talmudic lore about the antemundane creation of the Torah. On this both the Rabbanites, who accepted the authority of the Talmud, and the Karaites, who rejected it, are in agreement, though their attitude toward this bit of Talmudic lore differs. All of them, Rabbanites as well as Karaites, also discuss both the Christian and the Muslim doctrine of a pre-existent Word. We shall deal here, in chronological order, with the following authors: Saadia, the Karaites, Ḳirḳisānī and Joseph al-Baṣīr, Judah Barzillai, Judah Halevi, Abraham Ibn Ezra, the Karaite Judah Hadassi, and Maimonides.

2. SAADIA

In Saadia, just as there is no direct discussion of the orthodox Muslim doctrine of attributes, so there is no direct discussion of the orthodox Muslim doctrine of an uncreated Word in the sense of an uncreated Koran; there is in his work a discussion only of the Christian doctrine of an uncreated Word in the sense of an uncreated pre-existent Christ, which is included in his general discussion of the Trinity. But the objection raised by him against the Christian doctrine applies also to its corresponding Muslim doctrine, and it was undoubtedly meant by him to be taken as a criticism of its corresponding Muslim doctrine. Also with regard to the orthodox Muslim doctrine of attributes, as we have seen, he does not criticize it directly; his criticism of it is only implied in his criticism of the Christian doctrine of the Trinity.[1]

Saadia begins his discussion of the Christian belief in the

[6] In *Genesis Rabbah* 1, 4, the pre-existent Torah is taken to be an actually created Torah. In *Midrash Tehillim*, however, while in one place (on Ps. 90:3, § 12, p. 391) it is taken to be an actually created Torah, in another place (on Ps. 93:2, § 3, p. 414) it is taken to be pre-existent only in the thought of God.

[1] Cf. above, p. 13.

eternal generation of the Word in the sense of the pre-existent Christ by reproducing what the Christians consider as Old Testament proof-texts for this belief. He reproduces six such proof-texts.

The first proof-text, which follows immediately his refutation of what he terms the Christian rational arguments for the belief in the Trinity, including the belief in an uncreated Word used in the sense of the pre-existent Christ, is introduced by him as follows: "And if they derive their proof from Scripture, as perhaps some one of them (*ba'duhum*: *ḳeṣatam*) might say: 'I see that Scripture says that God is possessed of a spirit and a word, as it is implied in its statement: The spirit of the Lord spoke by me and His word was upon my tongue' (2 Sam. 23:2), our answer thereto, etc."[2] This verse, as far as I know, was not used in any Christian work available to Saadia as proof-text for the Trinity.

The second and third proof-texts are introduced by him as follows: "Similarly I find that one of them (*ba'ḍuhum*: *ḳeṣatam*) cites [the following two verses]: 'The spirit of God hath made me, and the breath of the Almighty giveth me life' (Job 33:4) . . . 'By the word of the Lord were the heavens made, and by the breath of His mouth [all the host of them]' (Ps. 33:6)."[3] Both these verses occur in Abucara as proof-texts for the Trinity.[4]

The fourth proof-text is introduced as follows: "I also encountered one of them who interpreted the verse 'The Lord created me at the beginning of His way' (Prov. 8:22) to mean that there is with God an eternal Word, which does not cease to create together with Him (*lam tazal ma'ahu taḫluḳ*)."[5] In Abucara, this verse is quoted in one place as proof-text that the second person of the Trinity, the Word, which in this verse is called Wisdom, is eternally generated and that through

[2] *Emunot* II, 5, p. 87, l. 20–p. 88, l. 3.

[3] *Ibid.*, p. 88, ll. 11–12.

[4] *Mayamar Theodur Abi Qurra*, III, 10 (for Job 33:4), and VII, 16 (for Ps. 33/32:6).

[5] *Emunot* II, 6, p. 89, ll. 10–12.

him God created the world,[6] and in another place he interprets the verse so as to make Wisdom say: "Before the ages have I created together with God." [7]

The fifth proof-text is introduced as follows: "Again I have seen others who, basing themselves on the declaration of God 'Let us make a man in our image' (Gen. 1:26), assert that that expression points to a plurality of creators." [8] This verse is taken by the Church Fathers [9] as well as by Abucara [10] to refer to the second person of the Trinity, the Word, who is God and through whom all things were made (John 1:1, 3).

The sixth proof-text, which he ascribes simply to "others," comprises the verses "And the Lord appeared to him by the teberniths of Mamre . . . And, lo, three men stood over against him" (Gen. 18:1–2). This verse does not occur in Abucara, but it is used by the Church Fathers as proof-text for the Trinity.[11]

It is to be noted how careful Saadia is in the use of his terms. The second, third, and fourth proof-texts, which he himself must have seen used by Abucara, are introduced by the words "I find that one of them" and "I also encountered one of them." The fifth proof-text, which he himself must have seen both in Abucara and in some work of the Church Fathers, he introduces by the words "Again I have seen others." The sixth proof-text, which he has not found in Abucara but must have seen in some works of the Church Fathers is simply ascribed to "others." But the first proof-text, for which he evidently had no source, is introduced by the words "And if they derive their proof from Scripture, as perhaps someone of them might say." In other words, Saadia himself supplied the Christians with a proof-text only to refute it.

Saadia refutes all these proof-texts one by one.

[6] *Mayamar Theodur Abi Qurra*, VII, 14.

[7] *Ibid.*, III, 20.

[8] *Emunot*, II, 6.

[9] Justin Martyr, *Dial.* 62.

[10] *Mayamar Theodur Abi Qurra*, III, 20; VII, 16.

[11] Justin Martyr, *Dial.* 56 and 126; Irenaeus, *Adv. Haer.* IV, 10, 1; Eusebius, *Hist. Eccl.* I, 2, 7.

In his refutation of the first four proof-texts, Saadia draws a distinction between two meanings of the term "word," as well as of the term "spirit" when ascribed to God.

In the case of the first proof-text, which deals with a divine communication to a prophet, he says that "the terms 'spirit' and 'word' are created things, referring to the articulate speech revealed by God to his prophets."[12] What Saadia means by this is explained by himself in a passage where, commenting on the oft-repeated scriptural expression "and the Lord spoke," he says: "The real meaning of the term speech (*al-kaul*: *ha-dibbur*) implied in this expression is that God created a word (*kalām*: *dibbur*) which He conveyed through the air [in which it was created] to the hearing of the prophet or the people,"[13] to which he later adds that, at the time the word is created in the air, "God has a special light which He creates and makes manifest to prophets."[13a] In the case of the second and third proof-texts, which deal with the divine creation of things, he says that the term "word," and by implication also the term "spirit," means only the command or the will of God. To quote his own comment: "By their statement that the Creator created things by His word (*ḳaul*: *ma'mar*) the Scriptures only mean that He created them by His command (*amr*: *ṣivvuy*) or by His wish (*murād*: *ḥefeṣ*) or by His will (*mashī'ah*: *raṣon*), that is to say, He created them with design, and not purposelessly, aimlessly, and under

[12] *Emunot* II, 6, p. 88, ll. 3–4, following Arabic text as corrected by Goldziher ("Mélanges Judéo-Arabes," *REJ*, 60: 32–33 [1910], on the basis of the Hebrew translation.

[13] *Emunot* II, 12, p. 105, ll. 9–10. A view similar to that of Saadia's is quoted by Baḥya in *Kitāb Ma'ānī al-Nafs* III, p. 15, ll. 9–11, from an Arabic work, with the Hebrew title *Megillat Setarim*, by Nissim ben Jacob, which reads as follows: "The Israelites perceived the voices and saw them glittering in the midst of the cloud and the darkness and their form and lettering appeared to them in the air in the manner of ordered speech." Cf. Goldziher, "Mélanges Judéo-Arabes," *REJ*, 47: 185–186 (1903). It is undoubtedly under the influence of Saadia that Dūnash ibn Tamīm interpreted the term *ḳol*, "voice," in *Sefer Yeṣirah* to mean "a voice which God creates in the air and which He directs towards the ear of him who merits to hear it" (*Perush Sefer Yeṣirah*, p. 36, ed. Grossberg). Cf. Altmann and Stern, *Isaac Israeli*, pp. 211–212.

[13a] *Ibid.*, p. 106, l. 19.

compulsion." [14] And just as the terms "spirit" and "word" in connection with the creative activity of God in the second and third proof-texts mean that God created things by design and purpose, so also the term "wisdom" used in connection with God's creative activity in the fourth proof-text means that God created all things "wisely, so that whoever saw them would testify that a wise being had made them." [15]

Here, then, we have in Saadia a distinction between two meanings of the term "word" of God in Scripture. When used in connection with God's communication to a prophet, it refers to a real thing created by God in the air at the time of the prophetic communication. But when used in connection with the creative activity of God it refers only to the will and wisdom and design with which God performs any of His acts of creation.

This distinction drawn by Saadia between two meanings of the Word of God used in Scripture reflects the view of certain Muʿtazilites in their opposition to the orthodox Muslim view of an uncreated Koran. His distinction between the communicative word of God and the creative word of God reflects the distinction I have quoted in the name Abū al-Hudlhayl between the word of God in the sense of the message communicated by God to the Prophet and the word of God in the sense of the word "Be" with which God created the world.[16] Saadia's description of the communicative Word of God as a word created by God and conveyed by Him "through the air" to the prophets or the people who were addressed by the prophets reflects the view of Naẓẓām, traceable, as we have suggested, to Philo.[17]

Saadia's statement with regard to the communicative word

[14] *Emunot* II, 5, p. 88, ll. 13–15. Cf. his Commentary on *Sefer Yeṣirah*, chap. iv, p. 70, ll. 2–4: "When the believers say that God created the universe by a word or by a spirit or by a desire or by a will, they mean thereby only that He created every thing without coercion and without trouble and without any of the other difficulties which we encounter in the course of action."

[15] *Emunot* II, 6, p. 89, ll. 15–16; Cf. I, 3, p. 43, ll. 17 ff., Fourth refutation of the Second Theory of Creation.

[16] *Kalam*, p. 141.

[17] *Ibid.*, pp. 274–276.

that "God created a word which is conveyed through the air to the hearing of the prophet or the people" occurs, as we have seen, as a comment on the scriptural expression "and the Lord spoke." [18] Now this expression occurs in connection with God's speaking to Noah (Gen. 8:15), for instance, as well as to Moses (Exod. 6:2) and to the entire people of Israel at the revelation on Mount Sinai (Exod. 20:1, 22). When, therefore, Saadia in his comment on this expression says that the created word was conveyed through the air "to the hearing of the prophet or the people," he includes under "prophet" also Moses. Elsewhere, however, Moses is said by him, after Deuteronomy 34:10, to have been addressed by God without an intermediary, in contradistinction to all the other prophets who have been addressed by God through angels.[19] Evidently, according to Saadia, while to both Moses and the other prophets God spoke by means of a created word conveyed through the air, in the case of Moses the created word was created directly by God, whereas in the case of the other prophets the created word was created by the angels. But one thing is quite clear, that, according to Saadia, it was at the revelation of the Torah on Mount Sinai, as well as at the various revelations of the special laws to Moses, that the word which was conveyed through the air to Moses and the people was created. This quite evidently means that the Torah was created at the time the word was created. Taken by itself, this view of Saadia could imply either that he rejected the rabbinic statements about the antemundane creation of the Torah or that he followed that version of the statements according to which only the plan to create the Torah was conceived by God prior to the creation of the world.[20]

However, a direct rejection of the antemundane creation of the Torah is expressly stated by Saadia in his introduction to his lost commentary on Genesis, of which a fragment has been preserved by Judah ben Barzillai in his commentary on

[18] Cf. above, p. 90.

[19] *Emunot* II, 10, p. 100, ll. 2–6.

[20] *Midrash Tehillim* on Ps. 93:2.

Sefer Yeṣirah.[21] In that fragment, Saadia discusses the Talmudic passage in which the Torah is said to be one of the seven things that were created before the creation of the world. The sages, he says, "did not mean that these seven things were literally created prior to the creation of the world; the statement of their having been created prior to the world only means that it is for their sake, or because of them, that all things have been created." [22] From a fragment of his lost commentary on another book of the Pentateuch, Exodus, which is preserved by Abraham ibn Ezra in his comment on the verse which says concerning the tables of the Law that "the tables were the work of God" (Exod. 32:16), it may be further inferred that Saadia similarly did not follow literally the Talmudic saying that ten things, including the tables of the Law, were created on the eve of Sabbath in the twilight,[23] maintaining that the tables of the Law were created out of nothing at the time they were handed down to Moses.[24]

So much for his refutation of the first four proof-texts.

In his refutation of the fifth proof-text, Saadia tries to explain the plural in the verse "Let us make man" as what grammarians call plural of majesty or excellence.[25] This, it may be noted, differs from the various explanations offered by the rabbis [26] as well as by the Fathers of the Church.[27]

In his refutation of the sixth proof-text, he tries to show by Genesis 18:22, where "the men" are definitely different from "the Lord," that the "three men" in Genesis 18:2 are also different from "the Lord" in Genesis 18:1.[28]

3. KIRKISĀNĪ

In Chapters 2 and 4 of *Anwār* III, *Ḳirḳisānī* deals with certain problems relating to the Christian doctrine of the Trinity.

[21] *Perush Sefer Yeṣirah*, pp. 89–92.
[22] *Ibid.*, p. 92, ll. 17–18.
[23] *Mekilta*, *Vayassa'* 6 (ed. Lauterbach, II, p. 124); *M. Abot* V, 6.
[24] Abraham Ibn Ezra's Shorter Commentary on Exodus 32:16; cf. Ḳol Yehudah on *Cuzari* I, 89.
[25] *Emunot* II, 6, p. 89, l. 18–p. 90, l. 2.
[26] *Bereshit Rabbah* 8, 3 ff.
[27] Cf., e.g., Justin Martyr, *Dial.* 62; Irenaeus, *Adv. Haer.*, Praef. 4.
[28] *Emunot* II, 6, p. 89, ll. 5–9.

In the chapter between them, of which the heading and the beginning are missing, he deals with the belief in an eternally pre-existent Word. From the position of the chapter between two chapters dealing with Christianity, one would surmise that the Word dealt with in it is the Word in the sense of the pre-existent Christ, the second person of the Trinity. Thus when in the preserved ending of the opening passage of this chapter Ḳirḳisānī challenges some interlocutor to answer a criticism he is about to raise against some view of his, it is quite evident that the interlocutor is a Christian and that the view of his is the Christian belief in an eternally pre-existent Word in the sense of the pre-existent Christ. When, however, at the end of the partly preserved criticism, Ḳirḳisānī adds that "this argument applies to all who assert that the Word of God is pre-existently co-eternal with Him, such as Ibn Kullāb and others,"[1] it means, as I shall try to show, that the same criticism can be also raised against those Muslims who believe in an eternally pre-existent Word of God in the sense of the pre-existent Koran and that the "Ibn Kullāb" mentioned is the famous Mutakallim whose views on such an eternally pre-existent Word of God are reproduced in great detail by Ashʿarī in his *Maḳālāt*.[2]

Right after this conclusion of the opening passage of the chapter, Ḳirḳisānī begins a new passage as follows: "Now suppose one who believes in the eternal pre-existence of the Word should ask us thus."[3] What follows then is a succession of questions in which this supposititious questioner and other supposititious questioners, each of whom is referred to as "one of them," try to force Ḳirḳisānī to admit, on account of his belief in the divine origin of the Torah, that the Torah is pre-existently eternal, evidently in order to justify thereby

[1] *Anwār* III, 3, 1, p. 190, ll. 12–13.

[2] Cf. *Kalam*, pp. 248–251. But see n. 32, on p. 523, in Leon Nemoy, "A Tenth Century Criticism of the Doctrine of the Logos (John I, 1)," *JBL*, 64:515–529 (1945), where the entire chapter is assumed to deal with the Christian Logos and hence "Ibn Kilāb" is "apparently" a "Christian."

[3] *Anwār* III, 3, 2, p. 190, ll. 13–14.

their own belief in a pre-existently eternal Word. Ḳirḳisānī, of course, in answer to each question, tries to show by various arguments that the Torah is created. And so the succession of questions and answers goes on to the end of the chapter.

Now it can be shown, I believe, that, unlike the interlocutor in the opening passage of the chapter, none of the supposititious questioners is a Christian, for Christianity, despite its belief that the Torah is of divine origin, never claimed that it is uncreated, and consequently it is unlikely that a Christian would try to argue that a Jew, because of his belief in the divine origin of the Torah, must also believe in its uncreatedness. In Islam, however, those who believed in the uncreatedness of the Koran also believed that the prophetic words of the Hebrew Scripture, or at least those of them which are quoted or referred to in the Koran, are equally uncreated. Thus in the fictitious debate between a Christian and a Muslim by John of Damascus, the Muslim is made to argue that "the words of God," that is, the divine words of the Hebrew Scripture, are uncreated, whereas the Christian maintains: "I acknowledge only one Word of God in hypostasis to be uncreated." [4] Accordingly, all these supposititious questioners are Muslims of the kind described in the concluding statement of the opening passage of this chapter as being, like Ibn Kullāb, believers in an eternally pre-existent Word. Corroborative evidence for this is to be found in the following similarities of expression. Of Ibn Kullāb it is reported by Ashʿarī that he believed that "the word of God is an attribute (*ṣifah*) of His, subsisting in Him, and He and His word are coeternal." [5] Similarly here Ḳirḳisānī, in the course of his argument against "those who assert that the word of God is coeternal with Him, such as Ibn Kullāb and others," makes his supposed opponent say that the word of God is "an attribute in Him." [6] Again, Ibn Kullāb is reported by Ashʿari to

[4] *Disputatio* (PG 96, 1344 AB).
[5] *Maḳālāt*, p. 584, ll. 9–10; cf. *Kalam*, p. 248.
[6] *Anwār* III, 5, p. 192, l. 18; III, 16, p. 198, ll. 3–4.

have said that "the Word [of God] has no letters (*ḥurūf*) or sound (*ṣaut*) to it" [7] and that it cannot be heard.[8] So also here Ḳirḳisānī makes his opponent say that "God's word cannot be heard" [9] and that it "has no sound (*ṣaut*) or letters (*ḥurūf*) to it." [10]

Let us then first study Ḳirḳisānī's opening argument against the Christian eternally pre-existent Word and then study his arguments against the Muslim eternally pre-existent Word and, after that, see what his own conception of the Jewish pre-existent Word is.

Unfortunately the beginning of the chapter, which must have contained a restatement of the Christian conception of the eternally pre-existent Word, against which he proceeds to argue, is missing. We, therefore, have to reconstruct what that restatement was from the argument which he raises against it. The argument reads as follows: "What would be your opinion if one should say . . . [that] one who is not in motion and is incapable [of motion, is nevertheless in motion] and that one who is not walking and is incapable [of walking] is nevertheless walking? Would there be any difference between him and you?" [11] This argument quite evidently calls attention to the generally admitted absurdity of such contradictory propositions as "A is not in motion" and "A is in motion"; "A is not walking" and "A is walking." Since this argument is raised against the Christian doctrine that the Word is eternally pre-existent, it is quite evident that, in the missing beginning of the chapter, this Christian doctrine was so restated by Ḳirḳisānī as to contain two contradictory propositions, which two contradictory propositions would also be contained in the orthodox Muslim doctrine that the Koran is eternally pre-existent. The question is, what two contradictory propositions could he find in the Christian conception of an eternally pre-

[7] *Maḳālāt*, p. 584, l. 12.
[8] *Ibid.*, p. 585, ll. 8–11.
[9] *Anwār* III, 3, 5, p. 192, l. 12.
[10] *Ibid.*, l. 13.
[11] *Anwār* III, 3, 1.

existent Word that would also apply to the Muslim conception of an eternally pre-existent Word?

The answer is that the two contradictory propositions which Ḳirḳisānī could find implied in the doctrine of the Christians is their assertion, on the one hand, that God is one and their assertion, on the other hand, that the Word is other than God the Father and that, because it is eternal, it is God. And the same argument would apply also to the orthodox Muslims who, on the one hand, assert that God is one and, on the other hand, assert that the Word is eternal, for even though they maintain that they do not call the eternal Koran God, logically, by describing it as eternal, they imply that it is God, for everything eternal is God. This, as we have seen, is the Muʿtazilite argument against the doctrine of the eternity of the Koran.[12] Thus the view of the Christian Trinitarians as well as the view of the Muslim Attributists consists of two contradictory propositions, one affirming that God is one and the other affirming that God is not one.

Having thus stated his argument against both the Christian and the Muslim conception of an eternally pre-existent Word, Ḳirḳisānī stages a debate on the subject with his supposititious Muslim questioners.

The debate is opened by a Muslim.[13] He asks Ḳirḳisānī to tell him whether he believes that "God's Writ, meaning the Pentateuch and the other books, is from God." Ḳirḳisānī answers in the affirmative, explaining that by his belief that the Scripture is "from God" he means that the Scripture, being, as it is said of the Tables, "the work of God" (Exod. 32:16), is "other" than God, and hence "it was created and made by Him," that is to say, it had a temporal beginning and is not eternal. The Muslim then challenges him as follows: "But surely you do not deny that the Writ might indeed be something other than God, and yet not made and created by Him." By this the Muslim tries to force Ḳirḳisānī to admit that, even though Scripture is the work of God and other than

[12] Cf. *Kalam*, p. 264.

[13] *Anwār* III, 3, 2.

God, it need not have had a temporal beginning, but could have been coeternal with God and at the same time dependent upon God as its cause; and, once the Jew admitted this, his admission could serve as an argument for the eternity of the pre-existent Koran. To this Ḳirḳisānī answers: "If Scripture were coeternal with God, it would be a God, but in that case there would be many Gods." This, we may repeat, is exactly the Muʿtazilite argument against the eternity of the Koran. Ḳirḳisānī then goes on to show how it is exactly by this kind of reasoning that Christians try to prove that the Word and the Holy Spirit are each God, "for," he says, "the Christians claim that the Word and the Spirit are coeternal with God and thereby they prove that God is three." This, we may recall, is exactly the argument by which John of Damascus tries to prove that the Word and the Holy Spirit are each God.[14]

And so the issue is joined. The Muslim argues that the Hebrew Scripture is uncreated and hence orthodox Islam is right in asserting the uncreatedness of the Koran. Ḳirḳisānī argues that the Hebrew Scripture had a temporal beginning. The rest of the debate is taken up by other arguments advanced by Ḳirḳisānī to prove that the Hebrew Scripture had a temporal beginning. Out of his arguments there emerges Ḳirḳisānī's own conception of the Word of God. Let us see what that conception is.

God, according to Ḳirḳisānī, does indeed speak, "speaking, of course, without tongue and lips and toil and movements,"[15] and His speaking indeed produces a word, which was "originated" (*muḥdath*) and "created" (*maḫluḳ*) and was "not eternal" (*ghair ḳadīm*).[16] This word is produced by God "in something other than himself and not in himself"[17] and "it takes position in a thing."[18]

All this reflects the general Muʿtazilite formula that the

[14] Cf. *Kalam*, p. 137.

[15] *Anwār* III, 3, 10, p. 195, l. 11.

[16] *Ibid.*, 5, p. 192, l. 10; III, 6, p. 193, l. 4.

[17] *Ibid.*, 10, p. 195, l. 1.

[18] *Ibid.*, 12, p. 196, l. 11.

Word of God in the sense of the Koran was created in an abode.[19] But as to what that abode is, according to the Muʿtazilites it is either the Preserved Tablet in heaven [20] or in the air [21] or in the prophet, in whom it is created only as a capacity.[22] In Saadia, as we have seen, the abode in which the word was created was the air.[23] Ḳirḳisānī describes the abode as being of a threefold kind. First, it is the human "ear" by which one hears this word of God.[24] This quite evidently refers to such events as that of the revelation at Mount Sinai, when God is said to have answered Moses "by a voice" [25] and that all the people "heard the voice of words." [26] Second, it is the burning bush, out of the midst of which God is said to have called unto Moses.[27] With reference to this Ḳirḳisānī says that God "created the word and placed it in the bush." [28] This reflects the statement quoted by Ashʿarī in the name of the Jahmiyyah [29] and by Ibn Ḥazm in the name of the Muʿtazilites in general.[30] Third, it is the tables of the Law, the writing upon which is said to have been "the writing of God." [31] With reference to this Ḳirḳisānī says that "in the case of the Ten Commandments, the verses were God's word, but their location was the two tables." [32]

4. JOSEPH AL-BASĪR

Another Karaite author, Joseph al-Baṣīr, discusses the communicative word of God both in his *Neʿimot* and in His *Maḥkimat Peti.*

In his *Neʿimot*, in a chapter bearing the heading "That God speaks and that His word is created and what may be of-

[19] Cf. *Kalam*, p. 264.
[20] *Ibid.*, pp. 267–273.
[21] Ibid., pp. 274–276.
[22] *Ibid.*, pp. 274–278.
[23] Cf. above, p. 92.
[24] *Anwār* III, 3, 5, p. 192, l. 11.
[25] Exod. 19:19.
[26] Deut. 4:12.
[27] Exod. 3:4.
[28] *Anwār* III, 3, 11, p. 196, l. 4.
[29] *Ibānah*, p. 26, ll. 2–4 (68); cf *Kalam*, p. 266.
[30] *Fiṣal* III, p. 5, ll. 3–5; *Ibid.*, p. 266–267.
[31] Exod. 32:16, quoted by Ḳirḳisānī in *Anwār* III, 3, 2.
[32] *Anwār* III, 3, 11, p. 196, ll. 5–6. Cf. reproduction of Ḳirḳisānī's view in *ʿEṣ Ḥayyim* 98, p. 166.

fered in justification of this,"[1] after an argument to prove that the word of God must be created, he states his conclusion as follows: "We therefore maintain that God creates a word by reason of the fact that the prophet, of blessed memory, heard His word and that God, blessed be His name, caused the prophet to benefit by that word of His."[2]

In his *Maḥkimat Peti*, prefatory to his chapter headed "Of the word, that it is created,"[3] he says: "There is a great difference of opinion among the learned[4] with regard to the word of God, some of them saying that God speaks [with a word] which has no beginning; some of them saying that His word is He and He is His word; some of them saying that He speaks with a created word."[5] He then goes on to explain why he rejects the first two views and accepts the third view.[6] Of these three views, the first is quite evidently the orthodox Muslim view of the uncreatedness of the Koran and the third agrees in a general way, as does the same view in his *Ne'imot*, with Saadia's and Ḳirḳisānī's and some of the Mu'tazilites' interpretation of the communicative word of God. As for the second view, its meaning becomes clear from his criticism of it. In his criticism of it, al-Baṣīr continues to force the proponents of this second view to tell him what they exactly mean by their statement that "His word is He and He is His word" and, in the course of his criticism, at one point he addresses the proponents of this view as those who believe that the word is incarnate in "Jesus the son of Mary," in whom there is also a soul,[7] and at another point he assumes that the proponents of this view believe that the word of God

[1] *Ne'imot*, Hebrew p. 24a, ll. 30–31; Arabic p. 48a, l. 17 – p. 48b, l. 1. See comment on it in *'Eṣ Ḥayyim* 98, p. 165, ll. 36–38.

[2] *Ibid.*, Hebrew p. 25a, ll. 11–12; Arabic p. 50a, ll. 13–15.

[3] *Maḥkimat* 22, Hebrew p. 118a, l. 1.

[4] The reading in the Hebrew translation is *ben ha-'olam*, "among [the people of] the world." But I take it that the missing Arabic term underlying the Hebrew *ha-'olam*, "the world," was *al-'ulamā'*, "the learned," which was corrupted to *al-'ālam*, "the world."

[5] *Maḥkimat* 21, p. 117b, ll. 27–29.

[6] *Ibid.*, p. 118a, l. 1–p. 121a, l. 12.

[7] *Ibid.*, p. 120b, ll. 4–5.

is God.[8] From all this we know that his second view refers to the Word of God in the sense of the second person of the Christian Trinity. But I do not think that the expression "His Word is He and He is His Word" should be taken literally as expressing a Sabellian conception of the Trinity. It is only al-Baṣīr's own way of trying to reproduce the Christian doctrine of the second person of the Trinity by saying in effect that, unlike the orthodox Muslims who, while believing that the Word is coeternal with God, do not call it God, the Christians not only believe that the Word, whom they call Son, is coeternal with God but they also believe that that Word is God like the God whom they call Father.

5. JUDAH BEN BARZILLAI

A refutation of those described as having misinterpreted the verse "The Spirit of the Lord spake by me, and His Word was in my tongue" (2 Sam. 23:2) is to be found in the work of Judah ben Barzillai.[1] The reference here, as in Saadia, is to the Christian interpretation of Spirit and Word in this verse as meaning the third and second persons of the Trinity. He similarly refutes those who took the term "wisdom" in the verse "The Lord by wisdom founded the earth" (Prov. 3:19) as referring to the second or third person through whom God made all things (John 1:3),[2] and argues that it is to mean that God created all things according to wise planning.[3] So also Saadia interprets this verse as referring to the wise planning of God.[4] Thus, like Saadia, he does not

[8] *Ibid.*, ll. 16–19.

[1] *Perush Sefer Yeṣirah*, p. 75, ll. 15–18.

[2] Thus Irenaeus takes "wisdom" in this verse to refer to the third person, the Holy Spirit, whom, like the second person, he considers as pre-existent and as an instrument of creation (*Adv. Haer.* IV, 20, 3). Clement of Alexandria, however, takes "wisdom" in the parallel verse, "The Lord who made the earth by His power, who established the world by His wisdom" (Jer. 10:12 LXX), to refer to the "Word," the second person (*Cohortatio ad Gentes* VIII, 80[3], PG 8, 192 A).

[3] *Perush Sefer Yeṣirah*, p. 75, ll. 19 ff.

[4] *Emunot* II, 8, p. 91, l. 21–p. 92, l. 3.

believe in a pre-existent word or wisdom, even a created word or wisdom, which was used by God as an instrument of creation. We may assume that, also like Saadia, while denying a created creative word, he believed in a created communicative word, even though he does not say so explicitly, for, like Saadia, he does believe in a created light which appears at the time God is said to speak to prophets in order to assure them that "the word heard by them is from God." [7] The word heard by the prophet is evidently taken by him to be a created word.

Again, like Saadia, he does not follow, in its literal sense, the Talmudic saying that the Torah, together with six other things, were created prior to the creation of the world, maintaining that the saying was meant to be taken "figuratively and metaphorically." [8] Unlike Saadia, however, he follows literally the rabbinic saying as to the creation of ten things on the sixth day of creation at twilight.[9]

6. JUDAH HALEVI

A distinction like that made by Saadia between the creative word of God, which is to be taken to mean God's design and will, and the communicative word of God, which is to be taken to mean a real created word, is also implied in Judah Halevi. With regard to the creation of the world and the creation of things out of the ordinary course of nature within

[7] *Perush Sefer Yeṣirah*, p. 16, l. 36–p. 17, l. 1; p. 20, ll. 33 ff.

[8] *Ibid.*, p. 85, ll. 26–27; p. 88, l. 36; p. 89, l. 10. Neumark (*Toledot ha-Pilosophiah be-Yisra'el*, I, 75) is wrong in his statement that on pp. 57–58 Judah ben Barzillai stresses the belief in the antemundane creation of the Torah. All he does on these pages is to quote the Talmud and then to conclude by saying (p. 58, l. 2) "all of which will be explained by us later." The reference is undoubtedly to pp. 85–89. Neumark is also wrong in saying (*loc. cit.*) that on pp. 74–76 Judah ben Barzillai mitigates that Talmudic statement about the antemundane creation of the Torah. On those pages he discusses not the antemundane creation of the Torah but rather the conception of "wisdom" as an instrument of creation Judah ben Barzillai, as we have seen, explicitly rejects the literalness of the antemundane creation of the Torah on pp. 85–89.

[9] *Perush Sefer Yeṣirah*, p. 89, ll. 21–25; p. 139, l. 13–p. 140, l. 5.

the world, he says that God "requires no instrument and no intermediary causes";[1] He creates all those things "by His will (*irādah*: *ḥefeṣ*) or command (*amr*: *dabar*) or by whatever other term you wish to use."[2] The last statement means that whatever other terms are used in Scripture in connection with the creation of the world, or in connection with the creation of things out of the ordinary course of nature within the world, such for instance as the terms "word" (*dabar*) or "wisdom" (*ḥokmah*), are to be taken to mean the "will" of God and not some created real thing. In the act of creation, therefore, he denies the creation by God of a word by means of which he created the world and by means of which he continues to create things.

But with regard to God's communication to men, in connection with which Scripture uses such terms as "voice" (Exod. 19:19) or "said" (Exod. 19:21) or "words" (Exod. 20:1) or "heard the voice of the living God speaking" (Deut. 5:23), he does not take these terms to mean "will" or "intention." He takes them to refer to a real word created by God which in some miraculous way was heard by Moses and the people, for, referring to these terms, he says: "We do not know how the intention (*al-maʿnā*: *ha-ʿinyan*) became corporealized so that it became a word (*kalām*: *dibbur*) which struck our ear nor do we know how He created something from that which was nonexistent or from that which was available to him from among existent things."[3]

In all this, Halevi is in agreement with Saadia. With Saadia, too, he agrees that the word was created in the air, which reflects the views of Naẓẓām and Philo.[3a] Thus in one place he says that by the will of God "the air which touches the prophet's ear is shaped into the form of letters which make up

[1] *Cuzari* I, 89, p. 42, l. 7; p. 43, l. 6.

[2] *Ibid.* II, 6, p. 76, ll. 2–3; p. 77, l. 1. Cf. *mashīʾah: maʾmar*, ḥefeṣ, *ibid.* I, 89, p. 42, ll. 2, 9; p. 43, ll. 1, 8.

[3] *Ibid.* I, 89, p. 40, l. 27 – p. 42, l. 1; p. 41, ll. 25–27.

[3a] For possible evidence that Halevi was acquainted with the Arabic version of Philo's *De Decalogo*, see my paper "Halevi and Maimonides on Prophecy," pp. 66–68, in *JQR*, N. S., 33(1943).

the words which God wishes to be heard by the prophet and the people" [4] and in another place he says that God by His will "caused the air to be giving the sound of the Ten Commandments and caused the writing to be graven upon the tables." [5]

From these passages, together with the passage in which he says that God "created the tables [of the Law] and engraved writing upon them," [6] it may be inferred that, according to Halevi, the Torah was created when the word of God was created and that the word of God was created when it was heard by Moses, and that similarly the tables of the Law themselves as well as the shape of the letters engraved in them and the act of the engravement itself were created at the time the Ten Commandments were heard by Moses and the people. Referring directly to the Talmudic saying about the seven things, including the Torah, that were created prior to the world, he says that, if taken literally, it would appear to be senseless, but it is to be taken figuratively as having some hidden meaning. With regard to the Torah, he says, the statement means that prior to the creation of the world God had already planned to reveal in it a Law by which men were to live.[7] Similarly, the Talmudic saying about the ten things that were created on the sixth day of creation at twilight should not be taken literally.[8] He thus, again, agrees with Saadia in not following literally the Talmudic saying about the creation of seven things prior to the creation of the world and the creation of ten things on the eve of Sabbath at twilight.

7. ABRAHAM IBN EZRA

Like Saadia, Judah ben Barzillai, and Judah Halevi, Abraham Ibn Ezra was aware of Abū al-Hudhayl's distinction between the created creative word of God and the created com-

[4] *Cuzari* II, 89, p. 42, ll. 9–10; p. 43, ll. 8–10.

[5] *Ibid.* II, 6, p. 76, ll. 1–2; p. 75, l. 28–p. 77, l. 2.

[6] *Ibid.* I, 89, p. 42, ll. 1–2; p. 41, l. 28.

[7] *Ibid.* III, 73, p. 322, ll. 14–23; p. 323, ll. 17–26. Cf. *Midrash Tehillim*, on Ps. 93:2, 3, p. 414.

[8] *Ibid.*, p. 222, ll. 23–28; p. 223, l. 6–p. 229, l. 3.

municative word of God — and he deals with them. With regard to the created creative word of God, it is given by him a nonliteral interpretation in his statement that "the word by which the world was created means only the simple will [of God]," namely, that "only by His will was the world created." [1] This is in agreement with the view of all his Jewish predecessors. But as for his view on the created communicative word of God, it requires investigation.

In one place, Ibn Ezra mentions three views on the communicative word of God.[2] First, he says, "there are those who say that the word of God is eternal." This undoubtedly refers to the orthodox Muslim belief in a pre-existent eternal Word. Second, "the Geonic sages say that God created a voice." This quite evidently represents the view which we have met with in Saadia. Third, "there are those who, assuming that the word of God is something miraculous which is past our understanding, declare that God uttered the commandment 'Remember the Sabbath day' (Exod. 20:8) and the commandment 'Keep the Sabbath day' (Deut. 5:12) simultaneously." This is a reference to a well-known Talmudic saying.[3] Of these three views, the third is explicitly rejected by him; the first is not commented upon by him at all, but it is quite evidently rejected by him as he would reject the belief in any other thing co-eternal with God; as for the second, it is commented upon by him as follows: "and inasmuch as voice is an accident, it will require a created body." This comment, I take it, is Ibn Ezra's explanation why Saadia departed from Abū al-Hudhayl and took the word to be created in the air [4] rather than in no abode, for immediately after this comment he adds that "they also say that God creates a light and a body for a prophet on the occasion of his prophesying," which quite evidently refers to Saadia's statement that "God

[1] *Sha'ar ha-Shamayim* in *Kerem Ḥemed*, IV, p. 8, and *Kitebe Ranak*, ed. Rawidowicz, p. 401. Cf. also Commentary on Exodus 31:18.

[2] *Shorter Commentary on Exodus* 19:17.

[3] *Rosh ha-Shanah* 27a; *Shebu'ot* 20b.

[4] *Emunot* II, 12, p. 105, ll. 9–10.

has a special light which He creates and makes manifest to prophets." [7] But while Ibn Ezra does not directly reject this view, he indicates toward the end of his comment on this verse that he has a view of his own on the subject.

Ibn Ezra's own view on the communicative word of God appears in his comment on the verse "And he said, Show me, I pray Thee, Thy Glory" (Exod. 33:18). In that comment, Ibn Ezra begins by rejecting Saadia's interpretation of the term "glory" to mean a created light and of the expression "show me" to mean to show Moses that created light so that he could see it with his eyes.[8] Then, in contradistinction to this, he interprets the term "glory" to mean God's essence and Moses' expression "show me" to mean to cause him to have a knowledge and understanding of God's essence. At the conclusion of that comment, he adds: "So also the verse 'And God spoke unto Moses face to face' (Exod. 33:11) does not mean speech by mouth; it rather refers to the true speech of which the speech of the mouth is a likeness." By "true speech" Ibn Ezra certainly does not mean the temporary "created word" which, according to Saadia, God creates especially for prophets and simultaneously with which He also creates that created light which is explicitly rejected by Ibn Ezra. His distinction between "the true speech" (*ha-dibbur ha-amitti*) and "the speech of the mouth" is quite evidently the same as the distinction in Judah Halevi between "intellectual speech" (*al-nuṭḳ al-ʿaḳlī*: *ha-dibbur ha-sikli*) and "corporeal speech" (*al-nuṭḳ al-jismī*: *ha-dibbur ha-gashmi*),[9] which ultimately is based upon the Stoic distinction between "internal speech" (λόγος ενδιάθετος) and "uttered speech" (λόγος προφορικός).[10] What Ibn Ezra means by his interpreting "God spoke" as meaning that He spoke with a "true speech" is, therefore, to be taken to be the same as what he means by his

[7] *Ibid.*, p. 106, l. 19; cf. p. 90, n. 13a.
[8] Shorter Commentary on Exodus 33:18.
[9] *Cuzari* IV, 25, p. 280, ll. 11–12; p. 281, ll. 12–13.
[10] Cf. *Kalam*, pp. 286–287.

interpretation of the expression "show me," namely, that God caused Moses to discover by his own reason what the divine will and design and purpose were.

But, while Ibn Ezra definitely rejects Saadia's conception of a created word in the air associated with every divine communication with a prophet, there are certain cryptic statements in his Commentaries on the Bible which lend themselves to the interpretation that the act of speaking which in certain scriptural passages is attributed to non-human beings is taken by Ibn Ezra to mean speaking by way of a created word in the air. One of these cryptic statements is his comment on the verse "And the Lord opened the mouth of the ass and she said unto Balaam" (Num. 22:28), where, after quoting two opposite views as to whether the ass did speak, he says "the right view is that the ass did speak, but if you understand the secret of the angels of Abraham (Gen. 18:1) and of [the angel] of Jacob (Gen. 32:25), you will then understand the true meaning of this." [12] According to David Rosin,[13] what Ibn Ezra means by this cryptic remark is that, while indeed the ass spoke, she did not speak with her own mouth but rather by means of a voice especially created in the air and that similarly the angels who appeared to Abraham and the angel who wrestled with Jacob were not permanent angels, like Gabriel and Michael, for instance, but rather temporary angels especially created on certain occasions for special missions, like those ephemeral angels spoken of by the rabbis.[14] Then, again, like Saadia and others, Ibn Ezra denies the creation of the Torah prior to the creation of the world, trying to show that the Talmudic sages who have asserted it could not have meant their assertions to be taken literally; they are, beyond doubt, he says, meant to be taken as mere figures of speech. He further explains that the statements about the pre-existence

[12] The "man" in Gen. 32:25 is traditionally taken to be an angel disguised as a man (cf. *Genesis Rabbah* 77, 2 ff).

[13] Cf. David Rosin, "Die Religionsphilosophie Abraham Ibn Ezra's," *MGWJ*, 42:113, 208–213, 241 (1898).

[14] *Ḥagigah* 14a; *Genesis Rabbah* 78, 1.

of the Torah only mean the ideal planning of the world, intimating that it is only another way of expressing the philosophic view that the intelligible world was prior to the corporeal world.[15] Similarly, like Saadia and Halevi, he denied that the tables of the Law were actually created on the sixth day of creation, taking the Talmudic saying about the ten things, including the tables of the Law that were created on the sixth day of creation at twilight, to mean that "God, at the time of the creation of the world [that is, on the sixth day at twilight], decreed the future creation of these wonderful [ten] events which are outside of the order of nature." [16]

8. JUDAH HADASSI

Like Ibn Ezra and unlike all the others, both Rabbanites and Karaites, the Karaite Judah Hadassi denies any created words, whether communicative or creative. Thus commenting on the verse "Out of heaven He made thee to hear His voice, that he might instruct thee" (Deut. 4:36), which refers to the communicative word, he says: "If His voice were something created by the Lord thy God, how could it have proclaimed and said, 'I am the Lord thy God'? (Exod. 20:2), for if His voice were created, it could not have called itself 'creator' or proclaimed, 'I am the Lord thy God.' Therefore, His voice is not something created but it is rather the wisdom of God, and the voice of His wisdom comes to you from God by means of the wisdom of your own knowledge." [1] Then, commenting on the verse "By the word of God were the heavens made" (Ps. 33:6), which refers to the

[15] *Sha'ar ha-Shamayim* (Kerem Ḥemed, p. 6 and p. 8; p. 400 and 401), Introduction to the French Recension of his Commentary on Genesis (M. Friedländer, *Essays on the Writings of Ibn Ezra*, Hebrew Appendix, p. 4; Rosin, *Reime und Gedichte des Abraham Ibn Ezra*, pp. 67–68).

[16] Commentary on Num. 22:28; cf. also Commentary on Exod. 32:16; Shorter Commentary on Exod. 32:16; Introduction to the French Recension of his Commentary on Genesis (Friedländer, Essays, p. 4; Rosin, *op. cit.*, p. 69); Friedländer, *op. cit.*, p. 81, and p. 82, n. 3.

[1] *Eshkol ha-Kofer* 27, p. 19b.

creative word, he interprets the term "word" here to mean the "wisdom" (*ḥokmah*) or "decree" (*gezerah*) of God.[2]

The term "voice" or "word" whether used in connection with creation or in connection with communication is thus not to be taken in the sense of a created voice or word, and still less, of course, in the sense of an eternal voice or word. It is to be taken in the sense of the wisdom of God or, as he also says, in the sense of the "decree"[3] or "power"[4] and "might"[5] of God. He therefore concludes that "he who has said that the word is created has said nothing worthy of consideration,"[6] adding that the denial of a created voice is not a fancy of his own but rather a view which he has been taught by his Karaite masters.[7] This last statement is rather strange. As we have seen, both Ḳirḳisānī and al-Baṣīr, while denying the existence of a created creative voice, admit the existence of a created communicative word.[8] The only one of those discussed by us in this section who denied also the existence of a created communicative word is the Rabbanite Abraham Ibn Ezra, and there seems to be a connection between him and Hadassi. As will be recalled, in his discussion of the communicative word, Ibn Ezra says that God speaks, not by the word of mouth but by a true word, that is, by the reason, which may mean that man comes into the knowledge of the wisdom of God by means of his own reason. Hadassi's statement quoted above that "the voice of His wisdom comes to you from God by means of the wisdom of your own knowledge" says the same thing.

The Talmudic saying about the antemundane creation of the Torah, the literalness of which, as we have seen, was rejected by the leading Rabbanites of that period, is taken up by Judah Hadassi and is used by him as an occasion for a

[2] *Ibid.*
[3] *Ibid.*
[4] *Ibid.*, 49, p. 26d.
[5] *Ibid.*
[6] *Ibid.*
[7] *Ibid.*
[8] Cf. discussion of Karaitic views on the subject of a created communicative word in *'Eṣ Ḥayyim* 98, p. 165, ll. 30 ff.

characteristic Karaite attack upon the Talmudic sages, whom he refers to as the "nonsense-mongering Pharisees" [9] and "thy oppressing Pharisees." [10] The Talmudic sources upon which he drew his knowledge of the antemundane creation of the Torah are three: [11] first, the interpretation of the speech of "wisdom" in Proverbs 8, especially the interpretation of the word *amon*, "nursling," in verse 30 as if it read *uman*, "artisan," and the statement that before the creation of the world God "took counsel with the Torah"; [12] second, the statement that the Torah was created two thousand years before the creation of the world; [13] third, the statement that seven or six things were created before the creation of the world which he confused and combined with the statement that ten things were created on the eve of the first Sabbath in the twilight.[14] He introduces his criticism of these views with the statement: "All these are false." [15] Some of his criticisms are as follows: First, Scripture says that "in the beginning God created the heaven and the earth" (Gen. 1:1), and there is no mention of anything created before them.[16] This reflects the proclaimed Karaitic view, not followed by the Karaites themselves literally, that one should adhere only to what is written in the text. Second, how can one speak of two thousand years before the creation of the world, when there was no time before the creation of the world? [17] This is a well-known argument against the conception of the creation of the world [18] which Hadassi had adopted and applied to the question at hand. The same argument, incidentally, had also been used by Abraham Ibn Ezra in his attempt to show that the Talmudic saying should not be taken literally.[19] Third, in connection with the reading *uman* for the written *amon*, Hadassi ridicules this exegetical device of the Talmudic sages, which he illustrates

[9] *Eshkol ha-Kofer* 47, p. 25c.
[10] *Ibid.*, p. 25d.
[11] *Ibid.*
[12] *Tanḥuma, Bereshit* 1.
[13] *Genesis Rabbah* 8, 2.
[14] *M. Abot* V, 6.
[15] *Eshkol ha-Kofer* 47, p. 25d.
[16] *Ibid.*
[17] *Ibid.*
[18] *Moreh* II, 13, 1st Theory.
[19] *Sha'ar ha-Shamayim* in *Kerem Ḥemed*, IV, p. 6, and *Kitebe Ranaḳ*, ed. Rawidowicz, p. 400.

by many other examples.[20] In connection with the term *amon* in question, it can be shown, I believe, that this Talmudic exegetical device had already been used by Philo.[21] Finally, against the statement that God took counsel with the Torah he cites the verse "With whom took He counsel, and who instructed Him?" (Isa. 40:14).[22] A similar objection, it may be remarked, could be raised against the Church Fathers who describe the Son as the counselor of the Father in the creation of the world, but I have shown how the Fathers would have answered such an objection.[23] A similar answer, I imagine, would have been given by the rabbis.

9. MAIMONIDES

A view like that of Saadia and Halevi, consisting of a denial of an uncreated word, an affirmation of a created communicative word, and a denial of a created creative word, is to be found in Maimonides.

His denial of an uncreated word is to be found in his statement to the effect that his exposition elsewhere of the impossibility of the existence in God of real attributes makes it unnecessary for him to explain to his reader why there cannot be in God a real attribute of word (*al-kalām*: *ha-dibbur*).[1] The reference here, as may be gathered from the context, is to those Muslim theologians who conceived of the eternal Koran as an uncreated word existing in God from eternity as a real attribute.

His affirmation of a created communicative word is to be found in his statement that the need of explaining the denial of such an eternal and uncreated word is all the more unnecessary for Jewish readers, in view of the fact that "our people are in general agreement that the Torah is something created, that is to say, that the word (*al-kalām*: *ha-dabar*, *ha-dibbur*)

[20] *Eshkol ha-Kofer* 47, p. 25d.
[21] Cf. *Philo* I, pp. 267–269.
[22] *Eshkol ha-Kofer* 47, p. 46a.
[23] *The Philosophy of the Church Fathers*, I, p. 193, n. 12.
[1] *Moreh* I, 65, p. 108, l. 23.

ascribed to God is created and that it is ascribed to Him only in the sense that the word (*al-ḳaul*: *ha-ma'mar*, *ha-dibbur*) which Moses heard was created and brought into existence by God in the same manner as He created all his other works of creation." [3] Though his mention of the common Jewish belief that the Torah was created quite evidently refers to the rabbinic statements about the creation of the Torah,[4] it may be reasonably assumed that, like Saadia and Halevi, he did not take literally that part of the statement in which the creation of the Torah is said to have taken place prior to the creation of the world. In his discussion of the revelation on Mount Sinai, where Maimonides distinguishes between the "word" heard by Moses and the "voice" heard by the people,[5] both of which are described by him as "created," [6] the implication is that both of them were created at the time of the revelation on Mount Sinai. Then also, in his discussion of the difference between the prophecy of Moses and that of the other prophets,[7] he does not say that there was also a difference between them in that the word heard by Moses was created before the creation of the world, whereas the word heard by any of the other prophets was created at the time it was heard, the implication thus being that there was no such difference between them; in both cases the word was created at the time it was heard.

So much for Maimonides' conception of the communicative word.

With regard to the creative word, like Saadia and all his other Jewish predecessors, he denies that there was such a created word. This is expressed by him unambiguously in the following statement: "Whenever the expression 'and He said' occurs in the story of creation, it signifies 'He willed' (*shā'*: *raṣah*) or 'He desired' (*irāda*: *ḥefeṣ*). This has already been

[3] *Moreh* I, 65, p. 108, ll. 24–26.

[4] *Pesaḥim* 54a, *et al.*

[5] *Moreh* II, 33, p. 256, ll. 6, 13.

[6] For "word," see *Moreh* I, 65, p. 108, ll. 24–26; for "voice," see *Moreh* II, 33, p. 257, ll. 15–16.

[7] *Moreh* II, 45, p. 286, l. 15–p. 287, l. 17.

stated by other authors, and is well known." [8] Accordingly, as was to be expected, the verse "By the word of the Lord were the heavens made" (Ps. 33:6) is interpreted by him "figuratively" to mean that "they have come into existence by His intention (*kaṣd*: *da'at*, *kavvanah*) and by His will (*mashī'ah*: *raṣon*)." [9]

More explicit is Maimonides in his view that one is not to take literally the rabbinic statement that the tables of stone were created on the eve of the first Sabbath in the twilight. This, as we have seen, is also the view of Saadia, Halevi, and others. As interpreted by Maimonides, that statement means that on the eve of the first Sabbath in the twilight God implanted in nature the power to produce those miraculous tables at the appointed time.[10] This is exactly like the explanation quoted above from Ibn Ezra.[11]

V. Pre-existent Throne, and Created Will

1. PRE-EXISTENT THRONE

Just as the Muslim discussion of the pre-existent Koran reminded the spokesmen of Judaism of that time of the rabbinic lore about the pre-existence of the Torah, so also the Muslim discussions of the pre-existent throne of God re-

[8] *Ibid.* I, 65, p. 109, ll. 25–26.

[9] *Ibid.*, p. 110, ll. 1–4.

[10] *Commentary on M. Abot* V, 6. Cf. *Philo* I, p. 351, n. 24.

[11] Cf. above, p. 108.

Similarly, Maimonides' explanation of the verse that "the tables were the work of God" (Exod. 32:16) as meaning that "they were the product of nature, not of art" (*Moreh* I, 66, p. 110, ll. 9–10) is the same as Ibn Ezra's explanation as meaning that, unlike the second tables (Exod. 34:1), they were not hewn out of stone, but they were originally created in that size (Commentary on Exod. 32:16). Both of them are against Saadia who takes the verse to mean that the tables were created out of nothing. So also Maimonides' explanation of the statement that the tables were "written with the finger of God" (Exod. 13:18) as meaning that they were produced by "the word of God," that is, "by His will and desire" (*Moreh* I, 66, p. 110, ll. 20–22), is the same as Ibn Ezra's explanation that the expression is used "as a figure of speech, since in ordinary language writing is done with a finger" (Shorter Commentary on Exod. 31:18).

minded them of the rabbinic lore as to the pre-existence of the throne of glory. The verse in the Koran narrating that after He had created the heavens and the earth, God "seated himself on the throne" (7:52; cf. 20:4) reminded them of the visions of Micaiah and Isaiah wherein God is described as "sitting on His throne" (1 Kings 22:19) or "sitting on a throne" (Isa. 6:1). The Muslim tradition as to the pre-existence of the throne [1] reminded them of the rabbinic lore about the pre-existence of the throne of glory.[2] The verse in the Koran stating that "those who bear the throne and those around it celebrate the praise of their Lord" (40:7; cf. 69:17), and the Muslim tradition that the bearers of the throne were four angels [3] reminded them of the rabbinic tradition that the *ḥayyot*, "living creatures" (Ezek. 1:5), a sort of angels,[4] were the bearers of the throne [5] and that some of them,[6] or angels round about God,[7] sing His praises. When they found that among the Muslims those who opposed the literal interpretation of the Koranic references to the throne of God [8] interpreted the throne as signifying the outermost all-encompassing celestial sphere,[9] which according to the astronomical views of the time was the ninth sphere, it reminded them of those sayings of the rabbis in which the highest heaven (*'arabot*), the seventh in their enumeration,[10] is identified with the throne of glory.[11] Similarly when they found that among the Mus-

[1] Wensinck, *The Muslim Creed*, p. 162.

[2] *Pesaḥim* 54a, *et alii*.

[3] Cf. Sale's and Wherry's notes in their translations of the Koran *ad loc*.

[4] Cf. Saadia, *Tafsīr Kitāb al-Mabādī* I, p. 20 (38); Maimonides, *Mishneh Torah, Yesode ha-Torah* II, 7. Cf. also Ginzberg, *Legends of the Jews*, VI, 82, n. 440.

[5] *Genesis Rabbah* 78, 2; *Exodus Rabbah* 23, 15; *Deuteronomy Rabbah* 2, 20.

[6] *Ḥagigah* 13b.

[7] *Ḥagigah* 14a; *Genesis Rabbah* 78, 1; *Exodus Rabbah* 15, 6.

[8] For the literalists on this problem, see *Ibānah*, pp. 42, ll. 18 ff.; *Maḳālāt*, p. 35, ll. 7–8.

[9] Cf. G. Flügel, "Scha'rānī und sein Werk über die muhammadanische Glaubenslehre," *ZDMG*, 20: 28, n. 20 (1866).

[10] *Ḥagigah* 12b.

[11] *Ibid*.; *Pirḳe de-Rabbi Eli'ezer* 18.

lims the throne of God was also interpreted as signifying God's mastery, His rule, His power, and in general the Providence which He exercises upon the world,[12] they were reminded of those sayings of the rabbis in which the highest heaven (*'arabot*), already identified with the throne of glory, is said to be the seat and source of "righteousness, judgment, and justice; the treasures of life and the treasures of peace and the treasures of blessing" [13] or in which the throne of glory is said to be ministered by seven qualities, namely, wisdom, righteousness, and judgment, grace and mercy, truth and peace" [14] or is said to have four banners, namely, "righteousness and judgment, grace and truth." [15] And so, in the light of these discussions in Islam about the throne, they began to re-examine their own traditions about the throne of glory, especially the rabbinic sayings about its pre-existence.

In Saadia, the pre-existent throne is treated in the same way as the pre-existent Torah. Just as the pre-existent Torah is taken by him to mean a real word created by God in the air and conveyed to Moses at the time of the revelation, so also the pre-existent throne is taken by him as a sort of form which God creates "out of fire" at the time of a prophetic revelation "for the purpose of assuring His prophet that it is He that revealed His word to him." [16] The same assurance could be given by God, according to Saadia, also by the appearance at the time of the prophetic communication of "a pillar of fire or a pillar of cloud or a light that did not emanate from the ordinary luminations." [17]

Saadia calls the "throne of glory" simply "the throne" (*al-'arsh*), referring to the use of this term in Scripture in such verses as "and over the heads of the living creatures there was the likeness of a firmament (*raḳi'a*) . . . and above the

[12] *Ibānah*, p. 43, ll. 15–17 (84). Cf. Sale's and Wherry's notes in their translations of the Koran on 2:256.

[13] *Ḥagigah* 12b.

[14] *Abot de-Rabbi Nathan*, Recension A, 37, p. 110 (ed. Schechter).

[15] *Ibid.*, Recension B, 43, p. 121.

[16] *Emunot* II, 10, p. 99, ll. 14–16.

[17] *Ibid.* III, 5, p. 123, ll. 6–7.

firmament . . . was the likeness of a throne" (Ezek. 1:22, 26) and "I saw the Lord sitting on His throne" (1 Kings 22:19), and identifying that term with scriptural "glory of the Lord" (Exod. 16:7) and the rabbinic *Shekinah*.[18]

The discussion of the throne in Saadia comes as a sequence of his contention that scriptural anthropomorphic expressions are not to be taken literally and while no reference is made in that discussion to the throne in Islam, it contains an undertone of criticism of those in Islam who insisted upon the literal acceptance of such verses in the Koran as those which speak of God as having mounted the throne (7:52) or as sitting on His throne (20:4).[19] Evidence for this may be found in the term Saadia uses in the statement by which he introduces his own view. It reads as follows: "Similarly *al-kursī w'al-'arsh* and its bearers have all been brought into existence, the Creator having brought them into existence out of fire for the purpose of assuring His prophet that it was He that had revealed His word to him."[20] Ibn Tibbon, in his Hebrew version, translates the words *al-kursī w'al-'arsh* by *ha-kisse veha-raḳi'a*, "the throne and the firmament," evidently taking the term *'arsh* here to correspond to the word *raḳi'a* in the verse "and above the firmament (*raḳi'a*) was the likeness of a throne" (Ezek. 1:26) and perhaps justifying his translation on the ground that among some Muslims, as we have mentioned above, the *'arsh* of the Koran is identified with the ninth sphere.[21]

But the translation of *'arsh* here by *raḳi'a* is wrong on three grounds. First, Saadia would not have used *'arsh* for *raḳi'a*, for in his Arabic version of the Pentateuch he translates *raḳi'a* by *jalad*. Second, in his subsequent explanation of the introductory statement which we have quoted, he speaks only of two created things by means of which prophets, with the exception of Moses, receive the divine revelations, namely, (1) the

[18] *Ibid*. II, 10, p. 99, ll. 16–20.
[19] Cf. *Maḳālāt*, p. 35, ll. 7 ff.; *Ibānah*, p. 42, ll. 18 ff.
[20] *Emunot* II, 10, p. 99, ll. 14–15.
[21] Cf. below, p. 117.

throne or glory of God and (2) angels, by which he means the *ḥayyot*, "living creatures" (Ezek. 1:5), which are described by the rabbis as the "bearers" of the throne[22] and which Saadia must have identified with a sort of angels which are especially created for the purpose of prophetic revelation. No mention is made by him of a "firmament" created for the purpose of confirming the divine origin of a prophetic revelation. Third, if Saadia followed those who interpreted the Koranic *'arsh* as the ninth sphere, he would have also followed them in interpreting the Koranic *kursī* as the eighth sphere.[23]

I therefore suggest that the term *w'al-'arsh* is used here as an explanation of the term *al-kursī*, the term *kursī* being the term which Saadia invariably uses in his Arabic version of the Scripture as a translation of the Hebrew *kisse*,[24] and *'arsh* being the term which the Koran, with only one exception, uses as a designation for the throne of God, the one exception being the verse where it uses the term *kursī* instead of *'arsh* (2:256). What Saadia, therefore, means to say is that the throne of God, the Hebrew *kisse*, of which the Arabic translation is *kursī* but for which the Koran uses mostly the term *'arsh*, is not to be taken, as it is by Muslims, either literally or as the ninth sphere or as divine Providence, but rather as a temporary creation out of fire which appears to prophets at the time of their prophetic experience. And so also the bearers of the throne, which in Judaism are spoken of as *ḥayyot*, "living creatures," which are a sort of angels, and in Islam are spoken of as "angels," are not to be taken in the sense of those angels which have a permanent existence but rather as angels in the sense of transient beings created by God on the occasion of his revealing to men a prophetic message.

A denial of the literalness of the throne and its pre-existence

[22] *Genesis Rabbah* 78, 2; *Exodus Rabbah* 23, 15; *Deuteronomy Rabbah* 2, 20.

[23] Cf. above, n. 9.

[24] Gen. 41:40; Exod. 11:5, 12:29, 17:16; Deut. 17:18; Isa. 14:9, 14:13, 22:23, 66:1; Prov. 20:28, 25:5, 29:14; Job 26:9, 36:7.

is to be found also in Judah ben Barzillai. Like Saadia, he takes the throne to mean something created at a prophetic revelation as evidence of its coming from God. He describes it as a "throne of glory for the Holy Spirit," which Holy Spirit he identifies with the scriptural term "glory" and the rabbinic term "Shekinah." [25]

In Ibn Gabirol, the "throne of glory" is identified with the universal matter in his philosophic system. Thus in his poem *Keter Malkut*, he describes it as that "where the dwelling-place of Concealment and Majesty is" or "where the Mystery and Foundation is," [26] and in his *Fons Vitae* he says that "universal matter is a *cathedra* for the One and the form-giving Will is seated in it and abides on it." [27] The word *cathedra* here undoubtedly stands for the Arabic *kursī*, which is used by Ibn Gabirol as a mental translation of the Hebrew *kisse* in the sense of "throne," for elsewhere he describes that universal matter by the term *locus*,[28] reflecting the Arabic *maḥall*,[29] which in turn reflects Plato's "place" (χώρα) and "seat" (ἕδρα).[30]

Though Judah Halevi does not directly discuss the "throne of glory," still, like Saadia, he mentions two things which appear to prophets during their prophetic experience, namely, (1) the glory of God or the Shekinah and (2) messengers of God or a special kind of temporary angels which appear only for the purpose of a particular prophetic revelation.[31] The Glory of God and Shekinah, as we have seen, are terms which Saadia has identified with the throne of glory, and so, we may assume, did also Halevi identify them, though he does not say so explicitly.

Ibn Ezra, unlike Saadia, Ibn Gabirol, and Judah Halevi, follows one of the Muslim interpretations of the throne men-

[25] *Perush*, p. 16, l. 36–p. 17, l. 8.

[26] *Keter Malkut*, ll. 320–231.

[27] *Fons Vitae* V, 42, p. 335, ll. 22–24.

[28] *Ibid.* VI, 31, p. 314, l. 1.

[29] Cf. my paper, "Goichon's Three Books on Avicenna's Philosophy," *The Moslem World* (1941), pp. 7–8.

[30] *Timaeus* 52 AB.

[31] Cf. my paper, "Hallevi and Maimonides on Prophecy," *JQR*, 33: 49–58 (1942).

tioned above. He takes it to mean the all-encompassing ninth sphere.[32]

The Karaite Judah Hadassi, unlike Saadia, Judah ben Barzillai, and probably also Judah Halevi, does not identify the "throne of glory" and the "glory of God" with temporary signs, or what Halevi calls temporary angels, created by God at special revelations. He takes the term "throne" as the abode of "glory" and the term "glory" as the designation of the order of angels that are fashioned from fire, as distinguished from those that are fashioned from winds (cf. Ps. 104:4), and he divides the former into four groups.[33] All these kinds of angels are permanent angels. As to when the "throne" and the angels called "glory" and all the other angels were created, he records three views current among the Karaite masters.[34] First, they were created on the fourth day, which is the view of Masliaḥ ha-Kohen [Abū Sahl]. Second, they were created on the second day, which is the view of Japheth ha-Levi Abū ʿAli, corresponding to the rabbinic view.[35] Third, "the glory and its throne, and all the glories and angels in His world" were created on the first day, which is the view of Benjamin ha-Nahāwandī as well as that of "the Karaite sages (*ḥakme ha-daʿat*) and the Greek sages of our country." [36] The reference to the "Greek sages" is to Christian theologians of Constantinople, the city in which Hadassi flourished in the middle of the twelfth century, who must have acquainted him with the view of those Greek Church Fathers who held that angels were created on the first day.[37] The identification of "throne" with angels ultimately goes back to Jewish pseudepi-

[32] Introduction to the French Recension of Abraham Ibn Ezra's Commentary on Genesis (Friedländer, *Essays*, p. 4, ll. 19–20; Rosin, *op. cit.*, p. 68, ll. 239–243).

[33] *Eshkol ha-Kofer* 47, p. 25c, and 51, p. 27bc.

[34] *Ibid*. 47, p. 25c.

[35] *Genesis Rabbah* 1, 3; 3, 8; 11, 9.

[36] I take *ḥakme ha-daʿat* here to be the equivalent of *ha-maskilim*, in the sense of the latter as Karaites.

[37] Cf. pseudo-Athanasius, *Quaestiones ad Antiochum Ducem* (PG 28, 601 AB); Basil of Seleucia, *Oratio* I, 2 (PG 85, 29 D–32 A). Cf. *Philo*, I, pp. 418–419.

graphic works,[38] but from his reference to the "Greek sages of our country," Hadassi must have been directly influenced by the New Testament identification of thrones with angels (Col. 1:16).

In Maimonides there are two discussions of the throne of God: first, of the term "throne" as used in various places in Scripture; second, of the throne of God which is said by the rabbis to have been created before the creation of the world. With regard to the scriptural use of the term "throne," he says that it means these three things: (1) the Sanctuary; (2) the heavens: (3) the divine attributes of greatness and power, which, like all divine attributes, are not distinct from God's essence.[39] For the first of these meanings he quotes as scriptural proof-text the verse reading "A throne of glory, on high from the beginning, is the place of our sanctuary" (Jer. 17:12).[40] For the second meaning he quotes as proof-text both the verse reading "Thus saith the Lord, the heaven is my throne" (Isa. 66:1) [41] and the rabbinic passages referred to by us above.[42] For the third meaning he quotes one of the rabbinic passages referred to by us above.[43] Thus, directly on the basis of Scripture and the Talmud, Maimonides arrived at two nonliteral interpretations of the "throne" which is to be found in Islam. With regard to the rabbinic saying about the preexistence of the throne of glory, he rejects its literalness [44] and interprets the rabbinic references to the throne of glory as meaning the divine attributes of the governance of the world.[45]

2. CREATED WILL

While, as we have seen, both Rabbanites and Karaites rejected the belief in a created creative word as it was held by certain Mutakallimūn, there were a mysterious Rabbanite and

[38] Testaments of the Twelve Patriarchs, Levi 3:8; Slavonic Enoch 20:1.
[39] *Moreh* I, 9.
[40] *Ibid.*
[41] *Ibid.*
[42] *Ibid.* 70; cf. above, n. 11.
[43] *Ibid.*; cf. above, n. 13–15.
[44] *Ibid.* II, 26.
[45] *Ibid.* I, 70.

a Karaite who followed certain Mutakallimūn in the belief in a created creative will.

The mysterious Rabbanite who admitted a created instrumentality of creation is an anonymous Gaon who is reported by Abraham Ibn Ezra as having believed that God created the world by a created will.[1]

The same view was also held by the Karaite Joseph al-Baṣīr. In a passage in his *Maḥkimat Peti*, after stating that such predicates as "powerful" and "knowing" and "living" and "existent" indicate the essence of God, he says that the predicate "willing," as well as its opposite, "detesting," refers to a "created cause." [2] Later, in a chapter entitled "That God wills with a created will which does not abide in an abode," [3] he tries to prove how God cannot be conceived of as willing "according to His own self" nor "according to a cause which is eternal," and hence that He must be willing according to a "cause," that is, a will which is "created" and which does not exist in an "abode," that is, in a substratum. The implication of this view is that before the creation of the world God had created an incorporeal being called "will," by means of which He created the world. We have already seen how a similar view is to be found in Islam, even among those who denied the reality of divine attributes, and we have traced the origin of this view to a Neoplatonic source.[4]

A detailed criticism of the theory of a pre-existent created will is to be found in Joseph ibn Ṣaddiḳ. This view with regard to will is at first ascribed by him to "a book entitled *Manṣūrī*," [5] a work by Joseph al-Baṣīr,[6] and then it is ascribed by him to "the masters of the wisdom of the Kalam" [7] in

[1] *Yesod Mora* I, p. 11, ll. 4–8 (ed. 1840). Cf. Kaufmann, "Muammar as-Sulamī und der unbekannte Gaon in Ibn Ezra's Jesod Mora," *MGWJ*, 33: 327–332 (1884).

[2] *Maḥkimat Peti* 15, p. 112a; Arabic, p. 96.

[3] *Ibid.* 25, pp. 122b–123a; Arabic, pp. 19b–20b. Cf. Kaufmann, *Attributenlehre*, p. 263, n. 29.

[4] Cf. *Kalam*, pp. 140–142.

[5] *'Olam Ḳaṭan*, p. 44, l. 20.

[6] Cf. Frankl, *Ein Mu'tazilitischen*, p. 9, l. 18.

[7] *'Olam Ḳaṭan* III, p. 44, l. 29.

general. It is reproduced by him as maintaining that "God is willing in virtue of a will which is created [not in a substratum] and God is detesting in virtue of a detestation which is created [not in a substratum]."[8] This view was first advanced by Abū al-Hudhayl, who, according to Shahrastānī, anticipated Modalism; it was followed by Jubbā'ī, who was an Antiattributist and an opponent of Modalism, and it was followed also by Abū Hāshim and al-Baṣīr, both of whom were Modalists.

Against this view Ibn Ṣaddiḳ raises four arguments:

First, against the first part of the formula, namely, that "God is willing by a will which is created," he argues that that would lead to an infinite regress of wills.[9] Against the second part of the formula, namely, that "God is detesting by a detestation which is created," he argues that (1) if the created detestation were created by a created will, then it would again lead to an infinite regress of wills and (2) if it were created by a detestation, then it would lead to the absurdity that God created something which was detestable to Him, and (3) if it were created by somebody else besides God, then it would lead to all the absurdities following on the assumption of two Creators.[10]

Second,[11] the will cannot be "without a substratum" and "created." If you insist that the will is "without a substratum," it means that it is incorporeal. But, being incorporeal, it must be either identical with God or something other than God. Now, if it is identical with God, then either the will is uncreated like God or God is created like the will, but the former alternative is contradictory to the assumption that the will is created, and the latter is contradictory to the assumption that God is eternal. And if you insist that the will is "created" and hence "other than God," then, being created, it must be either

[8] *Ibid.*, ll. 22–23; cf. p. 45, l. 16.
[9] *'Olam Ḳaṭan*, p. 44, l. 30–p. 45, l. 4.
[10] *Ibid.*, p. 45, ll. 3–15.
[11] *Ibid.*, ll. 16–23.

a "substance" or an "accident." But, if it is a created substance, it must, on the Kalam's own assumption, have accidents; and, if it is an accident, it must exist in a substance. In either case, the created will would be composed of substance and accident. But, being created and composed of substance and accident, it is like the world itself, and what need was there to create first a will and then by that will to create a world?

Third,[12] the belief that God created the world by a created will is tantamount to a belief that God needed the help of something to serve Him as "instrument" (*keli*) in the creation of the world, but such a belief, Ibn Saddik goes on to argue, besides its implication of a certain powerlessness in God, would by a chain of logical reasoning lead to the contradictory conclusion that the world was beginningless and hence uncreated.

This theory of a created instrumental will is restated by Maimonides in the name of "the most ancient" of the Mutakallimūn. It reads as follows: "The Creator wills by a will, which will is not something added to the essence of the Creator but is a will not in a substrate." [13] By the "most ancient" of the Mutakallimūn he undoubtedly meant Abū al-Hudhayl,[14] Jubbā'ī, and the latter's son Abū Hāshim, whose views on this subject we have discussed above.[15]

[12] *'Olam Ḳaṭan*, p. 45, l. 24–p. 46, l. 2.

[13] *Moreh* I, 75 (3).

[14] *Milal*, p. 34, l. 20–p. 35, l. 3.

[15] *Ibid.*, p. 54, l. 9.

A restatement of al-Baṣīr's view in the name of al-Baṣīr, together with a restatement of al-Baṣīr's three arguments in support of his view and a refutation of these arguments, followed by three objections raised directly against the view itself and a quotation from Ibn Tibbon's version of the *Moreh Nebukim* of that passage in which Maimonides attributes this view to "the most ancient" of the Mutakallimūn, is to be found in *'Es Ḥayyim* 75, pp. 93–96.

VI. Unapproved Theories of Creation

Through the various pseudepigraphic writings and doxographies that sprang up in the ancient oriental centers of Greek learning, such as Harran and Gondeshapur, prior to the translation of genuine Greek philosophic writings into Arabic early in the ninth century, Arabic-speaking peoples became acquainted with certain garbled cosmogonies attributed to Greek philosophers. These garbled cosmogonies continued to be quoted by Arabic authors, both Muslim and Jewish, even after the genuine writings of the Greeks became known to them, often being combined with some of the genuine Greek philosophic cosmogonies or being quoted by the side of them. It is such lists of cosmogonies, all of which were rejected, plus one cosmogony, based upon the Bible and the Koran, which was accepted, that are the subject of our study here.

As a framework of our discussion of the rejected theories of creation, I shall take twelve of the thirteen theories enumerated by Saadia in his *Emunot ve-De'ot*, beginning with the second theory and following the order in which he presents them. Within these twelve theories I shall incorporate the corresponding theories contained in the eight theories enumerated by Baghdādī in his *Farḳ*,[1] in the six theories enumerated by him in his *Uṣūl*,[2] and in the five theories enumerated by Ibn Ḥazm in his *Fiṣal*.[3] The theory of creation *ex nihilo*, which appears with approval at the beginning of Saadia's list and at the end of Baghdādī's two lists, will be dealt with separately in a special section under the heading "Creation *Ex Nihilo*." These thirteen theories are the subject of my study in this chapter. In justification of my limiting myself to these thirteen theories, I may quote Saadia who, toward the end of his enumeration of the thirteen theories of creation, says: "It behooves us now to explain that there exist theories other

[1] *Farḳ*, p. 346, ll. 7–16.
[2] *Uṣūl*, p. 59, l. 6 – p. 60, l. 11; p. 70, l. 3 – p. 71, l. 13.
[3] *Fiṣal* I, p. 9, l. 17; p. 23, l. 16; p. 24, l. 21; p. 34, l. 1; p. 65, l. 20.

than the twelve [false theories] just enumerated. However, these do not constitute principal theories, some of them being derivatives of one of these principal theories, while others are derivative of a combination of two or three of them, and hence it is not necessary to list them here." [4]

I. PLATO'S PRE-EXISTENT ETERNAL MATTER ATOMIZED

The second theory of creation in his list of thirteen theories is described by Saadia as "that of him who asserts that the bodies had a Creator, with whom there coexisted eternal spiritual things, out of which He created the aforementioned composite bodies; and in support of this theory its proponent alleged that a thing can come into existence only from something." [1] Subsequently, it is to be noted, Saadia speaks of this theory as having many proponents.

That this theory on the whole reflects the view of Plato that the world must have a creator and that the creation of the world was out of something which he describes by various terms that came to be referred to as matter is quite clear. But that it was not meant to be a direct reproduction of Plato's theory in its original form as found in the *Timaeus* is evidenced by two facts.

First, while the story of creation in the *Timaeus* begins with the statement that "what has come to be must be brought into being by some cause," [2] which corresponds to the opening statement of this theory here that "bodies had a Creator," there is nothing in the *Timaeus* to correspond to the statement here that the proponents of this theory have arrived at their belief as the conclusion of their allegation that "a thing can come into existence only from something." In the *Timaeus*, the existence of the so-called matter out of which the

[4] *Emunot* I, 3, p. 70, ll. 5–8. For studies of the theories of creation, as well as of the arguments for them, in Saadia, cf. Jacob Guttmann, *Saadia*, pp. 35–44; Neumark, *Geschichte*, I, pp. 438–448; *Toledot*, II, pp. 113–120; Ventura, *Saadia*, pp. 95–108.

[1] *Emunot* I, 3, 2nd Theory, p. 41, ll. 10–12.

[2] *Tim.* 28 C.

world was created is assumed without any explanation. In fact, the allegation ascribed here by Saadia to the proponents of this theory is a paraphrase of the principle that "nothing comes into existence from nonexistence," which is described by Aristotle as the common opinion of all the early Greek physicists and as one which is accepted by himself.[3] But neither the physicists nor Aristotle use this principle as the basis of a belief in the createdness of the world; they use it only as a description of the origination of things in this our world which they assume to be eternal. Who then were the proponents of this theory which, starting with the assertion that the world was created by God, made use of this Aristotelian principle to show that God's creation of the world had to be from something?

Second, in the *Timaeus* there is no mention of "spiritual things" out of which the composite bodies in the world were created. What then is meant by these spiritual things?

The answer to the first of these two questions will be found in a subsequent section of this chapter,[4] where I shall try to show (1) that the controversy reported in the name of certain Mutakallimūn as to whether "the nonexistent" is "something" or "nothing" originated as a controversy over the meaning of the term "nonexistent" in a formula describing creation as coming "from the nonexistent" as to whether it meant "something" or "nothing"; (2) that those who took it to mean "something" did so because they followed the Aristotelian teaching that in every form of coming into existence the coming into existence must be from something, which is the background of the statement here that "a thing can come into existence only from something"; (3) that that something out of which the world came into existence was identified by them with the Platonic pre-existent eternal matter.

As for the second question, several explanations have been advanced as to the meaning of the "spiritual things." (1)

[3] *Phys.* I, 8, 191a, 30–31; cf. I, 4, 187a, 27–29.
[4] Cf. *Kalam*, pp. 359–372.

Some identify them either (a) only with atoms [5] or (b) only with Platonic ideas,[6] whereas (2) others identify them either (a) with a combination of the Platonic pre-existent matter with atoms [7] or (b) with a combination of Platonic ideas with atoms.[8]

A close examination of Saadia's subsequent discussion of this theory makes it quite clear that it is based upon a combination of the Platonic pre-existent eternal matter with atoms. That it is based upon the Platonic pre-existent eternal matter is evidenced by the fact that Saadia's description of the process of the creation of the world from the "spiritual things" follows, with but a few slight variations, Plato's description in the *Timaeus* of the creation of the world from his pre-existent matter.[9] That the "spiritual things" are atoms is also evidenced by Saadia's statement that from those spiritual things God "collected small points, that is, indivisible particles" [10] and from his subsequent reference to those spiritual things as "spiritual particles." [11] This means that among those Mutakallimūn who adopted the Platonic theory of creation out of a pre-existent eternal matter there were some who combined that theory with their belief in atoms and thus made that pre-existent eternal matter to consist of atoms. There is a suggestion of an atomized Platonic pre-existent eternal matter in the second of Shahrastānī's two doxographic reports on Plato,[12] the one which is described as being based on the *Timaeus*.[13]

There is, however, no way of telling whether, according to this theory, the atomized Platonic pre-existent eternal matter

[5] J. Fürst, *Glaubenslehre und Philosophie* (1845), p. 69; A. Schmiedl, *Studien über jüdische, insonders jüdisch-arabische philosophie* (1869), p. 281; M. Lambert, *Commentaire sur le Sefer Yeṣira* (1891), French, p. 17, n. .3

[6] W. Bacher, *Die Bibelexegese der jüdischen Religionsphilosophen* (1892), p. 15, n. 2; M. Schreiner, *Kalām*, p. 9, n. 5.

[7] Guttmann, *Saadia*, p. 45; Malter, *Saadia*, p. 203; Ventura, *Saadia*, p. 117.

[8] Neumark, *Geschichte*, I, pp. 448–449; *Toledot*, II, pp. 120–121.

[9] *Emunot* I, 3, 2nd Theory, p. 41, l. 16 – p. 42, l. 3.

[10] *Ibid.*, p. 41, ll. 14–15.

[11] *Ibid.*, ll. 20–21.

[12] *Milal*, p. 287, ll. 6–7; cf. Guttmann, *Saadia*, p. 45.

[13] *Milal*, p. 286, l. 18.

was also idealized. On the one hand, the term "spiritual" (*rūḥāniyyah*) is used in Arabic texts as the equivalent of the term "intellectual" (*'aḳliyyah*) as a description of Platonic ideas. Thus in the so-called *Theology of Aristotle*, where in one place the term "pattern" (*mithāl* = παράδειγμα), that is, a Platonic idea, is in one place described as "intellectual" (*'aḳlī* = νοερόν),[14] whereas, in another place, the Platonic ideas in their totality are referred to as "the spiritual things" (*al-ashyā' al-rūḥāniyyah*).[15] So also Shahrastānī in the first of his two doxographic reports on Plato, speaks of the latter's ideas, as "the intellectual patterns and the spiritual forms" which are "in the intellectual world." [16] In both the foregoing passages quoted, it is to be noted, the ideas are assumed to be what may be described as extradeical [17] — exactly as what one would have to assume them to be in this second theory, if the term "spiritual" here was taken to mean "ideal." Then also, Saadia's own statement that "certain persons of our own people" identified the pre-existent "eternal spiritual things" in this theory with the pre-existent "wisdom" in Proverbs 8:22 [18] would seem to indicate that by "spiritual" is meant ideal, for the "wisdom" with which the "eternal spiritual things" were identified by them is taken to refer to the Platonic ideas [19] and, while Saadia refutes this identification, he refutes it only on the ground that the wisdom in that verse is not eternal and is not something out of which the world was created. It is to be noted that in the first of Shahrastānī's two doxographic reports on Plato there is a suggestion that the pre-existent eternal matter was an ideal matter,[20] though according to this suggestion that ideal matter did not eternally co-exist with God but was an eternal emanation from God

[14] *Uthūlūjiyya*, p. 51, l. 17.

[15] *Ibid*., p. 52, ll. 5–6.

[16] *Milal*, p. 284, l. 8.

[17] Cf. "Extradeical and Intradeical Interpretations of Platonic Ideas" in my *Religious Philosophy*, pp. 27–68.

[18] *Emunot* I, 3, 2nd Theory, p. 45, ll. 4 ff.

[19] Neumark, *Geschichte*, I, p. 449; *Toledot*, II, p. 121; cf. Guttmann, *Saadia*, pp. 47–48.

[20] *Milal*, p. 283, ll. 14–18.

and though also there is no suggestion that it consisted of atoms. But, on the other hand, in the corresponding second of the nine theories of creation in Saadia's Commentary on *Sefer Yeṣirah*, the pre-existent eternal matter is only atomized but is not idealized. One would therefore be inclined to take the term "spiritual" here to mean "subtle," "fine," "tenuous," and to be advisedly used here by Saadia in order to indicate that the atoms, according to the proponents of this theory, are unextended and thus to lay them open to his subsequent criticism of them.[21] That the Arabic term *rūḥānī*, like its corresponding Greek term *πνευματικός*, may have the meaning of "subtle," "fine," "tenuous," can be shown from Shahrastānī who, while in his report on Plato, as we have seen, uses the term *rūḥāniyyah* as a description of ideas, in his report on Anaximenes says that "that which comes from the clearness of the pure air is something subtle (*laṭīf*) and spiritual (*rūḥānī*)," [22] belonging to what he describes as "supernal bodies." [23] As for Saadia's reference to the anonymous "certain persons of our own people," there is no evidence that they took "wisdom" to refer to Platonic ideas; they may have taken it to refer directly to what Saadia describes as the "eternal spiritual things," meaning thereby simply eternal atoms.

Now for Saadia's second theory in his Commentary on *Sefer Yeṣirah*.

The proponents of this theory, he says, believe that all visible things in the world have their origin in "a simple thing" (*shay basīṭ*),[24] which "simple thing" is in the course of his exposition described by him (1) as "the simple root" (*al-aṣl al-basīṭ*) called by the exponents of this theory "mother"

[21] *Emunot* I, 3, 2nd Theory, p. 42, l. 12 – p. 43, l. 7.

[22] *Milal*, p. 259, l. 14; cf. Proclus's description of fire and air as "the *πνευματικά* of the elements" in his Commentary on the *Timaeus* (40 E). So also in the *Dictionary of Technical Terms in the Sciences of the Musulmans*, I, p. 547, l. 14, is the term *al-arwāḥ*, literally "the spirits," given the meaning of *ajsām laṭīfah*, "subtle bodies."

[23] *Milal*, l. 13.

[24] *Tafsir Kitāb al-Mabādī*, p. 4, ll. 5–6 (17).

(*al-umm*) and "clay" (*al-ṭīnah*) and "matter" (*al-hayūlā*),[25] terms used as descriptions of Plato's antemundane matter,[26] and (2) as "the root (*aṣl*) of these [visible] things" conceived by the exponents of this theory as consisting of "atoms." [27] Thus this theory is quite evidently a combination of the Platonic theory of an antemundane matter with the theory of atoms. The combined nature of this theory is also to be discerned in Saadia's statement that its exponents are divided into three groups: (1) "Those who maintain that that eternal element was completely combined and composed by the Creation, so that nothing remained of it in its original state; (2) those who maintain that the Creator did not combine it completely, that this world has used up only part of it, and that the remainder is still unused, subsisting in its state of simplicity and tenuity; (3) those who maintain that while all of it has been used up in composition, not all of it has been used up by this world, for there proceeded from it an innumerable number of worlds, of which this world of ours is only one." [28] Now of these three groups, the first reproduces what

[25] *Ibid.*, ll. 10–11 (18).

[26] The term "mother" (*al-umm*) as a description of Platonic matter occurs in *Timaeus* 51 A. The term "hyle" for Platonic matter is Aristotelian (cf. *Phys.* I, 4, 187a, 17–18). The term "clay" (*tinah*), I think, is here a translation of the Greek ἐκμαγεῖον, "that on which an impression is made," such as a lump of wax or clay or any other similar stuff, which is used by Plato in *Timaeus* 50 C as a description of matter. This is probably also the origin of the use of the Hebrew term *ḥomer* as a translation of the Greek *hyle*. Cf. my paper "Arabic and Hebrew Terms for Matter and Elements with especial Reference to Saadia," *JQR*, n.s., 38: 47–61. Cf. also the use of "clay" (πηλός) in the sense of "matter" (ὕλη) in Plotinus, *Enneads* II, 4, 8.

[27] *Tafsīr Kitāb al-Mabādī*, p. 4, l. 7 (17). The underlying Arabic statement of Saadia here is to be translated as follows: "And they conceived the root (*aṣl*) of these things as indivisible parts." The term *aṣl*, "root," here, I take it, is used in the same sense as the term *aṣl* in *al-aṣl al-basīṭ*, "the simple root," in l. 11, where quite evidently it refers to *shay basīṭ*, "a simple thing," in l. 6, and hence my translation. Lambert, however, translates this Arabic statement of Saadia as follows: "Et ils se représentent les corps dans leur principe [*aṣl*] comme des parties indivisibles."

[28] *Tafsīr*, p. 5, ll. 4–9 (pp. 18–19). In connection with this view about a plurality of worlds, Saadia remarks that certain Jews of the time thought this view the same as that expressed in the rabbinic statement (*'Abodah Zarah* 3b) about the existence of 18,000 worlds. This rabbinic statement, it is to be noted, is reflected in Baghdādī's reference to some "commentators"

Plato himself says of the four elements out of which the world was created, namely, that "the making of the universe took up the whole bulk of each of these four elements" so that "nothing was left over whereof another world should be formed." [29] The second and third groups represent two phases of the atomistic theory, first, that not all the atoms were used up at one time, so that in the infinite space atoms are still floating aimlessly, from which, worlds are from time to time being formed,[30] and, second, that our world is one of an innumerable number of worlds.[31] But, it will be noticed, throughout his entire discussion of this second theory in his commentary on *Sefer Yeṣirah*, Saadia makes no allusion at all to the theory of ideas. Moreover, the chief argument by which Saadia tries to refute this second theory in his Commentary on *Sefer Yeṣirah* seems to be aimed at the defense of the Platonic theory of a pre-existent eternal matter by certain religious philosophers against the charge that a matter coeternal with God would make it a god equal with God. The defense against this charge was that the mere eternity of matter would not make it a god equal with God, for God would still exercise His power over that matter, being its shaper and molder.[32] Evidently having this in mind, Saadia says: "If the matter were coeternal with God it would not allow itself to be acted upon by God so that He could administer it at His will, for their equality in eternity necessarily requires that they should also be equal in the fact either that neither of them acts upon the other or that either of them acts upon the other." [33]

A view like this second theory of creation in Saadia's

---

who, relying on the plural *'ālamīna* used in the Koran, said that "God has 18,000 worlds every one of which is like this perceptible one" (*Uṣūl*, p. 34, ll. 4–5).

[29] *Tim.* 32 C – 33 A.

[30] *Diogenes* X, 89.

[31] *Ibid.*, 45, 73–74.

[32] Tertullian, *Adversus Hermogenem* 5; *Moreh* II, 13, 2nd Theory, p. 197, ll. 19 ff.; *Milḥamot Adonai* VI, l. 18, ad 3, p. 373.

[33] *Tafsīr*, p. 4, ll. 12–15 (p. 18).

Commentary on *Sefer Yeṣirah*, and perhaps also like the second theory of creation in his *Emunot ve-Deʿot*, if the term "spiritual" there is not taken to mean ideal, was held by Muhammad b. Zakariyyā al-Rāzī (d. 923 or 932), an older contemporary of Saadia. According to him, the world was created out of eternal atoms, which eternal atoms are called by him "absolute matter" (*al-hayūlā al-muṭlaḳah*) — a combination of terms reflecting the Greek χωριστὴ ὕλη by which Aristotle refers to the Platonic pre-existent eternal matter.[34]

While the reports by Saadia and Muhammad b. Zakariyyā al-Rāzī deal with a special version of the Platonic theory of creation, a report on the original form of the Platonic theory is listed by Baghdādī as the fourth of the eight theories enumerated in his *Farḳ* and as the second of the six theories enumerated in his *Uṣūl*. In the *Farḳ* it is described as the theory of "those who believe in an eternal matter (*hayūlā*), while admitting the creation of the accidents (*aʿrāḍ*) thereof." [35] In the *Uṣūl* it is described as the theory of "the partisans of matter in their assertion that the matter of the world is eternal but its accidents are created." [36] That the theory so described in both works is meant to be that of Plato can be shown by the fact that in Shahrastānī's doxography of Greek philosophers the Platonic theory of creation is represented as an assertion that, while matter (*hayūlā*) is eternal, the forms (*ṣuwar*) are created." [37] The "accidents" in Baghdādī are only verbal variations of the "forms" in the doxography of Shahrastānī.

2. THE ETERNAL AIR OF ANAXIMENES EMANATIONALIZED

The third theory is said by Saadia to be "that of him who asserts that the Creator of the bodies created them from His own essence." [1]

[34] Cf. Pines, *Atomenlehre*, pp. 40–45.
[35] *Farḳ*, p. 346, ll. 9–10.
[36] *Uṣūl*, p. 59, ll. 10–11; cf. p. 70, ll. 9–10.
[37] *Milal*, p. 286, ll. 12–13.
[1] *Emunot* I, 3, 3rd Theory, p. 45, l. 20 – p. 46, l. 1.

From its phrasing, this theory quite evidently refers to a theory of creation based upon a theory of emanation, according to which bodies were emanated directly from God. This is either a report of an actually existent theory of creation known to Saadia or a theory which, according to the practice of the time, Saadia thought might have already been formulated by someone on the basis of that theory of emanation. As for that theory of emanation, it is to be found in a report on the teaching of Anaximenes by Shahrastānī,[2] which is quite evidently based upon some early doxography. The account of the teaching of Anaximenes in the underlying doxography as reported by Shahrastānī falls into two parts, an apocryphal part [3] and a historical part.[4]

In the apocryphal part, Anaximenes is represented as a sort of forerunner of the theory of emanation and as one who, like all Arabic emanationists ever since the appearance of the *Theology of Aristotle*, uses the term *ibdāʿ* in the sense of God's creating something out of Himself and hence as a designation of the act of emanation. Thus, starting out with the assertion that in God are the forms of all the things that successively emanate from Him,[5] he goes on to outline his view of the process of successive emanation. The first emanation is "the form of the *ʿunṣur*," which, he says, "God created out of Himself" (*abdaʿa*).[6] The second emanation is "the form of the Intelligence (*al-ʿaḳl*)," which, he says, "proceeded (*inbaʿathat*) from the *ʿunṣur* by God's act of creation out of Himself." [7] Then God combined the *ʿunṣur* and the Intelligence,[8] and out of that combination there arose two worlds, described as "this world" [9] and "that world." [10]

In the historical part, continuing to use the term *ibdāʿ* in the sense of God's creating something out of Himself, the doxographer quotes Anaximenes as saying that "the very first

[2] *Milal*, p. 258, l. 9 – p. 260, l. 5.
[3] *Ibid.*, p. 258, ll. 10 ff.
[4] *Ibid.*, p. 259, ll. 12 ff.
[5] *Ibid.*, p. 258, ll. 12–13 and 16.
[6] *Ibid.*, p. 258, l. 17.
[7] *Ibid.*
[8] *Ibid.*, l. 18.
[9] *Ibid.*, p. 259, ll. 5 and 7.
[10] *Ibid.*, l. 7.

of the things created by God out of Himself (*al-mubdaʿāt*) was air and therefrom all the upper and lower bodies in the world arose."[11] He then goes on to quote Anaximenes as distinguishing within the air between "pure" air and "impure" air[12] and as saying that from the pure air arose "the world of spiritual beings" and from the impure air arose "the world of corporeal beings."[13]

Thus the historical part contains a repetition of the same theory of emanation as that contained in the apocryphal part, except that instead of the terms *ʿunṣur* and Intelligence it uses two kinds of air, the impure air and the pure air. As to what in the mind of the doxographer was the relation between these two parts, it is not clear. Shahrastānī hesitatingly suggests that "perhaps" the apocryphal part deals with "the spiritual world" and the historical part deals with "the corporeal world."[14] More likely, the historical part was meant to be an interpretation of the apocryphal part, so that *ʿunsur* was to be taken to mean air and Intelligence was to be taken to mean that which proceeded from the pure air by God's act of creation out of Himself.

But whatever the relation between the two parts of the doxography was thought of by the doxographer, here we have in the historical part a statement to the effect that all bodies, air and whatever arises from it, were created by God's act of creation out of Himself. This, we may assume, is the theory of emanation underlying the theory of creation described by Saadia as asserting that "the Creator of the bodies created them from His own essence."

3. THE ETERNAL WATER OF A PARTLY NEOPLATONIZED THALES ATOMIZED

The fourth theory is said by Saadia to be "that of him who combines the two preceding theories and maintains that the

[11] *Ibid.*, ll. 12–13.

[12] *Ibid.*, ll. 14–15.

[13] *Ibid.*, ll. 16–18.

[14] *Ibid.*, p. 259, l. 20 – p. 260, l. 2.

Creator created all things from His own essence as well as from things coeternal with Him, for he takes the spirits to come from the Creator and the bodies from the eternal things." [1] By the "eternal things," it is to be taken, he means what in the second theory he described as "eternal spiritual things," that is, atoms.

Apart from the expression "the eternal beings" by which is meant the eternal atoms, this theory of creation is quite evidently based upon a theory of emanation in which the emanatory process is restricted to what is described as "spirits," whereas "bodies" are outside of that process. Here, again, this may be a report of an actual theory of creation known to Saadia or it may be a theory which Saadia, according to the practice of the time, thought had already been formulated by someone on the basis of that theory of emanation. As for that theory of emanation, while Plotinus suggests it only as a possibility,[2] it could be actually found, as I shall try to show, in what must be taken to have been the original reading of a statement in a doxography used by Shahrastānī in his report on the teaching of Thales. Again, the account of this teaching of Thales in the doxography as reported by Shahrastānī is divided into two parts, an apocryphal and a historical, but here it is made clear that the apocryphal part deals with "spiritual beings" residing in "the intelligible world," whereas the historical part deals with "corporeal beings" residing in "the sensible world."

In the apocryphal part, starting out with the assertion that the Creator "has no forms with Him in His essence" [3] and that "creation [as expressed by the term *al-ibdaʿ*] means to bring into existence that which did not exist," [4] by which is meant proceeding from an essence devoid of any forms, he goes on to say that "the Creator created out of Himself (*abdaʿa*) the *ʿunṣur*," [5] or rather "the first *ʿunṣur*." [6] In that

[1] *Emunot* I, 3, 4th Theory, p. 40, ll. 3–6.

[2] *Enneads* VI, 8, 6 (ll. 18–23).

[3] *Milal*, p. 254, ll. 7–8.

[4] *Ibid.*, ll. 1–10.

[5] *Ibid.*, l. 18.

[6] *Ibid.*, l. 20.

ʿunṣur are "the forms of all the existent and known things [in both the intelligible world and the sensible world]," though it is only in "the intelligible world" that "from every one of those forms proceeded (*inbaʿthat*) an existent thing." [7] Later, in the historical part, this first *ʿunṣur* is also described as "the *ʿunṣur* of the spiritual, simple things" [8] and as the *ʿunṣur* whose "depth is incomprehensible and whose light is invisible." [9]

In the historical part, "water," [10] which is called "the corporeal *ʿunṣur*," [11] is described as "the *ʿunṣur* of corporeal, bodily things." [12] As for the origin of water, Thales is quoted as saying, according to the printed text, that "the first *al-mbdʿ* was water." [13] From the use made by Shahrastānī subsequently of this statement [14] it is evident that the unvocalized four letters *mbdʿ* were vocalized by him *mubdaʿ*, "created," and thus, according to this reading, the quotation from Thales means that "the first created thing was water." [15] But the four-letter *mbdʿ* of the printed text is suspect for the following reasons: (1) In the Greek sources Thales' water is described as ἀρχή,[16] of which the Arabic is *mbdʾ*, (= *mabdaʾ*), and so one has reason to suspect *mbdʿ* to be a corruption of *mbdʾ*. (2) Shahrastānī himself applies to water the term *mabdaʾ*: (a) Thus, after quoting Thales as saying that water is "a beginning and an end," he adds: "that is, the principle (*al-mabdaʾ*) and the consummation." [17] (b) Thus, also, he says that "Anaxagoras differs from Thales with reference to the first principle (*al-*

[7] *Ibid.*, p. 254, ll. 18–19, plus p. 255, l. 1.

[8] *Ibid.*, p. 255, ll. 11–13.

[9] *Ibid.*, l. 181.

[10] *Ibid.*, l. 5.

[11] *Ibid.*, ll. 6–7.

[12] *Ibid.*, l. 12.

[13] *Ibid.*, ll. 4–5.

[14] *Ibid.*, p. 256, ll. 5–13.

[15] Haarbrücker evidently vocalized *mbdʿ* here as *mubdiʿ*, for he translated it by "Schöpfer" (vol. II, p. 83, l. 25).

[16] Cf. *Metaph.* I, 3, 983b, 18–21. The term ἀρχή, by which Thales' water is also described in pseudo-Plutarch's *De Placitis Philosophorum*, I, 3, p. 276, l. 5, is in its Arabic version translated by *awwal* (ed. Badawi, p. 97, ll. 4–5).

[17] *Milal*, p. 255, ll. 11–12. This seems to be based upon the statement "all existence is from water and into water it is resolved" in *De Placitis Philosophorum* (Greek, p. 276, ll. 12–13; Arabic, p. 97, ll. 7–8).

mabda' al-awwal)," [18] where from the context it is clear that "the first principle" refers to both Anaxagoras' homoeomeries and Thales' water. On the basis of all this we may conjecture that Shahrastānī had before him two readings, *mbd'* and *mbd'*, and while he chose the latter in order to be able to say that Thales' view of a created water was borrowed from the story of Creation in Genesis and a verse in the Koran (11.9),[19] the other reading still lingered in his mind and he used it.

We may thus assume that Saadia had before him this doxography about the teaching of Thales with its original term *mbd'*. Thus according to that doxography spirits emanated from God, but bodies arose out of water which was described as "the first principle," that is to say, an eternal principle.

4. DUALISM

The fifth theory is said by Saadia to be "that of him who asserts the existence of two creators." [1] The particular kind of dualism dealt with here by Saadia, it has been shown, is that of Manichaeism.[2] Baghdādī mentions dualism as the third in his list of six theories, describing it as that of "the Dualists in their belief in the eternity of light and darkness." [3] Ibn Ḥazm, after referring to the fourth in his list of five theories as the theory of "those who maintain that the Agent of the world and its Ruler is more than one," [4] says that those who maintain so "fall into various groups, all of whom are reducible to two groups," [5] and, in the course of his description of the first of these groups, the Magians, he says that, according to them, "Ahriman is the doer of evil and Ormazed is the doer of good." [6]

[18] *Milal*, p. 256, l. 15.
[19] *Ibid.*, ll. 5–13.
[1] *Emunot* I, 3, 5th Theory, p. 48, ll. 12–13.
[2] Guttmann, *Saadia*, pp. 53–54; Neumark, *Geschichte*, I, p. 452; *Toledot*, II, p. 155; Ventura, *Saadia*, pp. 127–137.
[3] *Ibid.*, p. 59, ll. 10–11.
[4] *Fiṣal* I, p. 34, l. 1.
[5] *Ibid.*, ll. 2–3.
[6] *Ibid.*, ll. 13–14.

5. THE FOUR ELEMENTS OF EMPEDOCLES

The sixth theory is described by Saadia as that "of him who professes four natures (*ṭabā'i'*; Hebrew: *yesodot* = elements)."[1] Its proponents, says Saadia, maintain that "all bodies are composed of four natures, namely, heat and cold and moisture and dryness; that each of these four natures existed at first in isolation, then they united, and as a result there originated from them the bodies."[2] In the course of his discussion, instead of heat and cold and moisture and dryness he speaks of fire, air, water, and earth,[3] which means that he identifies the "four natures" with what is generally known as the "four elements."

In the form in which it is thus represented by Saadia, it reflects the view of Empedocles as that which could have been gathered by him from Greek philosophic works already translated into Arabic, which, by the way, is different from the view of the Neoplatonized Empedocles to be found in the pseudepigraphic doxography preserved in Shahrastānī.[4] The Greek philosophic sources of the teachings of Empedocles already available to Saadia and Baghdādī are the various works of Aristotle and the pseudo-Plutarch's *De Placitis Philosophorum*. From these sources they could have gathered the following main points in the teaching of Empedocles: (1) "The elements (στοιχεῖα: *ustuksāt*) are four, fire, air, water, earth. The principles are two, Love and Strife, of which one produces union and the other separation."[5] (2) These four elements of Empedocles "always remain and are not generated."[6] (3) The world was constructed out of the segregated elements after they had been combined by Love.[7] It is on the

[1] *Emunot* I, 3, 6th Theory, p. 55, l. 7.

[2] *Ibid.*, ll. 7–10.

[3] *Ibid.*, p. 55, l. 20 – p. 56, l. 5; p. 57, ll. 2–5.

[4] *Milal*, p. 260, ll. 6 ff.

[5] *De Placitis* I, 3, 20 (Arabic, p. 103, ll. 7–9). The term *al-ījād* in the Arabic is a misprint of *al-īḥād* = ἑνωτική; cf. *Metaph.* I, 7, 988a, 27–28; *De Gen. et Corr.* II, 1, 329a, 1–3.

[6] *Metaph.* I, 3, 984a, 8–10.

[7] *De Caelo* III, 2, 301a, 16–20.

basis of these statements, or statements like these, that Saadia has reproduced the essential points in Empedocles' theory needful for his purpose, namely, that at first the elements or natures were segregated, that then they became aggregated, and that as a result of that aggregation the world was formed.

The indiscriminate use of the terms "elements" and "natures," or rather their identification, by both Saadia and Baghdādī, has its origin in Aristotle. In Aristotle, each of the four elements is characterized by the qualities "hot" and "cold" coupled with the properties "dry" and "moist." [8] These qualities are sometimes each of them described by Aristotle as a "nature" (φύσις),[9] but sometimes they are all of them described by him as "elements" (στοιχεῖα).[10] So also Galen, referring to Hippocrates' discussion of heat and cold and dryness and moisture in his *De Natura Hominis*, designates them by the term "elements," [11] even though Hippocrates himself does not use that term, and evidently it is on the basis of Galen's statement that Isaac Israeli, similarly referring to Hippocrates, also designates these four qualities by the term "elements." [12]

Since Empedocles is criticized by Aristotle, it was quite natural for Saadia to draw upon Aristotle's criticism for his own criticism of the same theory.

Aristotle in his criticism tries to show that Empedocles' theory fails to explain how compound natural bodies are generated from the elements. They cannot be generated from a mere chance coming together of elements. They must be generated from a coming together according to a certain proportion. "What, then, is the cause of this proportional coming together?" The cause cannot be any of the four ele-

[8] *De Gen. et Corr.* II, 3, 330a, 30 – 330b, 5.

[9] *De Part. Animal.* I, 1, 640b, 9; *Metaph.* I, 3, 983b, 26.

[10] *De Gen. et Corr.* II, 3, 330a, 30, 33–34.

[11] *De Elementis ex Hippocrate* I, 9, in *Galeni Opera Omnia*, ed. Kühn, I, p. 481; cf. Zeller, *Phil. d. Griech.*, II, 2³, p. 441, n. 2 (English, *Aristotle*, I, p. 479, n. 5).

[12] Isaac Israeli, *De Elementis*, fol. VIIb, ll. 67–68; *Sefer ha-Yesodot*, pp. 36–37. Cf. Jacob Guttmann, *Isaac ben Salomon Israeli*, p. 60, n. 5.

ments, nor even Love and Strife. The cause of this would necessarily have to be what is called the "nature" of each thing, but about this, complains Aristotle, Empedocles in his poem "On Nature" "says nothing" and what he does say "is no explanation of 'nature.'" [13] From Aristotle's subsequent discussion it may be gathered that Aristotle could conclude his argument by saying that if Empedocles had tried to explain what that "nature" is he would have arrived at Aristotle's own view that that "nature" is what Aristotle calls the formal, final, and efficient cause, which ultimately leads to his own prime mover.[14]

Similarly Saadia in his criticism of this theory tries to show that its proponents failed to explain how the elements changed from a state of separation to a state of union. He challenges them to tell him whether the state of union in which the elements came to exist and similarly the state of separation in which they originally existed was due to "their own essence (*li-ʿaynihā*: *le-ʿaṣmam*) or to something other than this." [15] He rejects the first alternative on the ground that if their own essence were the determining cause for their being either in a state of separation or in a state of union, then by their own essence they should have either remained in a state of separation or they should have always been in a state of union. Then, taking up the second alternative, namely, the assumption of the existence of "something other" than the four elements, he rejects it as follows: If, on the one hand, that "something other" is assumed to have caused the original state of separation of the elements, then "this would bring into play a fifth [element] of a causative nature,[16] which the proponents of this theory should be called upon to explain what it is, but this they will find themselves unable to do." [17] If, on the other hand, that "something other" is assumed to

[13] *De Gen. et Corr.* II, 6, 233b, 3–18.

[14] *Ibid.*, 9, 335a, 24 ff.

[15] *Emunot* I, 3, 6th Theory, p. 56, ll. 5–7; cf. l. 11.

[16] Aristotle calls Empedocles' Love and Strife "elements" which cause motion (*De Gen. et Corr.* I, 1, 314a, 17); hence my translation.

[17] *Emunot* I, 3, 6th Theory, p. 56, ll. 12–13.

have caused their subsequent state of union, then "this is exactly what we were aiming at when we said that the elements had a Creator, who had created them in a state of union." [18]

Thus by the very same reasoning by which Aristotle forces Empedocles to admit the existence of a prime mover, Saadia forces him and his followers to admit the existence of a Creator.

In connection with this theory of four eternal elements, Saadia refers to a certain unnamed person "of our own people," who had a partly similar view. That unnamed person of the Jewish people, who undoubtedly believed in the scriptural teaching that the world was created by God, is said by Saadia to have believed in the eternity of two pre-existent elements, "water" and "air," for which he claimed to have found support in Scripture.[19] The support which he claimed to have found in Scripture was probably due to the fact that, like Philo,[20] he interpreted the terms "heaven" and "earth" in the opening verse in Genesis to mean the elements of "fire" and "earth" and, inasmuch as in that opening verse the creation of only "heaven" and "earth" is mentioned, he inferred that the elements of "water" and "air" were eternal. It may be remarked that in the old rabbinic speculations on the creation of the world from some pre-existent element, fire or light and snow,[21] or water and earth,[22] usually come into play. However, none of these pre-existent elements are said by the rabbis to be eternal.

Corresponding to this sixth theory in Saadia is the seventh in Baghdādī's list of seven erroneous theories in his *Farḳ* and the fourth in his list of five erroneous theories in his *Uṣūl*. In the *Farḳ* it is described as the theory of "the philosophers who assert the four natures (*ṭabā'i'*) and the four elements (*'anāṣir*), which are earth and water and fire and air." [23] In

[18] *Ibid.*, ll. 9–10.

[19] *Ibid.*, p. 57, ll. 2–13.

[20] Cf. *Philo*, I, pp. 306–307.

[21] *Genesis Rabbah* 10, 3; *Pirḳe de-Rabbi Eliezer* 3; cf. *Moreh* II, 26.

[22] *Exodus Rabbah* 13, 1.

[23] *Fark*, p. 346, ll. 14–15.

the *Uṣūl* it is described as the theory of "the advocates of natures, who assert the eternity of earth and water and fire and air." [24] In neither of these works is the name of the author of this theory given. But in the *Farḳ*, just prior to this sixth theory, at the conclusion of the description of the fifth, which is that of Neoplatonic emanationism, there is the statement: "This was the opinion of Empedocles." This statement is probably misplaced and should be transferred to the end of this sixth theory.

6. THE INFINITE OF ANAXIMANDER

The seventh theory is said by Saadia to be that "of him who professes four natures and matter (*hayūlā*)." [1] On the face of it, this would seem to mean the assertion of four eternal elements underlying which was an eternal matter. So taken, this would seem to refer to Aristotle's theory of the four elements, for it is exactly in these terms that Aristotle himself states the difference between his own theory of the four elements and that of Empedocles. According to himself, he says, believing as he does that the elements are transformed into one another, there is something common to all the elements,[2] namely, "a single matter" (*μία ὕλη*),[3] whereas, according to Empedocles, believing as he does that the elements are not transformed into one another, there is nothing common, that is, a single matter, to all of them.[4] The fact that the theory preceding it, the sixth in Saadia's list, is that of Empedocles would seem to corroborate the impression that this is the view of Aristotle. But this interpretation of Saadia's theory is impossible, for Aristotle's theory of eternity, as we shall see, is dealt with by Saadia right after this theory, the eighth in his list, so that this theory must be that of somebody else. What we need here

[24] *Uṣūl*, p. 59, ll. 12–13.

[1] *Emunot* I, 3, 7th Theory, p. 57, ll. 13–14.

[2] *De Gen. et Corr.* II, 7, 334a, 15–17.

[3] *Ibid.*, 334b, 3.

[4] *Ibid.*, 334a, 18–20, and II, 6, 333a, 16–17. Cf. Joachim's Commentary (p. 239) on 334a 15 – b, 7.

is a theory which, like that of Empedocles, believes in four elements, but, while unlike that of Empedocles and like that of Aristotle, believes that underlying the four elements there is a common matter, still this common matter is unlike Aristotles common matter.

That there was such a theory may be gathered from Aristotle, who, in one of his works, after mentioning Empedocles as having postulated the four elements,[5] refers to "those who postulate, besides the four elements we have mentioned, a single matter (μίαν ὕλην)," [6] which is subsequently described by him by the term "infinite" (ἄπειρον),[7] that is, Anaximander's theory of the infinite.[8] But, then, in his further descriptions of that "infinite" of Anaximander, which he calls "matter," he points, by implication, to certain differences between that matter as conceived of by Anaximander and his own conception of matter. One of the differences between them is implied in his description of Anaximander's "infinite," or "matter," as "body," [9] for his own matter is not a body. Another difference between them is implied in his description of Anaximander's "infinite," or "matter," as being the "principle," that is, the "cause," of other things, beside which there are no other "causes," as being that which "steers" all things, and as being "the divinity," [10] for his own matter, while described as a cause, is not the only cause, for beside it there are three other causes; moreover, his own matter does not "steer" all things and is not "the divinity," for his own matter is pure potentiality which is acted upon by a succession of forms ultimately arriving at a pure form or prime cause or prime mover who is God.

It is thus this theory of Anaximander, which is described by Aristotle himself as being unlike both his own theory and the theory of Empedocles, that is meant by Saadia's seventh theory.

[5] *De Gen. et Corr.* II, 1, 329a, 2–3.
[6] *Ibid.*, 2, 329a, 8–9.
[7] *Ibid.*, 12.
[8] *Phys.* III, 4, 203b, 14; *De Placitis* I, 3, 3 (Arabic, p. 98, ll. 1–8).
[9] *De Gen. et Corr.* II, 2, 329a, 11.
[10] *Phys.* III, 4, 203b, 10–15.

Corroborative evidence that Saadia's seventh theory is the theory of Anaximander, which, according to Aristotle, is only a variation of the theory of Empedocles, may be gathered from Saadia's criticism of these theories when compared with Aristotle's common criticism of the theories of Anaximander and Empedocles.

The theory of Anaximander is criticized by Aristotle both directly and indirectly. Directly, he tries to show that that single matter or infinite of Anaximander cannot be something underlying the four elements, concluding that it is "either any one of the elements, or else it is nothing." [11] He thus finds that Anaximander's view is logically the same as that of Empedocles. Indirectly, both Anaximander and Empedocles, believing as they do in material causes only, are undoubtedly included by Aristotle in his general criticism of all those materialists who explain generation and motion and change by only material causes. This general criticism of his contains the following points: (1) "It is characteristic of matter to suffer action and to be moved, but to move and to act belongs to another power." [12] (2) Using "water" and "fire" and a "saw" as examples, he argues that (a) "water does not of itself produce an animal out of itself"; [13] that (b) "even fire [which acts and sets things moving] is itself moved and suffers action"; [14] that (c) "they (that is, the materialists) act in a manner resembling him who would attribute to the saw the cause of those things that come-to-be," [15] concluding with an assertion of his own view that "if there is to be movement, there must be something which moves" [16] and that all movements "must be under one principle," [17] that is, under one Prime Mover. A restatement of this criticism, especially applied to Anaximander, is to be found in pseudo-Plutarch's *De Placitis Philosophorum*, which reads as follows: "Besides Anaximander is wrong in that, while setting forth matter,

[11] *De Gen. et Corr.* II, 5, 332a, 20–25.
[12] *Ibid.*, 9, 235b, 29–31.
[13] *Ibid.*, 32–33.
[14] *Ibid.*, 236a, 7; cf. 11–12.
[15] *Ibid.*, 7–9.
[16] *Ibid.*, 10, 237a, 17–18.
[17] *Ibid.*, 22.

he makes no mention of the efficient cause, for the infinite can be nothing but matter, but matter cannot become actual, except an agent be annexed." [18]

Reflecting this Aristotelian common criticism of the theories of Anaximander and Empedocles is Saadia's common criticism of his seventh and sixth theories, which are respectively those of Anaximander and Empedocles. The main points in his criticism are as follows: (1) Their admission that "no act is produced except by an agent" refutes their own view that "an inanimate object could produce anything"; [19] (2) using "water" and "fire" and a "saw" as examples, he argues that (a) "water" is only an intermediary cause which is used by God in the production of fruit from a tree; [20] that (b) "fire" burns not of itself but by its being moved by the air, "which is in turn moved by the Creator . . . who is the Prime Mover"; [21] and that (c) in the scriptural verse, "should the saw magnify itself against him that moveth it?" (Isa. 10:15), there is evidence for the belief that "all acts are to be traced back to the Prime Mover." [22]

7. THE ARISTOTELIAN ETERNITY OF THE WORLD

The eighth theory is said by Saadia to be that "of him who asserts that the heavens are the makers (*fāʿilah*: *poʿalim*) of the bodies and who regards the heavens as eternal and as not being composed of those four natures but rather of another thing, a fifth [nature]." [1]

On the face of it, this statement would seem to mean that only the heaven, which is not composed of the four elements, is eternal and, being eternal, is the maker, that is to say, the creator, of the bodies, which, being composed of the four elements, are not eternal, and consequently that part of the

[18] *De Placitis* I, 3, 3, p. 278, ll. 1–7 (Arabic, p. 98, ll. 5–8).
[19] *Emunot* I, 3, 7th Theory, p. 57, l. 19 – p. 58, l. 2.
[20] *Ibid.*, p. 58, ll. 2–7.
[21] *Ibid.*, ll. 7–11.
[22] *Ibid.*, ll. 11–16.
[1] *Emunot* I, 3, 8th Theory, p. 58, ll. 16–18.

world under the heaven, which is composed of those bodies, is not eternal. But, inasmuch as the view that heaven consists of a fifth element is identified with the name of Aristotle,[2] who is its author,[3] we have reason to assume that the anonymous author of this theory is Aristotle and that it is to Aristotle to whom Saadia ascribes the view that the heaven is eternal and that it is the maker of the bodies, which would seem to imply that the subcelestial bodies are not eternal and that they are made or created by the eternal heaven. But here is the rub. Aristotle, as known from his own writings, did not regard the subcelestial part of the world as not eternal nor did he regard it as being made or created by the eternal heaven. Let us then try to find out exactly what Aristotle's view was about the distinction between the heaven and the part of the world below it and also exactly what his view was about the relation of the heaven to the part of the world below and, in the light of what we find, let us see whether we cannot harmonize the statements of Saadia here with the known views of Aristotle.

To begin with, Aristotle, we find, draws a distinction between things under the heaven, which he describes as "generable and corruptible," [4] and things in the heaven, which he describes as "eternal and primary." [5] Still, despite the generability and corruptibility of things under the heaven, he believes that the subcelestial part of the world is eternal, for, as he says, though individual things are generable and corruptible, "generation and corruption will always be continuous and will never fail," [6] and this unfailing process of generation and corruption implies, according to him, something eternal underlying that process. As for the cause of this unfailing continuity of the process of generation and corruption of the individual things which constitute the sublunar part of the world, he says that it is "the circular motion [of the heaven]." [7] But with regard to the heaven, whose circular motion causes the unfailing continuity of the subcelestial in-

[2] *Diogenes*, V, 32; *Milal*, p. 318, ll. 1–2.
[3] *De Caelo* I, 2, 268b, 14 ff.
[4] *De Gen. et Corr.* II, 9, 335a, 24.
[5] *Ibid.*, 29.
[6] *Ibid.*, 10, 336b, 25–26.
[7] *Ibid.*, 336b, 34 – 337a, 1.

dividual things, as well as with regard to anything else that causes motion, Aristotle says that "in all things, alike in the products of nature and in the products of art, we are accustomed to give the name the maker (τὸ ποιοῦν) to that which is causing motion (κινητικόν)," [8] for "the mover (τὸ κινοῦν) is said to make something and the maker (τὸ ποιοῦν) to cause motion." [9]

This, then, is what we find in Aristotle with regard to the distinction between the heaven and the part of the world below it and also with regard to the relation of the heaven to that part of the world below it. In the light of all this, when Saadia uses the term "eternal" as a description only of "the heavens," he does not mean to imply that the subcelestial part of the world is not eternal; he only means that the subcelestial "bodies" individually are, as described by Aristotle, generable and corruptible, and, when he describes "the heavens" as "the makers of the bodies," he does not mean that the heaven is the creator of the bodies; he uses the term maker as used by Aristotle, in the sense of mover. Thus it is the view of the genuine Aristotle, as found in his genuine writings, that is reproduced here by Saadia.[10] While in his exposition here of Aristotle's theory of the eternity of the world Saadia did not feel it was necessary for him to refer to Aristotle's prime mover, his statements in the preceding theory, the seventh, that a verse in Isaiah is evidence for the belief that "all acts are to be traced back to the Prime Mover" [11] and that "the Creator . . . is the Prime Mover" [12] show that the Aristotle used by him here is likewise the Aristotle of the genuine Aristotelian writings and not the Neoplatonized Aristotle.

[8] *Ibid.*, 9, 335b, 27–29.

[9] *Ibid.*, I, 6, 323a, 15. Cf. the discussion of this 8th theory of Saadia by Ventura in his *Saadia*, p. 142.

[10] It is Saadia's 8th Theory that Moses Ibn Ezra identifies with that of Aristotle (*'Arugat ha-Bosem* in *Zion*, 2 (1842–43): 158. Dukes, in his note *ad loc.* (*ibid.*, n. 1) erroneously takes Ibn Ezra's statement to refer to Saadia's 7th Theory.

[11] Cf. above, p. 145, n. 22.

[12] Cf. above, p. 145, n. 21.

Just as his reproduction of the theory of the eternity of the world reflects specific statements or views of Aristotle, so also his three arguments against this theory are aimed at specific statements or views of Aristotle.

The first argument is aimed at a solution offered by Aristotle of two difficulties raised by himself. The two difficulties are as follows: First, why is there a difference in the number of motions between the outermost sphere and the five planets below it and also between these five planets and the sun or the moon below them? [13] Second, why are there a multitude of stars in the outermost sphere and only one single star in each of the spheres below it? [14] The solution of these difficulties offered by Aristotle is that there is a difference in the perfection of these three kinds of celestial spheres, the outermost sphere being the most perfect, the spheres between the outermost sphere and the solar and lunar spheres being next in perfection, and the solar and lunar spheres being the lowest in perfection.[15] With this evidently in mind Saadia argues as follows: "Of that which is eternal one part cannot be higher in degree of importance than another. Consequently, whether [as in the explanation of difference between the motions of the solar and lunar spheres and those of the spheres between them and the outermost spheres] the inner group of spheres be assumed to be of greater importance [than those below them] or whether [as in the explanation of the difference between the motion of the outermost sphere and the motion of the five planets below it] the outer sphere be assumed to be of greater importance, his solution is refuted. The same refutation applies to his explanation of the order of the distribution of the stars, some of which are located in the inner spheres, while most of them are situated in the outermost sphere." [16]

The second argument reflects two statements in Aristotle:

[13] *De Caelo* II, 12, 291b, 28 – 292a, 9.
[14] *Ibid.*, 292a, 10–14.
[15] *Ibid.*, 292a, 22 – 292b, 25; 292b, 27 – 293a, 4.
[16] *Emunot* I, 3, 8th Theory, p. 60, ll. 3–6.

(1) that the view of the eternity of the heaven and the view that the heaven consists of a fifth element are logically connected with each other;[17] (2) that he is inclined to accept the view that our sensory organs are perceptive of external objects because in each of them there is one of the four elements of which the eternal objects are composed.[18] Evidently with these two statements in mind, Saadia argues that in view of the fact that the heaven is perceived by our eyes, even though there is not in them the fifth element, the heaven cannot be said to consist of the fifth element and hence the heaven cannot be said to be eternal.[19]

The third and fourth arguments[20] are based upon the principle of the impossibility of one infinite being greater than another. This principle, though not directly stated by Aristotle, is clearly implied in some of his statements. Thus Averroes, commenting upon Aristotle's statement that "the same [infinite] thing cannot be many infinites,"[21] remarks that it is so because "it is impossible that one infinite should be greater than another."[22] Thus also Crescas, commenting upon Aristotle's statement that there cannot be "two infinites, that which moves and that which is moved, differing in their form and power,"[23] remarks: "This is impossible, for since the sum of these two will be greater than either one of them, it would follow that one infinite would be greater than another."[24]

Corresponding to this eighth theory in Saadia is the seventh in Baghdādī's list of seven erroneous theories in his *Farḳ* and the fifth in his list of five erroneous theories in his *Uṣūl*. In the *Farḳ* it is described as the theory of "those [philosophers] who believe in the eternity of the four elements and also in

[17] *De Caelo* I, 2–3.
[18] *De Sensu* 2, 438b, 17–19.
[19] *Emunot* I, 3, 8th Theory, p. 60, ll. 6–11.
[20] *Ibid.*, p. 60, l. 11 – p. 61, l. 6.
[21] *Phys.* III, 5, 204a, 25–26.
[22] Averroes in III *Phys.*, Comm. 37 (vol. IV, p. 102 C).
[23] *De Caelo* I, 7, 275b, 27–29.
[24] *Crescas' Critique of Aristotle*, p. 117.

the eternity of the celestial spheres together with their stars, maintaining that the celestial sphere[s] consist of a fifth nature and are not subject to generation and corruption either in their entirety or in part." [25] In the *Uṣūl* it is described as the theory of "those who believe in the eternity of the four elements and also in the eternity of the celestial spheres." [26]

8. EPICUREAN ATOMISM AND CHANCE

The ninth theory is described by Saadia as "the theory of chance (*ittifāḳ*: *miḳreh*), according to which there had existed from eternity "bodies not known what they are," except that some of them were "light" and some of them "heavy," and these bodies in their motion "converged toward the space now occupied by our world and crowded and pressed together" and out of this "by chance, without the design of a designer, nor as the act of an agent, whether that agent is acting with choice or is inanimate," the world came into being, the lighter bodies having become the heaven and the stars, the heavier parts having become earth and water, and the bodies of medium weight having become air.[1]

This theory reflects Greek atomism as it was known to Arabic readers from various doxographies, such as the Arabic translation of pseudo-Plutarch's Epitome of Aetius' *De Placitis Philosophorum* and as the doxography of Greek philosophers reproduced by Shahrastānī. Saadia's reference to the atoms as "bodies not known what they are" reflects the description of the atoms in Shahrastānī as being only "apprehensible by the mind" [2] or as being "intelligible, that is, apprehensible by the imagination but not by sense perception." [3] In pseudo-Plutarch the atoms are similarly said to be "conceivable only by reason" (λόγῳ, Arabic: *ʿaḳlan*).[4] Saadia's statement that

[25] *Farḳ*, p. 346, ll. 15–17.
[26] *Uṣūl*, p. 59, ll. 13–14.
[1] *Emunot* I, 3, 9th Theory, p. 61, ll. 12–19.
[2] *Milal*, p. 277, l. 9.
[3] *Ibid.*, l. 12.
[4] *De Placitis* I, 3, 18, p. 285a, ll. 3 and 8 (Arabic, p. 102, ll. 11 and 13).

some of the atoms are "light" and some "heavy" is to be taken to mean that they all have weight but that some of them are heavier than others, thus reflecting the statement in pseudo-Plutarch that the Epicurean atoms, in contradistinction to Democretean atoms, have weight.[5] Saadia's statement that the atoms "converged" toward the space now occupied by the world and "crowded and pressed together" alludes to the Eupicurean theory of the "swerve" (*παρέγκλισις*, *clinamen*) as it is described in pseudo-Plutarch's statement that "all atoms are moved, some perpendicularly and some obliquely."[6] Saadia's statement that out of this collision the world arises "by chance, without the design of a designer, nor as the act of an agent," reflects the pseudo-Plutarch's description of the formation of the world out of the "unprovident (*ἀπρονόητον*, *ghayr mudabbarah*) and fortuitous" motions of the atoms.[7]

9. THE DAHRIYYAH'S ETERNITY OF THE WORLD AND WHO THE DAHRIYYAH WERE

The tenth theory is described by Saadia as "the theory known as that of eternity (*dahr*: *ḳadmut*),"[1] of which the proponents, he says, are of three types. Some of them speak simply of "eternity" and mean thereby the eternity of the world as a whole; others add to their assertion of the eternity of the world as a whole the assertion of the eternity of "matter"; still others add to it the assertion of the eternity of "the four natures," that is, the four elements.[2] Then, describing the view of those who speak only of the eternity of the world as a whole, he says: "Its proponents assert that all things, namely, the heaven and the earth and plants and animals and the other phenomena, have always been as we see

[5] *Ibid.*, I, 3, 18 (Arabic, p. 102, l. 15); I, 12, 5 (Arabic, p. 117, l. 6).
[6] *Ibid.*, I, 12, 5 (Arabic, p. 117, ll. 6–7); I, 23, 4 (Arabic, p. 120, ll. 8–10).
[7] *Ibid.*, I, 4 (Arabic, p. 105, ll. 6 ff).
[1] *Emunot* I, 3, 10th Theory, p. 63, l. 6.
[2] *Ibid.*, p. 63, ll. 6–8; p. 65, ll. 14–15.

them, having neither beginning nor end, and their foremost argument in support of this theory is that they believe only in what is subject to the perception of their senses." [3]

Now this description of the view of the proponents of this theory certainly does not mean that they who are said to boast of believing only in what is observed by them with their senses denied the universally observed transitoriness of individual plants and animals and all other individual phenomena. Undoubtedly what the description means is that, despite the universally observed transitoriness of individual plants and animals and all other individual phenomena, the proponents of this theory believed that the process of generation and corruption to which all things in the world are seen to be subject is never seen to have a beginning or end.[4] Since this is what their conception of eternity must mean, it is exactly the same as the conception of eternity described by Saadia in his eighth theory, which, as we have seen, is that of Aristotle. So also the same as the view of Aristotle would be the view of those who had added to their assertion of the eternity of the world as a whole the assertion of an eternal matter underlying the eternal process of the generation and corruption of individual things. And if those who had added to their assertion of the eternity of the world as a whole the assertion of the eternal four elements meant by it the eternal cyclical transformation of those elements, then their view, again, would be the same as that of Aristotle.[5] Thus on the mere showing of Saadia's description of it, this tenth theory is the same as Aristotle's theory listed by Saadia as the eighth theory. Still the very fact that it is listed apart from the eighth theory quite clearly indicates that Saadia meant it to be different from the eighth theory. The question therefore is: Why did he not state what the difference between these two theories was?

[3] *Ibid.*, p. 63, ll. 8–10.

[4] It is in this sense that Baghdādī represents the view of the Dahrites in his *Uṣūl*.

[5] Cf. *De Gen. et Corr.* II, 11, 338a, 5 ff.

An answer to this question that suggests itself is that Saadia did not think it was necessary for him to explain how the eternity of the tenth theory differed from the eternity of the eighth theory, and this probably because he thought that the particular term used by him for the eternity of the tenth theory would be self-explanatory for its difference from the eternity of the eighth theory. It happens that in Arabic two terms are used for eternity in its application to the world and to things within the world, namely, *ḳidam*[6] and *dahr*, and Saadia himself has used the term *ḳidam* in such expressions as "if that from which existent things are assumed to have been created is eternal, then it is equal in its eternity with the Creator"[7] and "the eternity of visible things."[8] Here, however, in the tenth theory, he uses the term *dahr* for "eternity." Now the use of the term *dahr* for the eternity of the world at once suggests that its proponents are the Dahrites, *al-dahriyyah* or *al-dahriyyūn*[9] and *aṣḥāb al-dahr*,[10] as Saadia refers to them, namely, a group of people who constantly turn up in the pages of Arabic works as archrepresentatives of believers in the eternity of the world and as those whose conception of eternity is different from that of the Aristotelians. Consequently Saadia in his tenth theory, having used the term *dahr* for eternity, did not feel the need of explaining how this conception of eternity differed from that of his eighth theory.

What the difference was between the Dahrite eternity and the Aristotelian eternity is most clearly stated by Ghazālī in the contrast drawn between "the philosophers" and "the Dahrites." Though by "the philosophers" he means the Neoplatonized Aristotelians, such as Alfarabi and Avicenna, to whom God is both the cause of the emanation of the world and the cause of the motion of the world, rather than the

[6] Cf., for example, *Luma'*, p. 7, l. 12; *Tahāfut al-Falāsifah* I, 1, p. 21, l. 3; *Cuzari* I, 62, p. 26, l. 24; *Nihāyat*, p. 11, l. 6; *Moreh* II, 13, p. 196, l. 3.

[7] *Emunot* I, 2, p. 39, ll. 14–15.

[8] *Tafsīr Kitāb al-Mabādī*, p. 5, l. 1.

[9] *Tafsīr* of Job 22:15: *Sharḥ* on Prov. 7:27; *Tafsīr Kitāb al-Mabādī*, p. 2, ll. 16–17.

[10] *Emunot* I, Exordium, p. 31, l. 11.

followers of the genuine Aristotle of Saadia's eighth theory, to whom God is only the cause of the motion of the world, the distinction drawn by Ghazālī here between the Neoplatonized Aristotelians and the Dahrites equally applies, as we shall see, to the genuine Aristotelians of Saadia and the Dahrites.

As represented by Ghazālī, the Dahrites are Aristotelians in one respect and non-Aristotelians in another respect.

They are Aristotelians in respect of their conception of the eternal process of generation and corruption within the world, which is summarized by Ghazālī as follows: "A cause is required only by that which originates in time. No body in the world, however, originates in time, nor does a body perish; it is only the forms and accidents that originate in time. Bodies are either the heavens, and they are eternal, or they are the four elements, which are the stuff of the sublunar part of the world; but, as for these four elements, their bodies and matters are also eternal, and it is only the forms that are continuously changed upon them as a result of mixtures and alterations, in the course of which there arise human souls [as well as animal] and vegetative souls. The series of the causes of all these things which originate in time terminate in the circular motion [of the heaven], which circular motion is eternal." [11]

But the Dahrites are non-Aristotelians in respect of their explanation as to what is the ultimate cause of the eternal process of generation and corruption within the world. The difference between them is represented by Ghazālī as follows: The Neoplatonized Aristotelians, or "the philosophers" as he calls them, believe that the world, though eternal, has a God, who is "the maker or agent of the world," [12] by which he means (1) that He is the emanative cause of the existence of the world and of all beings within it,[13] including the souls

[11] *Tahāfut al-Falāsifah* X, 1, p. 206, l. 6 – p. 207, l. 2.
[12] *Ibid.*, III, 1, p. 95, ll. 6–7; IV, 1, p. 133, ll. 8–9.
[13] *Ibid.*, III, 15, p. 102, ll. 4; IV, 2, p. 134, ll. 2–5.

that move the celestial spheres,[14] and (2) that He is also the final cause of the motion of the world.[15] In contradistinction to these "philosophers," the Dahrites deny that there is a God beyond the world, who is a cause in any sense of either the existence of the world or of the motion of the world.[16] To them, the eternal existence of the world has no cause; only the eternal motion of the world has a cause; but that cause is not beyond the world, it is within the world; it is "the eternal soul of the celestial sphere." [17]

Thus the essential difference between the Neoplatonized Aristotelians and the Dahrites is that, according to the former, there is a God beyond the world, who is both the emanative cause of its existence and the final cause of its motion, whereas, according to the latter, the world has no cause at all for its existence, and the cause which it has for its motion is within it. This essential difference also exists between the Dahrite and the genuine Aristotle, for, though the God of the genuine Aristotle is not the emanative cause of the existence of the world, He is still, in the words of Aristotle himself, "a substance which is eternal and immovable and separate from sensible things" and "produces movement through infinite time." [18] This, we may assume, is the difference between Saadia's eighth theory, the Aristotelian, and his tenth theory, the Dahrite, for, as we have seen above, Saadia makes reference to Aristotle's prime mover as well as to Aristotle's identification of his prime mover with God.[19]

But who were those Dahrites who substituted for Aristotle's God beyond the world a soul within the world? Saadia refers to this theory as one held by some people of his own time.[20] In Baghdādī, their theory is included among those theories which, he says, were held by "infidels before the days of

[14] *Ibid.*, III, 30, p. 110, l. 6; 37, p. 114, ll. 4–13; XIV, 1, p. 239, ll. 4–7.
[15] *Ibid.*, XIV, 1, p. 239 ll. 6–7; XV 1, p. 247, ll. 4–7.
[16] *Ibid.*, IV, 1, p. 133, ll. 6–7; X, 1, p. 206, ll. 5–7.
[17] *Ibid.*, X, 1, p. 207, ll. 1–4.
[18] *Metaph.* XII 7, 1073a, 3–7.
[19] Cf. above, p. 147.
[20] *Tafsīr Kitāb al-Mabādī*, p. 2, ll. 11–12 (p. 15).

Islam." [21] An account of them is given by Shahrastānī, who calls them "the Dahrite philosophers" (*al-falāsifah al-dahriyyah*),[22] or simply "Dahrites" (*dahriyyah*),[23] or "the Dahrites" (*al-dahriyyūn*).[24] Lumping them together with "the Naturalists" (*al-ṭabī'iyyah; ṭabī'iyyūn*), he describes them as those "who acknowledge sensible objects but do not acknowledge intelligible objects." [25] He contrasts them, on the one hand, with the Sophists (*al-sūfastā'iyyah*), "who acknowledge neither sensible objects nor intelligible objects," [26] and on the other hand, with "the theistic philosophers" (*al-falāsifah al-ilāhiyyūn*),[27] "who acknowledge both sensible and intelligible objects, but do not acknowledge divine ordinances (*ḥudūd*) and judgments based thereon (*aḥkām*)." [28] Then, lumping them together with "Sabians and astrologers and idolaters and Brahmans," Shahrastānī describes them as "people of desires (*ahwā'*) and opinions (*arā'*)." [29]

From all these descriptions we gather four facts about the Dahrites. First, from Baghdādī's statement that "they were infidels before the days of Islam" and from Shahrastānī's description of them as "philosophers" and as those who did not believe in a revealed law, we gather that the Dahrites were a group of heathen philosophers who flourished before the rise of Islam evidently in such oriental centers of Greek philosophy as Harran and Gondeshapur. Second, from Shahrastānī's statement that unlike "the theistic philosophers," by which he means Plato and the Neoplatonized Aristotle,[30] these Dahrites are like "the Naturalists" in that "they acknowledge sensible objects and do not acknowledge intel-

[21] *Fark*, p. 346, l. 6.

[22] *Milal*, p. 2, l. 16.

[23] *Ibid.*, p. 202, l. 8.

[24] *Ibid.*, p. 201, l. 6.

[25] *Ibid.*, ll. 6–7.

[26] *Ibid.*, p. 202, l. 13.

[27] *Ibid.*, l. 15. The text reads here *al-falāsifah al-dahriyyah* and Goldziher (*EI*, s.v. "Dahriya," vol. I, p. 894a) finds a contradiction between this statement and the statement on p. 201, ll. 6–7, where the Dahriyyah are said to deny intelligible objects. But a comparison of this statement here with the statement on p. 201, ll. 7–11, shows that *al-dahriyyah* here is a corruption of *al-ilāhiyyah* or *al-ilāhiyyūn*.

[28] *Milal*, p. 202, ll. 14–15.

[29] *Ibid.*, p. 2, ll. 16–17.

[30] See Shahrastānī's exposition of the views of Plato and Aristotle in *Milal*, pp. 283 ff. and pp. 311 ff.

ligible objects," we gather that on this point they followed the Stoic view that "what the senses represent is true" [31] but that "ideas are nothing else but conceptions of our mind." [32] Third, from both Saadia's and Ghazālī's statements that the Dahrites believed that this world of ours is eternal we gather that on this point they followed the Aristotelian view of the eternity of this world of ours rather than the Stoic view that this world of ours, being one of an infinite succession of worlds, is only of temporal existence. Fourth, from Ghazālī's contrast between the Aristotelian God, who is separate from the sensible world, and the Dahrite "eternal soul of the sphere," which is within the sensible world, we gather that on this point the Dahrites, again, followed the Stoics, who indifferently gave the name God to "the world, the stars, the earth, and above all these to the mind in the ether," [33] that is, to the soul in the sphere. The Dahrites were thus a group of ecclectic philosophers, holding views unlike those of any particular Greek philosophers or of any particular group of Greek philosophers or even of any of those groups of Greek philosophers nowadays called eclectics.

It is also to be noted that, according to Shahrastānī, "there is a tradition that a small group of *al-dahriyyah* said that from eternity the world had been scattered atoms, moving without perpendicularity (*ghayr istiḳāmah*), then these atoms collided fortuitously and therefrom the world emerged in the shape in which thou now seest it." [34] Thus a small group of Dahrites became followers of Epicurean atomism and chance.

Originally, we may assume, this entire group of eclectic philosophers was not known by any special name. The name *Dahriyyah*, by which it is referred to in Muslim writings, was quite evidently given to it by Muslims. As for the origin of that name, Goldziher suggested that it was the term *dahr*

[31] *De Placitis* IV, 9 (Arabic, p. 162, ll. 20–21).

[32] *Ibid.* I, 10, 5 (Arabic, p. 116, ll. 3–5).

[33] *Ibid.* I, 7, 33, p. 306a, ll. 8–11 (Arabic, p. 114, ll. 11–12). For the Greek "earth" the Arabic has "ether," which is quite obviously due to a scribal error.

[34] Cf. Goldziher, "Dahriya" in *EI*, vol. I, pp. 894–895.

as used in a certain Surah in the Koran.[35] In that Surah, after commanding the belief in the existence of God (45:2–4) and in revelation (45:1 and 15) and in punishment for sins (45:10) and in the creation of the world (45:21) and in reward for good deeds, including the promise of resurrection (45:21 and cf, 25), the Prophet goes on to say of one "who takes his desires (*hawāhu*) for God" (45:22) and of those who claim that "there is only this our present life: we die and we live, and nought but *al-dahr* destroys us" (45:23) that "they have no knowledge; they only express an opinion (*yaẓunnūna*)" (45:23). Presumably the Muslims, on coming in contact with members of this group and finding them opposed to everything taught in that Surah of the Koran, began to refer to them in the language of that Surah as claiming that nothing but *al-dahr* destroys them and as taking their "desires" for God and as having no knowledge but only expressions of "opinion."

It is, however, to be noted that, while the Koranic text would explain how the term Dahrites came to be used as a designation of deniers of the belief in resurrection[36] or even of deniers generally of any other established Muslim belief,[37] it does not explain the most common use of the term "Dahrites" as a designation of those who affirmed their belief in the eternity of the world nor does it explain the use of the term *dahr* in the sense of eternity, for the term *al-dahr* in the verse quoted, as well as in the other verse (76:1) in which it occurs, means "time." This most common use of "Dahrites" as well as this new use of *dahr* is undoubtedly due to the influence of the Arabic translations of Greek philosophic works, where the term αἰών, "eternity," in contradistinction to χρόνος, "time," was translated by *dahr*[38] in contradistinc-

[35] Cf. Lane's *Lexicon*, *s. v.*, p. 924, col. 1.

[36] *Nihāyat*, p. 123, l. 8 – p. 124, l. 1.

[37] See, e.g., the use of *dahriyyah* in *Intiṣār* 2, p. 14, 1. 20, *et passim*, and in *Maḳālāt*, p. 430, 1. 1.

[38] *De Placitis* I, 21, 2 (Arabic, p. 119, l. 11); *Metaph.* XII, 9, 1075a, 10 (Arabic, Text. 51, p. 1693, l. 8).

tion to *zaman*.[39] As to how the Arabic translators of Greek philosophic works came to use *dahr* as a translation of *αἰών* in the sense of eternity, it is to be explained on the ground that *dahr* means not only "time" but also "a space of time," and *αἰών*, too, means, originally, "a space of time." [40]

A theory corresponding to the tenth theory in Saadia's list occurs also in the lists of Baghdādī and Ibn Hazm. In Baghdādī's *Farḳ* it occurs as the third and as the fifth in the list of nine theories. As the third it reads simply: "The Dahrites (*al-dahriyyah*) who believe in the eternity (*ḳidam*) of the world." [41] As the fifth it reads: "The philosophers who profess the eternity (*ḳidam*) of the world and deny the Maker. This is the view of Pythagoras and Codrus." [42] In Baghdādī's *Uṣūl*, where it is the first in the list of six theories, it reads: "The Dahrites known as Eternalists (*al-dahriyyah al-maʿrūfah bi'l-azaliyyah*) because of their claim that from eternity the world has been existing in its present form as to its celestial spheres and stars and the rest of its constituent parts and [also] that [from eternity] living beings have been descending from other living beings as they are now." [43] In Ibn Ḥazm's *Fiṣal*, where it is the first of the five theories discussed there, it is at first presented simply as the theory of "him who says that the world is eternal and has no ruler (*mudabbir*)," [44] but in the course of the subsequent discussion the Dahrites (*al-dahriyyah*) are mentioned as its proponents.[45]

[39] *De Placitis* I, 21, 1 (Arabic, p. 119, l. 10); *Metaph.* XII, 6, 1071b, 7 (Arabic, Text. 29, p. 1556, l. 6).

[40] A survival of *dahr* in its original sense of time may be discerned in the expression *ḳidam al-dahr*, "the eternity of time *a parte ante*," in Ibn ʿAsākir's *Tabyīn*, p. 128, l. 18. But see McCarthy's comment on this expression in his book *The Theology of al-Ashʿarī*, p. 212, n. 3: "*al-dahr* is a famous Arabic word. Here it is perhaps the equivalent to 'the world'."

[41] *Farḳ*, p. 346, ll. 8–9.

[42] *Ibid.*, ll. 10–11. On the Arabic spelling of the name "Codrus" and its reading, see Flügel's note on *Fihrist*, p. 239, l. 26.

[43] *Uṣūl*, p. 59, ll. 7–9.

[44] *Fiṣal* I, p. 9, l. 17.

[45] *Ibid.*, ll. 19–20.

10. THE "KNOW-NOTHINGISM" OF PROTAGORAS, PYRRHO, AND CARNEADES

The last three theories — the eleventh, twelfth, and thirteenth — are ascribed by Saadia to those who for various reasons refuse to commit themselves to any view with regard to the origin of the world. Of these three theories, the eleventh is ascribed to those "according to whom the truth (*ḥaḳīkah*: *amitah*) of things depends solely upon opinions (*al-iʻtiḳādāt*: *ha-deʻot*)";[1] the twelfth is ascribed to those "who maintain that it is proper for man to suspend judgment (*yaḳif*: *yaʻamod*) and not believe in anything, for they say that speculation is full of uncertainty";[2] the thirteenth is ascribed to those "who assert that there is no truth (*ḥaḳīḳah*: *emet*) to anything at all."[3] Similarly in Baghdādī's *Farḳ*, the first of the eight cosmogonical theories enumerated by him is described as that of "the Sophists (*al-sūfistāʼiyyah*) who deny truths (*al-ḥaḳāʼiḳ*),"[4] a description which corresponds to Saadia's description of the proponents of his thirteenth theory; but, in another place of his *Farḳ* the Sophists are divided by him into the following three groups: (1) those who "deny the truths (*al-ḥaḳāʼiḳ*) of all things";[5] (2) "those who are in doubt about the existence of truths";[6] (3) "those who assert that the truths of things depend upon opinion (*al-iʻtiḳād*),"[7] which correspond exactly to Saadia's eleventh, twelfth, and thirteenth theories in reverse order. So also Ibn Ḥazm, immediately before his enumeration of the four cosmogonical theories, enumerates three classes of Sophists (*al-sūfistāʼiyyah*), which are described as follows: "One class of them deny truths (*al-ḥaḳāʼiḳ*) altogether; a second class of them are in doubt concerning truths; a third class of them

[1] *Emunot* I, 3, 11th Theory, p. 65, l. 20.
[2] *Ibid.*, 12th Theory, p. 67, ll. 14–16.
[3] *Ibid.*, 13th Theory, p. 69, l. 3.
[4] *Farḳ*, p. 346, l. 6.
[5] *Ibid.*, p. 311, l. 3; cf. *Uṣūl*, p. 6, l. 7.
[6] *Farḳ*, p. 311, ll. 4–5; cf. *Uṣūl*, p. 6, l. 17 – p. 7, l. 1.
[7] *Farḳ*, p. 311, ll. 5–6; cf. *Uṣūl*, p. 7, l. 3.

maintain that things are true for him according to whom they are true and false for him according to whom they are false," [8] which, again, correspond exactly to Saadia's eleventh, twelfth, and thirteenth theories in reverse order. The same threefold classification of the Sophists, differently arranged, is to be found in Ṭūsī [9] and Taftāzānī.[10]

Let us now, on the basis of Saadia's descriptions of these three theories, try to identify their historical proponents, thereby identifying also the historical proponents of the three types of Sophists enumerated by Baghdādī, Ibn Ḥazm, Ṭūsī, and Taftāzānī. The proponents of Saadia's eleventh theory, those described as advocating a subjective conception of truth, quite evidently represent the view of the Sophist Protagoras, whose characteristic teaching was that man is the measure of all things.[11] The proponents of Saadia's twelfth theory, those described as advocating a suspension of judgment and a doubting of everything, are quite evidently followers of Pyrrho, who are known as Ephectics (ἐφεκτικοί), "suspensors of judgment," [12] and as Aporetics (ἀπορητικοί), "doubters." [13] The proponents of Saadia's thirteenth theory, those described as denying and disavowing any possible knowledge of truth, quite evidently are the members of the New Academy, the followers of Carneades, who are characterized as treating truth as "inapprehensible" (ἀκατάληπτος) [14] and as maintaining that "there is absolutely (ἁπλῶς) no criterion of truth." [15] Thus it is only with reference to Protagoras that the term "Sophist" could have been used in these Arabic texts in its technical sense as a designation of one belonging to the pre-Socratic school of Greek philosophers known as Sophists. With reference to the other two, Pyrrho and Carneades, the term could

[8] *Fiṣal* I, p. 8, ll. 3–5.
[9] Ṭūsī on *Muḥaṣṣal*, p. 23, n. 1.
[10] Taftāzānī, p. 20, l. 2 – p. 23, l. 3.
[11] Cf. Diels, *Fragmenta der Vorsokratiker*, under Protagoras, Fr. I.
[12] *Diogenes*, IX, 69, 70.
[13] *Ibid.*; Sextus, *Pyrrh. Inst.* I, 7.
[14] Sextus, *Pyrrh. Inst.* I, 2–3, 226.
[15] *Id.*, *Adv. Logic.* I, 159.

be used only in the sense of "sophistical" or "fallacious." It is in this latter sense that the term *sūfasṭā'iyy*, "Sophist," is explained by Ṭūsī in the following passage: "This word is of the language of the Greeks. *Sūfā* in their language means 'knowledge' or 'wisdom' and *asṭā* means 'error,' so that *sūfasṭah* means 'the knowledge of error.' "[16] Taftāzānī similarly explains "*sūfasṭā*" as "a name given to falsified wisdom and specious knowledge, because *sūfā* means knowledge and wisdom, and *asṭā* means the specious and false."[17]

VII. Theory of Atoms

In commenting on the generalization of Maimonides that, "regarding the subject of the unity of God and whatever is dependent upon this subject," the "Geonim" and the "Karaites" followed the "Mutakallimūn of Islam," whereas "the Andalusians from among the people of our religion" followed the "philosophers," I have inferred from Maimonides' own words that this generalization did not include the problem of atomism.[1] In my discussion here of the attitude of these Jewish philosophers toward atomism, I shall first deal with those to whom Maimonides refers as "Geonim," taking this term to refer loosely to all those of the Orient, then I shall deal with those whom he describes as the "Andalusians," and finally with the "Karaites."

The problem of atomism is introduced by Israeli in the course of his discussion of the meaning of Galen's definition of the term "element," which is quoted by him as reading

[16] *Muḥaṣṣal*, p. 23, n. 1, ll. 6–7 of the note.

[17] Taftāzānī, p. 23, ll. 1–2. This explanation is traceable to Alfarabi, in his *Iḥṣā' al-'ulūm* (ed. A. G. Palencia), p. 24, ll. 14 ff., who rejects the explanation by some people that Sophists are so called after the name of a person. This passage of Alfarabi is quoted in the name of Alfarabi by Moses Ibn Ezra in his *Kitāb al-Muḥāḍarah wa'l-Mudhākarah* (cf. Halper's Hebrew translation *Shirat Yisrael*, p. 79). It is also quoted, without mentioning the name of Alfarabi by Shem-tob b. Joseph Falaquera in *Reshit Ḥokmah*, p. 36.

[1] *Moreh* I, 71, p. 122, ll. 1–2.

that "the element is the minimum of the parts of a thing." [2] In that discussion, after showing that the element as defined by Galen means the same as what Aristotle means by element, he introduces a fictitious interlocutor whom he imagines as saying that by "parts" he means "those parts into which a body is divided naturally and of which it is composed, just as a body is divided into planes and planes into lines and lines into points." [3] Israeli then goes on to imagine how that fictitious interlocutor, once he had expressed his view, continued to defend it. To quote: [4] "And he adduced proof [5] for his view from a statement by Democritus, for Democritus had said that a body is composed of planes and planes are composed of lines and lines are composed of points, and as further proof he quoted [6] the agreement (disagreement) [7] of Ibrāhīm al-Naẓẓām and his fellow members of the Muʿtazilite sect [8] on

[2] *Sefer ha-Yesodot* II, p. 40, l. 8; *Liber De Elementis* II, p. 7d, l. 13. Cf. Galen, *De Elementis ex Hippocrate* I, 1 (*Opera*, ed. Kuhn, I, p. 413); *De Hippocratis et Platonis Placitis* VIII, 2 (V, p. 661).

[3] *Yesodot*, p. 43, ll. 3–5; *Elementis*, p. 8a, ll. 8–11.

[4] *Yesodot*, p. 43, ll. 5–10; *Elementis*, p. 8a, ll. 11–17.

[5] Latin: *et certificet*; Hebrew: "and I adduce proof," in which the Hebrew ואביא, "and I adduce," is to be taken as a corruption of והביא, "and he adduced." The underlying Arabic term here, we take it, was *wa-ḥaḳḳaḳ*.

[6] Latin: *et attulit*; Hebrew: *ve-zakar*, of which the Arabic quite evidently was *wa-ḍakar*.

[7] In Hebrew, the reading here is *haskamah*, "agreement"; in Latin, it is *inconvenientia[m]*, "disagreement." Though actually Naẓẓām is known to have disagreed with his fellow Mu'tazilites on the problem of atomism (see *Kalam*, pp. 495f), the original Arabic reading here, I take it, was a term meaning "agreement," and this for the following reason: The Latin term *convenientia*, which is used here with the negative prefix *in* and later without this negative prefix (see below at n. 11), is a literal translation of the Arabic term *ijmā'*, "agreement." So also does the Hebrew term *haskamah*, which is used both here and later (see, again, below at n. 11), occur as a translation of *ijtimā'*, which is another form of the same Arabic term (cf. Baḥya, *Ḥobot ha-Lebabot* II, 5, p. 119, l. 14). Now, if the underlying Arabic text here used a term meaning "disagreement," then on the basis of the Latin *inconvenientia* it would be the unusual combination of some such negative particle as *la* or *ghayr* with the term *ijmā'* or *ijtimā'* instead of the ordinary Arabic term *iḫtilāf*, meaning "disagreement," which would naturally be expected here. We may, therefore, assume that the negative prefix *in* in the Latin *inconvenientia* was added either by mistake or in an attempt to harmonize the statement with the actual fact of Naẓẓām's disagreement with his fellow Mu'tazilites on the problem of atomism.

[8] Latin: *abrae ordinatoris et sociorum eius qui sunt desperati* — (1) *or-*

this [view of Democritus], for from their words it is to be understood that a body is composed of atoms, that is to say, of points." [9]

In his answer to the fictitious interlocutor, Isaac Israeli makes the following statements: "That which thou hast related of the statement of Democritus to the effect that, when points are put together, there arises a line is a statement which lends itself to two interpretations"; [10] so also "that which thou hast inferred with regard to the agreement (*convenientia*: *haskamat*) of the Muʿtazilites [on this view of Democritus] from what is to be understood of their assertion that bodies are composed of atoms" [11] lends itself to the same two interpretations, for the points of Democritus as well as the atoms of the Muʿtazilites must be either extended or not extended.[12] He then goes on to show how neither of these interpretations is admissible, for, if they are not extended, then they cannot form a body; and, if they are extended, then they are bodies, and, as such, they are divisible and hence are neither points nor atoms.[13] It is to be remarked that Israeli's statement that the atoms of the Muʿtazilites lend themselves to two interpretations actually corresponds to the difference of opinion between the two Muʿtazilite schools of Baṣra and Baghdad as to whether the atoms are magnitudes or not.[14] It is also to be remarked that Israeli's argument against the two alternative interpretations of the term "points" in the statement attributed to Democritus reflects the argument used by Aristotle against

---

dinator is a literal translation of al-Naẓẓām; (2) *desperati* = *de separati*, *separati* being a literal translation of *muʿtazilah*. Cf. Goldziher, "Mélanges Judéo-Arabes," *REJ*, 47:43 (1903); Jacob Guttmann, Die philosophischen Lehren des Isaac ben Salomon *Israeli* (1911), p. 16.

[9] Latin: *praedicta*; Hebrew: *ha-neḳudot*, "the points."

[10] *Yesodot*, p. 43, ll. 10–11; *Elementis*, p. 8a, ll. 17–19.

[11] *Yesodot*, p. 49, ll. 14–15; *Elementis*, p. 8c, ll. 53–55.

[12] *Yesodot*, p. 43, ll. 11–13; p. 49, l. 15 – p. 50, l. 1; *Elementis*, p. 8a, ll. 19–21; p. 8c, ll. 55–58.

[13] *Yesodot*, p. 43, ll. 13–18; p. 50, ll. 1–10; *Elementis*, p. 8a, ll. 21–30; p. 8c, ll. 58–70.

[14] Cf. *Kalam*, pp. 472–473.

the following two alternative views, namely, either a body is composed of indivisibles or indivisibles are extended bodies.[15]

In this passage, the statement of Democritus quoted by Israeli's hypothetical interlocutor is quite evidently a quotation from some source, probably an Arabic translation of some Greek doxography of philosophers, no longer extant. We have already suggested above how such a restatement of Democritus' theory of atoms could have arisen out of certain statements in Aristotle and how, while in the original doxography the term "points" was not necessarily used in a mathematical sense, in the Kalam it was taken to mean mathematical points and thus gave rise to the conception of the unextendedness of atoms.[16] So also the statement about the agreement, or disagreement, between Naẓẓām and his fellow Muʿtazilites, quoted, again, by Israeli's fictitious interlocutor, is quite evidently based on some report in which Naẓẓām was represented incorrectly as agreeing, or perhaps correctly as agreeing, with his fellow Muʿtazilites in their affirmation of atoms.

While Israeli deals with atomism as reported in the name of Democritus and in the name of the Muʿtazilites, Saadia deals with three types of atomism derived from entirely different sources.

The first type of atomism is referred to by him in the course of his discussion of an argument raised by a certain "heretic" against one of his proofs for creation.[17] That argument was evidently recognized by him as being similar to the first of the four arguments raised by Zeno against Aristotle's theory of the infinite divisibility of space,[18] and so, without mentioning the name of Zeno, Saadia goes on to enumerate three answers to Zeno's argument that were known to him. As he phrases them, the answers read as follows: "Some of the speculative thinkers (*al-naẓẓārīn*), therefore, have resorted to

[15] *De Gen. et Corr.* I, 2, 316b, 14–18; *Metaph.* XIII, 8, 1083b, 13–16.
[16] Cf. *Kalam*, pp. 479–483.
[17] *Emunot* I, 1, 1st Theory, 4th Argument, p. 36, ll. 14–18.
[18] *Phys.* VI, 2, 233a, 22–23; cf. *Kalam*, p. 515.

the theory of atoms; others of them propounded the theory of the leap; still others of them proposed the theory of the coincidence of an infinite number of particles of time with an infinite number of particles of space." [19] Of these three answers, the second is that of Naẓẓām's theory of the leap, which, as we have seen, was devised directly as an answer to Zeno's first argument,[20] and the third is Aristotle's own answer to that first argument of Zeno.[21] As for the first answer, we may assume that it refers to the theory of atoms as held by the generality of the Mutakallimūn, which theory, we may further assume, is taken by Saadia to have been adopted by the Mutakallimūn because of their opposition to any kind of infinite divisibility — an opposition which, as I have tried to show, was primarily due to religious considerations.[22] Saadia then goes on to answer the heretic's argument and thus also indirectly Zeno's argument, the latter with especial reference to the use made of it by the heretic as a refutation of Saadia's argument for creation.[23]

The second type of atomism is dealt with by Saadia in his second theory of creation,[24] according to which Plato's pre-existent eternal matter was conceived by some Mutakallimūn as consisting of atoms. Though the atoms in this second theory are described by Saadia as "points" qualified by the term "small" [25] and compared to "dust and strands of hair," [26] this does not mean that the atoms in this theory are, as in Greek philosophy, conceived of as extended bodies, for his subsequent statement that these pre-existent eternal atoms have "no boundary and no dimensions" [27] and do not exist "in place" [28] and are "neither long nor wide nor deep" [29] shows quite

[19] *Emunot*, *loc. cit.*, ll. 18–20.
[20] Cf. *Kalam*, pp. 515–517.
[21] *Phys.* VI, 2, 233a, 24–31; cf. *Kalam*, p. 516.
[22] Cf. *Ibid.*, pp. 468–471.
[23] *Emunot*, *loc. cit.*, p. 36, l. 20 – p. 37, l. 4.
[24] Cf. above, pp. 125–132.
[25] *Emunot* I, 3, 2nd Theory, p. 41, l. 15.
[26] *Ibid.*, p. 42, ll. 11–12.
[27] *Ibid.*, ll. 15–16.
[28] *Ibid.*, l. 16.
[29] *Ibid.*, p. 43, ll. 2–3.

clearly that the atoms in this theory are assumed to have no extension. So also are these atoms said by Saadia to be devoid of such qualities as "hot and cold and moist and dry" [30] and "color and taste and smell." [31] Now in Greek philosophy, there is Aristotle's argument against the assumption of a magnitude arising out of the combination of nonmagnitudinous points [32] and there is also Plutarch's criticism that the atomists have failed to show "how bodies (that is, atoms) which have not any quality can bring all sorts of qualities to others only by their meetings and joining together, as, for instance — to take that which comes next to hand — whence does that which we call heat proceed, and how is it engendered in the atoms, if they neither had heat when they came, nor are become hot after their being joined together?" [33] This is exactly what Saadia argues against those in the Kalam who held atoms to be without qualities. He says: "I consider it remote — nay, as utterly untenable — the notion that a thing that is formless can be changed so as to assume the form of fire and water and air and earth . . . and that what is not circumscribed by any condition can be so altered so as to become circumscribed by all those conditions that are at present visible [in things]." [34]

The third type of atomism, that of the Epicureans, is dealt with by Saadia in his ninth theory of creation.[35] As described by him, the atoms in this ninth theory have the following characteristics: they can be conceived only by the intellect; they are magnitudinous bodies; they vary in weight; they move not perpendicularly, but in every direction; they collide by chance, and thus form the world. He rejects this theory on philosophic grounds by specific arguments.[36] Even the theory

[30] *Ibid.*, p. 42, ll. 13–14.

[31] *Ibid.*, l. 15.

[32] *De Gen. et Corr.* I, 2, 316a, 29–31; *Metaph.* XIII, 8, 1083b, 15–16; cf. *Kalam*, p. 485.

[33] *Adversus Coloten* 8.

[34] *Emunot* I, 3, 2nd Theory, p. 42, l. 19 – p. 43, l. 4.

[35] Cf. above, pp. 150–151.

[36] *Emunot* I, 3, 9th Theory, p. 62, ll. 9–20.

of chance, which is connected with it, is rejected by him not on the general religious principle that it implies a denial of the existence of God, but rather on the ground of certain specific philosophic arguments.[37]

When we come to those Jewish philosophers to whom Maimonides refers as "the Andalusians of our religious community," we find that all of them, as Maimonides says, "adhered to the teachings of the philosophers."[38] All of them show their rejection of atomism by espousing, in one way or another, the Aristotelian theory of matter and form. Some of them give more definite evidence of their rejection of atomism. Thus Ibn Gabirol, in his *Fons Vitae*, makes the Master declare that "it is impossible to find a part which is indivisible, for all the dimensions of a body are infinitely divisible."[39] Thus also Baḥya, as we have shown, in reproducing the Kalam argument from composition for the creation of the world substituted in it the composition of matter and form for the composition of atoms.[40] Judah Halevi — wishing to show that in matters of religious laws one must not rely upon one's own arbitrary opinion but one must examine them and trace them back to their sources, and that one must follow the result of such an examination, even if it may appear strange to one's own preconceived notions — says: "Thus opinion and common belief deny the nonexistence of the void, whilst logical conclusion rejects its existence; opinion denies the infinite divisibility of a body, whilst logical conclusion affirms its necessity."[41] In this passage he thus directly

[37] *Ibid.*, p. 62, ll. 1–9; p. 62, l. 20 – p. 63, l. 4.

[38] *Moreh* I, 71, p. 122, ll. 9–10.

[39] *Fons Vitae* II, 18, p. 57, ll. 6–8.

[40] Cf. *Kalam*, pp. 389–390.

[41] *Cuzari* III, 49, p. 198, ll. 24–27; p. 199, ll. 24–27. In one place Halevi speaks of "naturally generated things composed of minute proportions which are too minute to have an opinion formed of them" (*Cuzari* I, 99, p. 52, ll. 14–15, and p. 53, ll. 14–15) have been erroneously taken by David Cassel in his *Das Buch Kuzari* I, 99, p. 71, n. 3, to refer to atoms and this erroneous interpretation is followed by Klatzkin, *Oṣar ha-Munaḥim ha-Pilosofiyim*, s.v. *Yaḥas* 2 (II, p. 34). See the correct interpretation in the commentaries *Ḳol Yehudah*, *Oṣar Neḥhad*, and Zifroni *ad loc.*

rejects the void and indirectly, by accepting the infinite divisibility of a body, he rejects atoms. Similarly, when he tells the reader, through the Rabbi's address to the king of the Khazars, that "I will not lead thee the way of the Karaites, who ascend the heights of theology without intermediate steps," [42] the intermediate steps which follow consist of topics taken from the Aristotelian philosophy, including matter and form.[43] Here, too, by mentioning matter and form as one of his approved topics of philosophy, he indirectly rejects atoms. Abraham Ibn Ezra, in his brief essay entitled *Aruggat ha-Hokmah u-Pardes ha-Mezimah*, expounded the atomistic theory of the Kalam. But this does not mean that he approved of that theory. As suggested by Krochmal, this brief essay may have been a mere literary exercise written in his youth or it may have been a composition written at the request of a friend during his migratory years.[44] Maimonides rejects both Epicurean atomism, with its belief in the eternity of the atoms [45] and their chance collision,[46] and the Kalam atomism, with its belief in the creation of the atoms and the world by the will of God,[47] but in his rejection of Epicurean atomism, only its theory of chance is stigmatized by him as being against religious beliefs.[48] Its theory of the eternity of the atoms, like Plato's theory of the eternity of matter [49] and Aristotle's theory of the eternity of the world,[50] we may assume, would not have been considered by him as being against religious beliefs; his rejection of it would be on purely philosophic grounds. It is also on purely philosophic grounds that he rejects the Kalam type of atomism, his philosophic criticism of it being scattered throughout his exposition of it

[42] *Cuzari* V, 2, p. 294, ll. 18–19; p. 295, ll. 18–19.
[43] Cf. *Kalam*, p. 87.
[44] Cf. *Kerem Ḥemed* 4 (1839), pp. 1–5 (*Kitebe Ranaḳ*, ed. Rawidowicz, pp. 397–399); Schreiner, *Kalam*, pp. 35–41.
[45] *Moreh* I, 73, Prop. 1, p. 135, ll. 27–28.
[46] *Ibid.*, II, 13, 3rd Theory, p. 198, ll. 28–30.
[47] *Ibid.*, I, 73, Prop. 1, p. 135, ll. 28–29.
[48] *Ibid.*, II, 13, 3rd Theory, p. 198, ll. 28–30.
[49] *Ibid.*, 2nd Theory.
[50] *Ibid.*, II, 25.

in his twelve propositions.[51] In a general way, he dismisses it as belonging to the teachings of the "ancient philosophers," that is, the antiquated philosophers, which "the later philosophers have shown to be false." [52]

While among the Rabbanites there was no one who espoused atomism, among the Karaites this theory had its followers. Joseph al-Baṣīr, both in his *Ne'imot* [53] and his *Maḥkimat Peti*,[54] preliminary to his discussion of theological problems, has a special chapter in which he presents his conception of the structure of the physical world as based on atomism. Jeshua ben Judah in his *Bereshit Rabbah*, which is a commentary on the story of creation in the Book of Genesis, enumerates five proofs for the creation of the world, all of them assuming the existence of atoms. Of these five proofs, the first is the Kalam proof from accidents,[55] which is reproduced in its original Kalam form based on the assumption of atoms.[56] In addition to the indirect use of atomism in these proofs for the creation of the world, Jeshua ben Judah discusses directly problems related to the theory of atomism.[57] Both Joseph al-Baṣīr and Jeshua ben Judah assume that the atom has magnitude, al-Baṣīr expressing himself explicitly on the subject by saying that the atom occupies space,[58] and Jeshua ben Judah referring to it indirectly by calling the atom a body.[59] Both of them speak of atoms as being the substrata of accidents,[60] which probably means that they follow that school of the Kalam which maintained that the atoms cannot be devoid of accidents.[61] Judah Hadassi, however, is opposed to atomism,

[51] *Ibid.*, I, 73.

[52] *Ibid.*, 71, p., p. 122, ll. 26–28.

[53] *Ne'imot*, chap. 3, fol. 3b ff.

[54] *Maḥkimat Peti*, chap. 1, fol. 105a ff.

[55] Cf. *Kalam*, pp. 392–409.

[56] See analysis of these arguments in M. Schreiner, *Studien über Jeschu'a b. Jehuda*, pp. 25–38.

[57] *Ibid.*, pp. 45–53.

[58] *Ne'imot* 3, p. 3a; *Maḥkimat Peti* 1, p. 105a.

[59] Jeshua b. Judah's *Bereshit Rabbah*, p. 74a (quoted in Schreiner, *Studien*, p. 45, n. 2).

[60] *Ibid.*

[61] Cf. *Kalam*, p. 488.

expressing his view as follows: "Bodies are of four natures, according to some philosophers, but, according to others, they are of atoms. But against those who say that bodies are composed of atoms the following objections may be raised: First, by definition an atom is that which is indivisible, but that which is indivisible has no extension, but that which has no extension cannot be joined with another atom to form a body. Second, an atom has not the quality of moisture or hotness or coolness or dryness. Consequently a body formed by the combination of such atoms would have to be devoid of these four qualities. But since body is not devoid of these qualities, we conclude that bodies are composed of the four natures mentioned before." [62] It will be noticed that the first argument is like that used by Aristotle and Israeli and that the second argument is like that used by various Greek philosophers and Saadia. Aaron ben Elijah of Nicomedia, after quoting these arguments of Hadassi against atomism, adds: "He has thus shown that our [Karaite] sages are divided on this question, some of them believing that body is composed of four natures, while others believe that it is composed of atoms." [63] Still, while Hadassi in the passage quoted is outspokenly against atomism, in another place in his work he expounds the theory of atoms,[64] without any comment of disapproval.

VIII. Causality

In our discussion of atomism, we started with the Rabbanites, all of whom we found to be opposed to atomism, and then we took up the Karaites, among whom we found some who favored atomism. Similarly now, in our discussion of causality, we shall start with the Rabbanites, all of whom we shall show were opposed to the denial of causality, and then we shall take up those Karaites who favored atomism

[62] *Eshkol ha-Kofer* 28, p. 19c–d.
[63] *'Eṣ Ḥayyim* 4, pp. 17–18.
[64] *Eshkol ha-Kofer* 67, p. 31b–c.

and try to find out whether they also favored the denial of causality.

I. SAADIA AND BAḤYA

No direct reference to the Mutakallimūn's denial of causality is to be found in Saadia. But there is a passage in which he quite evidently argues against the Mutakallimūn's denial of fixity in the order of nature and of their belief that every event in the world is directly and arbitrarily created by God. The passage occurs amidst his discussion of the miracles reported in Scripture, which he describes as consisting either of "the subjection of the natures of things" [1] or of "the transformation of a substance." [2] Saadia begins it with the following statement: "At this point I find it necessary to make an observation for the purpose of safeguarding [our belief] in the [usual] fixity [of things]." [3] Then, after explaining that God does not change any of the ordinary things in the world unless there is a "cause" (*'illah*), that is, a reason or purpose, for His doing so,[4] he goes on to argue as follows: "For if we were to assume [that God changes things arbitrarily for no reason or purpose at all], then our confidence in the fixity of things would be shaken. None of us could then be sure, upon his returning to his dwelling and family, whether the All-Wise had not changed their essences and whether they were not different from the way in which he had left them." [5]

There are also passages in Saadia which contain expressions of belief in causality or in nature as a causal principle, but

[1] *Emunot* III, 4, p. 121, ll. 4–5. The expression "the [usual] fixity [of things]" is Rosenblatt's happy translation of the Arabic term *al-ḥaḳā'iḳ* (Hebrew *ha-amitot*), literally: "the verities." Cf. Ghazālī's use of this term in the following statement in his *Tahāfut al-Falāsifah*, Intr. 12, p. 10, ll. 10–11: "It is improper for you to confuse the verities of things (*ḥaḳā'iḳ al-umūr*) with customs (*al-'adāt*) and manners (*al-marāsim*)."

[2] *Emunot* III, 4, p. 120, l. 13.

[3] *Ibid.*, l. 14.

[4] *Ibid.*, p. 121, ll. 5–7.

[5] *Ibid.*, ll. 7–10. Cf. *Kalam*, p. 547 n. ll.

whether they are aimed at the Mutakallimūn's denial of causality and nature is not clear. Thus in his discussion of the various types of natural human knowledge, in contrast to divinely revealed knowledge, he says that, "as far as all created beings are concerned, they cannot acquire knowledge except by the mediation of a cause." [6] This is in contrast to the Kalam deniers of causality who believed that human knowledge was continually created by God from instant to instant.[7] Similarly, his statement that the conception of certain things is "impossible from the standpoint of nature" [8] and his contention against the Epicureans that to conceive of something as having come to pass by chance implies the existence of something "by nature" [9] are also in contrast to the Kalam deniers of nature as a causal principle.[10] But the causality and nature which is thus affirmed by Saadia is that kind of causality and nature which is shared by all scriptural philosophers ever since Philo [11] — a causality or nature which, having been implanted by God in the world at the time of its creation, continues to be governed by His will and is subject to the possibility of being upset by His creation of what is called miracles. Accordingly, in his argument against those who deny miracles, Saadia describes them as those who "reject whatever contradicts nature (*al-ṭabʿ*: *ha-ṭebaʿ*) and custom (*al-ʿādah*: *ha-minhag*) and always draw their arguments in support of their opinions from nature and regularity (*al-rasm*: *ḥok*)." [12]

In the last passage quoted, it will be noticed, the term "custom" is used by Saadia as the equivalent of the term "nature." So also in other passages does he use these two terms as equivalents. Thus in his reference to miracles, he

[6] *Emunot*, Introduction 3, p. 10, l. 13.

[7] *Moreh* I, 73, Prop. 6; cf. *Tahāfut al-Falāsifah* XVIII, 10, p. 303, l. 12, quoted *Kalam*, p. 549.

[8] *Emunot* I, 1, 1st Theory, First Argument, p. 33, ll. 12–13.

[9] *Ibid*. I, 3, 9th Theory, p. 62, ll. 2–3.

[10] Cf. *Kalam*, pp. 559, 560.

[11] Cf. *Philo*, I, pp. 325–359.

[12] *Emunot* I, 3, 5th Theory, p. 53, ll. 2–3.

describes them as coming about "only through the creation of what is not in accordance with nature (*al-ṭabʿ*: *ha-ṭebaʿ*) and custom (*al-ʿādah*: *ha-minhag*)." [13] Thus also in his discussion of the doctrine of resurrection, he raises the hypothetical question whether resurrection is not impossible by "nature" (*al-ṭabʿ*: *ha-ṭebaʿ*),[14] but in the course of his discussion he substitutes for the term "nature" the expressions "the current and familiar customs" (*al-ʿādāt al-jāriyyah al-mutaʿālimah: ha-minhagim ha-nehugim ha-nodaʿim*) [15] and "the customs of nature" (*ʿadāt al-ṭabʿ. minhag ha-ṭebaʿ*).[16] In this coupling of "nature" and "custom" one should not detect a defiance to the Mutakallimūn who, in their theory of custom, use the term "custom" in contrast to the term "nature," for the Mutakallimūn's theory of custom, as we have seen, arose among the Ashʿarites [17] and could not have been known to Saadia. The technical sense in which these two Arabic terms are used here by Saadia comes from their having been employed as translations of the Greek terms φύσις and ἔθος as used by Aristotle. Now it happens that in Aristotle, despite the formal distinction made by him between "nature" and "custom," [18] there are such statements as that custom "resembles nature" [19] and that custom "becomes nature" [20] and that "frequency," which in one place is said by him to result in "custom," [21] in another place is said by him to produce "nature." [22] It is to be remarked that, with regard to miracles, Philo, who in one place speaks of miracles as being contrary to that which is "by nature," [23] in another place speaks of

[13] *Ibid.*, ll. 1–2.

[14] *Ibid.* VII, 1 (Arabic text published by W. Bacher in *Festschrift zum achtzigsten Geburtstage Moritz Steinschneiders*, 1896, p. 99, ll. 15, 16, 17, 18, 19).

[15] *Ibid.*, p. 99, l. 21.

[16] *Ibid.*, p. 99, l. 22.

[17] Cf. *Kalam*, pp. 544–551.

[18] *Metaph.* I, 1, 981b, 3–5; *Rhet.* I, 10, 1369a, 35 – b, 1, 1369b, 6–7.

[19] *Eth. Nic.* VII, 11, 1152a, 31.

[20] *Magna Moralia* II, 6, 1203b, 31–32.

[21] *Rhet.* I, 10, 1369b, 6–7.

[22] *De Memoria et Reminiscentia* 2, 452a, 30.

[23] *Qu. et Sol. in Gen.* IV, 51.

them as God's frequent creations of effects contrary to "those arising from customs." [24] So also Alfarabi, a contemporary of Saadia, defines miracles as being "outside nature (*al-jibillah*) and customs (*al-'ādāt*)." [25] It is to be further remarked that any philosophically trained Arabic-speaking Jew who was brought up on the Talmud and was familiar with its use of the Hebrew term *minhag*, "custom," in its quotable saying, "The world continues in its custom," [26] would be apt to use its Arabic equivalent *'ādah* as a description of the established order of the world and hence to couple it with the term "nature." All this will explain, I believe, why some other Jewish philosophers writing in Arabic or in Hebrew sometimes similarly use the term "custom" as the equivalent of the term "nature."

Baḥya refers to the Mutakallimūn's denial of causality incidentally when, in his reproduction of the view of the Predestinarians among them, he mentions not only their denial of causality in the actions of men but also their denial of causality in the movements of all the inanimate things in the world.[27] His assertion of his own belief in causality is to be found in his long description of the organic structure of the world and its orderly processes and "its causes and effects," [28] all of which he uses as evidence of the existence and unity and wisdom of God.

2. JUDAH HALEVI AND ABRAHAM IBN DAUD

Judah Halevi's discussion of causality contains, as I have shown elsewhere,[1] two statements aimed at Ghazālī.

In one place, arguing against the belief in continuous creation and hence the denial of causality, and bearing in mind

[24] *Quod Deus Immut.* 19, 88.
[25] *Fuṣūṣ al-Ḥikam* 28.
[26] *Abodah Zarah* 54b.
[27] *Ḥobot* III, 8, p. 163, ll. 16–19.
[28] *Ibid.* I, 2, p. 100, ll. 5–9 ff.
[1] Cf. my paper "Judah Halevi on Causality and Miracles," *Meyer Waxman Jubilee Volume* (1966), pp. 137–153.

his own view that miracles constitute the proofs for the veracity of Scripture,[2] he says: "If all the events in the world were effected by the primary intention of the Prime Cause [without any intermediate causes],[3] they would, each in its turn, be created anew at each instant. We might then say concerning the world, with all that there is in it, that God created it this very instant, the result thus being that there would be nothing about miracles to cause man to be affected with wonder by them and still less to lead him to believe [in what one is commanded to believe] on account of them."[4] This quite clearly is aimed at Ghazālī who, in his defense of the denial of causality, argues that upon the denial of it "depends the possibility of affirming miracles the characteristic mark of which is an infringement of custom."[5]

In another place, trying to show how natural events come to pass by a series of causes leading up to God, who is the Prime Cause, he uses as an example the burning of a piece of wood by fire.[6] Inasmuch as the preceding statement is quite clearly aimed at Ghazālī, we have reason to assume that the example of the burning of a piece of wood by fire was deliberately chosen by Judah Halevi because the opponent he visualized here was Ghazālī who, in his defense of the denial of causality, says that he will use "only one example, namely, the burning of cotton through contact with fire."[7] The substitution of a "piece of wood" for Ghazālī's "cotton" may be explained by the consideration that the use of "cotton" as a common example of something that is burned by fire would be rather unusual for an author living in Spain and writing for readers in Spain — a country where cotton did not grow and had to be imported.

No direct criticism of the Kalam denial of causality is to

[2] *Cuzari* I, 9; I, 11; I, 25.

[3] Cf. Halevi's description of "primary intention" in *Cuzari* V, 20, p. 336, ll. 28 ff.; p. 337, ll. 27 ff.

[4] *Ibid*., p. 340, ll. 12–14; p. 341, ll. 8–12.

[5] *Tahāfut al-Falāsifah*, Phys., 6, p. 271, ll. 10–11.

[6] *Cuzari* V, 20, p. 338, ll. 5–13; p. 339, ll. 2–9.

[7] *Tahāfut al-Falāsifah* XVII, 2, p. 278, l. 6.

be found in Abraham Ibn Daud, but in his discussion of the antinomy of free will and the foreknowledge of God, upon which we shall comment later, there is what appears to be a disguised criticism of the denial of causality by the extremely orthodox in Kalam. Wishing to show how people sometimes, owing to ignorance, speak of two alternatives as being equally possible, when in reality there are no two alternative possibilities, he says: "As, for instance, speculation as to whether an eclipse of the moon will occur during a certain given month or not. To those who are ignorant of astronomy the eclipse may possibly occur or not occur, whereas with reference to itself one of these alternatives must necessarily occur. God knows the alternative which is necessary and astronomers have been enabled by God to know it, so that the eclipse to them is not something that is only possible, as it is to the common people." [8] Now it happens that in Islam there were — as we gather from Ghazālī's arguments against them — [9] those who denied the astronomical explanation of eclipses, both of the eclipse of the moon as being caused by the interposition of the earth between it and the sun and of the eclipse of the sun as being caused by the interposition of the moon between it and the earth, and hence they denied also the predictability of eclipses, and both these denials of theirs were due to their belief that "eclipses are a bowing down in reverence at the manifestation of God," [10] and hence, of course, not predictable. It is therefore quite possible that in selecting this example of an eclipse and his emphasis that astronomers consider it as a necessary event which can be predicted, whereas the common people consider it as a possible event which is unpredictable, Abraham Ibn Daud had in mind the discussion in Ghazālī of the belief about eclipses among certain orthodox elements in Islam.

[8] *Emunah Ramah* II, vi, 2, p. 96.

[9] *Tahāfut al-Falāsifah*, Intr., 13–16, p. 11, l. 6 – p. 13, l. 3. Cf. *Kalam*, pp. 549, 550.

[10] *Ibid.*, 15, p. 12, ll. 6–7.

3. MAIMONIDES

In Maimonides [1] there are: a direct exposition of the Mutakallimūn's views on duration and destruction, a statement of the implication of these views as a denial of causality in the sense of efficient causation, an exposition of the Mutakallimūn's theory of custom, and a criticism of their denial of efficient causation. In addition, Maimonides also mentions the Mutakallimūn's denial of causality in the sense of final causation and criticizes this denial.[2]

In his exposition of the Mutakallimūn's views on duration and destruction, Maimonides mentions two views. These two views, as we shall see, correspond to four of the eight views on duration and destruction which we have found to have been held by those Mutakallimūn who denied causality. Their reduction by Maimonides to two views was quite evidently due to his dividing those four single views into two composite views, each of them containing certain common elements by which it differed from the other. In his characterization of each of these composite views, Maimonides mentions, as we shall see, only those elements which are shared in common by its component parts, leaving out any mention of anything by which they differ.

The first of these two views, in so far as it concerns the duration and destruction of accidents only, is described by Maimonides as "the view of some of the Mutakallimūn who are the majority." [3] Later, the view which is contrasted by him with this view, is described by him, as we shall see, as the view of "some of the Mutakallimūn from among the Muʿtazilites." [4] Inasmuch as the term Muʿtazilites in his historical sketch of the Kalam [5] as well as elsewhere [6] is contrasted by him with the term Ashʿarites, we may identify this view "of some of the Mutakallimūn who are the majority"

[1] *Moreh* I, 73, Props. 6 and 10.
[2] *Ibid.* III, 17 and 25.
[3] *Ibid.* I, 73, Prop. 6, p. 140, l. 1.
[4] *Ibid.*, l. 2.
[5] *Ibid.* I, 71, p. 122, ll. 4–6.
[6] *Ibid.* I, 73, Prop. 6, p. 141, ll. 12 and 20.

with the view of "the Ash'arites" [7] and the view of the Ash'arite "Bāḳillānī," [8] which we have listed respectively as the first and the second of our list of eight. In his description of this view, Maimonides mentions all the characteristics that we have found in the description of the corresponding view of the Ash'arites and hence also of the view of Bāḳillānī, namely, that accidents do not endure for two instants, that they are continuously created at every instant, and that they cease to exist by their ceasing to be created again.[9] It will be noticed that Maimonides does not mention the different views held by the Ash'arites [10] and by the Ash'arite Bāḳillānī [11] with regard to the destruction of "body" and "substance." But he does ascribe to the Ash'arites a common view with regard to the destruction of "substance." Thus starting with a restatement of well-known Ash'arite views, by saying that the majority of the Mutakallimūn, that is, the Ash'arites, believe that God never creates a substance without an accident, that no accident endures for two instants, and that, when God wishes an accident to endure, He continuously creates the same accident at every instant, he concludes by saying "so that, if He wishes to create in the substance another kind of accident, He does so; and, if He refrains from creating and does not create any accident, the substance in question ceases to exist." [12] It is not quite clear whether the concluding statement just quoted is based upon some definite Ash'arite source which Maimonides had in mind or whether it is a conclusion which he himself has arrived at on the basis of the Ash'arite views restated by him. In the latter case, it is quite possible that the term "accident" is used by Maimonides here as a general designation both of "the *ma'nā* of duration" of the Ash'arites and of "the modes of existence" of the Ash'arite Bāḳillānī, for, as we have seen, both the *ma'nā* of duration

[7] Cf. *Kalam*, pp. 552–526.
[8] *Ibid.*, pp. 526–528.
[9] *Moreh* I, 73, Prop. 6, p. 139, ll. 26–29.
[10] Cf. *Kalam*, pp. 523–526.
[11] *Ibid.*, pp. 527–528.
[12] *Moreh* I, 73, Prop. 6, p. 139, l. 23–p. 140, l. 1.

and the modes of existence are described as accidents[13] and also as being durationless and continuously created, so that the substance in which they exist ceases to exist when they cease to be created.[14]

The second view is described by Maimonides as that of "some of the Mutakallimūn from among the Muʿtazilites," who "maintain that some accidents endure for a certain extent of time, whereas others do not endure for two instants."[15] This is a restatement of the views of Abū al-Hudhayl[16] and Jubbāʾī,[17] which we have listed as the fourth and the last of the eight views. But here, again, it will be noticed that nothing is said by Maimonides about the difference between them as to how the duration is created by God in those durational accidents. Thus, again, he reproduces only that which is common to the two views combined by him into this one second view. Commenting upon this view of the Muʿtazilites, Maimonides says: "But with regard to this they have no established rule to which they could refer so as to be able to say, Such and such a kind of accident endures and such and such a kind of accident does not endure."[18] By this Maimonides means to say that, inasmuch as ultimately, according to both Abū al-Hudhayl and Jubbāʾī, the duration in the durational accidents is created by God, neither of them has any explanation why some accidents are durational and others are durationless other than the arbitrary will of God.

Then, in contrast to the view on destruction held by the "majority" of the Mutakallimūn, Maimonides says vaguely that "according to some of the Mutakallimūn," by which he quite evidently means Muʿtazilites, "when God wishes to destroy the world, He will create an accident of destruction, which will not be in a substratum, and that [accident] of destruction will be opposed to the existence of the world."[19]

[13] Cf. *Kalam*, pp. 524, 527.
[14] *Ibid.*, pp. 526, 528.
[15] *Moreh* I, 73, Prop. 6, p. 140, ll. 2–3.
[16] Cf. *Kalam*, pp. 530–533.
[17] *Ibid.*, pp. 537–540.
[18] *Moreh* I, 73, Prop. 6, p. 140, ll. 3–4.
[19] *Ibid.*, ll. 16–17.

This, again, is a restatement of what is common to both Abū al-Hudhayl and Jubbā'ī with regard to the destruction of bodies. For both of them believe that the destruction of bodies is brought about by the creation of a substratumless accident of destruction, even though they differ on the question whether God would destroy some bodies in the world without destroying the whole world. Of Jubbā'ī it is explicitly reported that he and his son Abū Hāshim asserted that "when God wishes the destruction of bodies, He creates for them a destruction not in a substratum, which destruction is an accident contrary to all bodies, so that thereby the totality of bodies are destroyed," [20] and also "God has no power to destroy some bodies, while allowing others to endure." [21] No such limitation of God's power to destroy occurs in Abū al-Hudhayl's statements on destruction,[22] from which it is to be inferred that, according to him, God has the power both to destroy the whole world and to destroy only certain bodies in it. So also it is both Abū al-Hudhayl and Jubbā'ī that are meant by "the Mu'tazilites" to which "the philosophers," as quoted by Ghazālī, attribute the view that God will destroy the world by the creation of a substratumless act of destruction.[23]

The implication of these views on duration and destruction, says Maimonides, is the Mutakallimūn's belief that "it is not to be said that there exists some kind of nature and that in every given body it is its nature that determines that such and such accidents should accrue to it. Nay, they rather maintain that it is God who has created those accidents at this present instant without the intermediacy of any nature and without any other thing." [24] They thus also maintain that "there is no nature necessitating the existence or the non-existence of a thing," [25] that "it should not be said that this is

[20] *Uṣūl*, p. 231, ll. 12–14.
[21] *Farḳ*, p. 319, ll. 10–12; cf. *Uṣūl*, p. 45, ll. 11–13; p. 231, ll. 14–15.
[22] Cf. *Kalam*, pp. 531, 532.
[23] *Ibid.*, p. 539.
[24] *Moreh* I, 73, Prop. 6, p. 140, ll. 4–8.
[25] *Ibid.*, ll. 13–14.

in any respect the cause of that,"[26] and that, "in the last analysis, God is the sole agent."[27] This denial of causality with its corollary that God is the sole agent has further led to a theory of which Maimonides says that the Mutakallimūn speak as "admissibility" (*al-tajwīz*: *ha-haʿabarah*) and which he himself explains in philosophic terms as meaning that "everything that is imaginable is admissible for the intellect."[28]

These views of the Mutakallimūn are contrasted by Maimonides with the views of the philosophers. To the philosophers, he says, there are things in the world which are necessary, for, as Aristotle says, things that always come to pass in the same way come to pass by necessity,[29] which things are also described by him as those which cannot be otherwise.[30] Examples of such necessary things are the motion of earth downwards and of fire upwards and the like, for, even though one could conceive of earth as moving upwards or of fire as moving downwards, such a conception is contrary to what is of necessity, and consequently is to be considered as impossible, for, as says Aristotle, "the impossible is that of which the contrary is of necessity true."[31] The possible to the philosophers, as again Aristotle says, is that which "may either be or not be; the same thing, then is possible both to be and not to be."[32] Examples of such possible things are things which happen by chance, for, once more as says Aristotle, "chance is an accidental cause"[33] and "the accidental is not necessary but may possibly not exist."[34] To the Kalam, on the other hand, even if something is in conformity with reality, that is to say, with what always comes to pass in the same way, it is still not to be called necessary, it is to be called possible, inasmuch as its contrary can be conceived

[26] *Ibid.*, p. 141, l. 10.

[27] *Ibid.*, l. 8. Literally "the last agent is God." But the description of God as "the last agent" by those who do not believe in intermediate agents is quite impossible. Hence my free translation.

[28] *Ibid.*, Prop. 10, p. 144, ll. 3–4.

[29] *Phys.* II, 5, 196b, 10–12.

[30] *Metaph.* V, 5, 1015a, 34.

[31] *Ibid.* V, 12, 1019b, 23–24.

[32] *Ibid.* IX, 8, 1050b, 11–12.

[33] *Phys.* II, 5, 197a, 5–6.

[34] *Ibid.* VIII, 5, 260b, 9–10.

by the imagination, for it is possible to form in our mind an image of earth as moving upwards or of fire as moving downwards. Only that is considered by them as impossible of which even an image cannot be formed, and of this they give a number of examples.[35] To quote Maimonides' own brief characterization of the view of the Mutakallimūn: "That which can be imagined is according to them possible, whether existence corresponds to it or not, and that which cannot be imagined is impossible." [36]

In further contrast between the Mutakallimūn and the philosophers, Maimonides goes on to say that those things which, on account of their always occurring in the same way are described by the philosophers as things which cannot be otherwise, can according to the Mutakallimūn be otherwise, for their occurring always in the same way, they argue, is not due, as is claimed by the philosophers, to a concatination of causes which is not subject to change but rather to a "continuance (*jary*: *hemshek*) of custom" [37] in the successive creations of God, from which, however, He may deviate and act in some other way. Maimonides explains the Mutakallimūn's conception of this continuous but changeable course of God's customary acts of creation by the analogy of the customary course of action of a human being, say, a king, which, while seen always to be the same, may still be changed.[38] Continuousness and changeableness are thus, according to Maimonides, characteristic of the custom which the Mutakallimūn attribute to God's successive acts of creation. It is the continuousness of God's custom that explains not only the regularity of succession of the newly created things in the world but also why these newly created things appear to us as a continuously existent one thing. Thus when a garment dyed black by its contact with a certain dye seems to us to continue to be black with the same blackness, it is

[35] Cf. *Kalam*, pp. 578–589, and below section on "Impossibilities."
[36] *Moreh* I, 73, Prop. 10, p. 145, ll. 5–7.
[37] *Ibid.*, p. 144, l. 17.
[38] *Ibid.*, ll. 17–19.

only because it is the custom of God, who has created the blackness in the garment on its coming in contact with that certain dye, to continue to create the same kind of blackness in the garment at every instant.[39] Thus also when the knowledge of an object acquired by us under certain circumstances seems to us to continue to be the same knowledge we have of the object for some length of time, it is only because it is the custom of God, who has created in us that knowledge of the object under those certain circumstances, to continue to create in us the same kind of knowledge of the object at every instant.[40] And it is the changeableness of God's custom by which the Mutakallimūn explain their belief that things which appear always to occur in the same way are things which can be otherwise. Thus fire and water, which by the continuousness of God's custom cause combustion and coolness respectively, may have their actions changed by God so that fire would cause coolness and water would cause combustion.[41]

In his criticism of the Mutakallimūn's denial of causality, Maimonides takes as the target of his attack his own formulation of it as a view which maintains that "everything imaginable is admissible for the intellect." Drawing upon the meaning of the terms imagination and intellect as technically used in philosophy, he tries to show that not everything conceived by the imagination is intellectually admissible. And here are the main points in his criticism.

To begin with, referring the reader to Aristotle's classification of the faculties of the soul, two of which are imagination and intellect, he reminds him of the fact that "man is not distinguished [from other living beings] by having imagination," expecting the reader to complete the sentence by adding "but rather by having an intellect;" and, from the fact that imagination may exist in living beings without an intellect, he himself concludes for the reader that hence "the function of

[39] *Ibid.*, Prop. 6, p. 140, ll. 17–25.
[40] *Ibid.*, ll. 25–28.
[41] *Ibid.*, Prop. 10, p. 144, ll. 21–23.

imagination is not the function of the intellect but rather its contrary." [42]

Then he goes on to describe the essential differences between the function of the intellect and the function of the imagination, with a view to showing that, while the intellect has the power to distinguish within its conceptions between those which are true and those which are false, the imagination possesses no such power. In fact, he shows how the function of the imagination is twofold and how, while in one respect it reproduces images of things as they really exist, in another respect, known in the formal classification of the internal senses as "compositive imagination," it constructs false images, such, for instance, as the image of a man with the head of a horse and with wings.[43]

Finally, Maimonides shows by concrete examples borrowed from the mathematical sciences how things, which to the imagination appear to be impossible, have been proven by means of intellectual reasoning to be possible and, conversely, how things, which to the imagination appear to be possible, have been proven by means of intellectual reasoning to be impossible.[44]

So much for Maimonides' discussion of the Mutakallimūn's denial of efficient causes.

His mention of the Mutakallimūn's denial of final causes occurs in two places. In one place, amidst his restatement of the view of "the Islamic sect of the Ashʿarites" that reward and punishment are not in accordance with one's actions, he says: "It also follows from this view that His [God's] actions have no end," [45] that is, have no final cause. In another place, after dividing all actions into futile and sportlike and vain and good [46] and after ascribing to both Scripture [47] and philosophy [48] a belief in final causes, he refers to a "sect from among the people of speculation," [49] that is, a sect of the

[42] *Ibid.*, p. 146, ll. 11–15.
[43] *Ibid.*, ll. 15–26.
[44] *Ibid.*, p. 146, l. 27 – p. 147, l. 19.
[45] *Ibid.* III, 17 (3), p. 337, ll. 17–18.
[46] *Ibid.* III, 25, p. 365, ll. 5–6.
[47] *Ibid.*, p. 366, ll. 1–5.
[48] *Ibid.*, ll. 8–9.
[49] *Ibid.*, ll. 10–11.

Mutakallimūn, whose view he describes as follows: "All of God's actions correspond to His will, so that one should not seek an end for them and say, Why did He do so? for He does what He wills and that which He does is not consequent upon wisdom." [50] He then goes on to criticize this view in two ways.

In his first criticism, after showing that the Mutakallimūn's denial of final cause in God's actions means that His actions are "futile" and hence it is inconsistent with their own belief that God has knowledge of His actions,[51] Maimonides adds that, "as the assumption that anything among His actions is by way of sport (*al-laʿb*: *ha-ṣeḥok*), the impossibility thereof is manifest at first thought." [52] What he means by this is that such an assumption, which is implied in the Mutakallimūn's denial of final causes in God's actions, is contradicted by their own Scripture, in which God proclaims (44:38; cf. 21:16): "We have not created the heavens and the earth in sport (*lāʿibīna*)."

In his second criticism, he refutes the reason by which, he tries to show, the Mutakallimūn were led to their denial of final causes in God's actions. They were led to this view, he says, by reasoning from an analogy between God's creation of the world as a whole and His creation of the particular things within the world. Having in mind his own earlier discussion of the problem of the purpose of the creation of the world and his own conclusion that all those who believe in creation are bound ultimately to admit that it "depends upon the divine will," [53] he says: "They ask, What is the end of the existence of the world as a whole? To this they necessarily answer, like all those who believe in the creation of the world, that it was created because God willed it so, and for no other reason. The same answer they then apply to the particular things in the world." [54] In his refutation of that reason for the Mutakallimūn's denial of final causes, having

[50] *Ibid.*, ll. 12–14.

[51] *Ibid.*, ll. 14–16.

[52] *Ibid.*, ll. 17–18.

[53] *Ibid.* III, 13, p. 329, l. 14.

[54] *Ibid.* III, 25, p. 366, ll. 23–26.

in mind his concluding remark in that earlier discussion of his, namely, that for "divine will" one may use "divine wisdom," [55] he now tries to show at great length that that "divine will" is not an arbitrary will; it is a will which is identical with wisdom and design and purpose, though a wisdom and a design and a purpose which are incomprehensible to us.[56]

This is how Maimonides criticized the Mutakallimūn's denial of causality. In both form and substance, it will be noticed, his criticism differs from that of Averroes.[57]

[55] *Ibid.* III, 13, p. 329, l. 14.

[56] *Ibid.* III, 25, p. 367, l. 1 – p. 368, l. 16.

[57] Cf. *Kalam*, pp. 551–558. On the question whether Maimonides was acquainted with the works of Averroes at the time of his writing *The Guide of the Perplexed*, the following are the facts.

In a letter to Joseph Ibn Aknin, written in October 1189, Maimonides says that he has just recently received Averroes' commentaries on the works of Aristotle, except the *De Sensu et Sensibili*, but that he has not yet found time to study them; see S. Munk, "Notice sur Joseph Ben-Iehouda," *Journal Asiatique*, 3e Série, 14 (1842), p. 31. *The Guide of the Perplexed* was completed in 1185 (see Z. Diesendruck, "On the Date of the Completion of the Moreh Nebukim," *HUCA*, 12–13: 461–497 [1937–38]) or sometime between 1185 and 1190 (cf. D. H. Baneth in his edition of *Iggerot ha-Rambam* I 1946, p. 2).

Erroneous, therefore, is the legend, given currency by Leo the African in the 16th century, that Maimonides was a pupil of Averroes (cf. Munk, *op. cit.*, p. 31, n. 1, and Renan, *Averroès et l'Averroïsme*, 2nd ed., 1861, p. 20). It is on the basis of this erroneous legend that Schmölders describes Maimonides as "fidèle disciple d'Aboù [*sic*] Roshd" in his *Essai sur les Écoles Philosophiques chez les Arabes*, 1842, p. 135, n. 1.

Equally erroneous is Shem-Tob ben Joseph Falaquera's assumption that Averroes was acquainted with Maimonides' *Guide of the Perplexed* and made use of it in his own works. Thus in his *Moreh ha-Moreh* pp. 56–57, with reference to *Moreh Nebukim* I, 73, Prop. 6), on finding that a passage dealing with the Mutakallimūn's denial of causality quoted by him from Averroes (= *Tahāfut al-Tahāfut* XVII, 3–12, p. 519, l. 12 – p. 524, l. 11) is similar to passages in which Maimonides deals with the same subject, he introduces his quotation from Averroes as follows: "It seems to me that it was that which the aforementioned philosopher [Averroes] had learned from the discussions of our master [Maimonides] concerning this subject that led him to say what he did say, as will become clear from his own words to be quoted" (*ibid.*, p. 56 end). It may be added that, in the light of this explicit statement by Shem-Tob that it was Averroes who was influenced by Maimonides, an earlier statement by him in the Introduction of his work (p. 8, ll. 3–5) is to be slightly emended to read as follows: "There is no doubt that he [Averroes] came to know the discussions of our master [Maimonides]; perhaps it was that which he had learned from the latter's various discussions concerning the views of the Mutakallimūn

But among the Mutakallimūn there were "some" who, as Maimonides himself says, "professed belief in causality." [58] The anonymous "some," as we have shown,[59] are Naẓẓām and Muʿammar, both of whom discarded the Mutakallimūn's belief in continuous creation and adopted that particular theory of causality according to which God at His creation of the world implanted in it the principle of causality, whereby events in the world continue to follow one after another without each of them being a new creation by God. But Naẓẓām and Muʿammar differed as to how that principle of causality operates in the world. According to Naẓẓām, that principle of causality operates in the world under the supervision of God. According to Muʿammar, however, the world, after its creation by God, was abandoned by Him and left to itself, so that the principle of causality operates in it without any supervision by God, the implication thus being that, once the world was created by God, it can dispense with God as the supervisor of the manner of its existence, which really means that it can dispense with God as the preserver of its existence.

It is this view of Muʿammar, we take it, that Maimonides has reference to in the following passage: "Know that one of the people of speculation from among the Mutakallimūn went so far in his ignorance and recklessness as to say that, even if it were possible to assume that the Creator had ceased

---

that led him to write that which he did write; he thus drew the water of wisdom and found pearls." In the printed edition, the reading is to the effect that it was Maimonides who came to know the discussions of Averroes and hence made use of them. The emendation suggested requires only the deletion of one letter, the letter *vaw*, at the end of one word, so that in l. 3 the word דבריו would read דברי. See also my discussion of the relation between Maimonides and Averroes in *Crescas' Critique of Aristotle*, p. 323.

With all this compare the restatement of Averroes' and Maimonides' criticisms of the Mutakallimūn's denial of causality in Majid Fakhry's *Islamic Occasionalism*, pp. 83 ff., introduced by the following words: "The debt of Maimonides to Averroes in the formulation of his criticism of Ash'arite occasionalism can be readily perceived by whoever peruses their respective anti-Ash'arite writings, however cursorily" (p. 83).

[58] *Moreh* I, 73, Prop. 6, p. 141, l. 11.

[59] Cf. *Kalam*, pp. 559–578.

to exist, it would not necessarily follow that the thing created by Him, namely, the world, would have to cease to exist, for a production need not necessarily cease to exist when the producer, after having produced it, has ceased to exist." [60]

In his criticism now of Muʿammar's conception of causality, just as in his preceding criticism of the Mutakallimūn's denial of causality, Maimonides, again, tries to show that it is at variance with the view of the philosophers. His argument may be restated as follows: When the philosophers describe God as the Prime Cause, they mean thereby that He is the efficient and formal and final cause of the world, and by His being the formal cause of the world they mean that He is the cause of the perseverance and permanence of things in the world, so that without the continuance of the ultimate causality of God, the proximate causes of things in the world could not function.[61]

4. JOSEPH AL-BAṢĪR AND JESHUA BEN JUDAH

Aaron ben Elijah of Nicomedia, who, as we have seen, would seem to suggest that the Mutakallimūn's adoption of atomism was due to their denial of causality,[1] would also seem to suggest that any affirmation of atomism implies a denial of causality. In our study of the Kalam, however, we have found that at least one Mutakallim, Muʿammar, who believed in atomism, believed also in causality.[2] We therefore have to investigate whether Joseph al-Baṣīr and his pupil Jeshua ben Judah, both of whom believe in atomism, do deny causality or not. As in the case of the Mutakallimūn, their view on causality has to be derived from whatever they happen to say about duration and destruction, as neither of them deals directly with causality. Then also, as we may assume that Joseph al-Baṣīr and his pupil Jeshua ben Judah share the same

[60] *Moreh* I, 69, p. 117, ll. 21–15.
[61] *Ibid.*, p. 117, l. 15 – p. 118, l. 2.
[1] Cf. *Kalam*, p. 468 n. 21.
[2] Cf. *Ibid.*, p. 566.

view on causality, so we may also assume that whatever may be inferred from statements of either one of them is to be taken to represent also the view of the other.

Both Joseph al-Baṣīr and Jeshua ben Judah divide accidents into those which endure and those which do not endure. Joseph expresses himself directly on the subject by saying: "Accidents fall into two classes. Some of them endure and some do not endure. As for those which do not endure, . . . they are such as voices, that is, speech . . . and, as for that which endures two instants or more, it is such as blackness and its like."[4] Jeshua expresses himself indirectly on the subject when, in answer to the question whether "it is possible for blackness to endure," he says that "blackness belongs to those [accidents] which endure."[5] Both of them also explain that the destruction of durational accidents comes about by contrary accidents. Thus Joseph al-Baṣīr says that, "with regard to those accidents which endure, their destruction is brought about by their opposite (*be-ḥillufam*)"[6] and Jeshua ben Judah says that, "with the coming into existence of whiteness, the continuously existent blackness ceases to exist."[7]

Now these statements quite evidently reflect Abū al-Hudhayl's and Jubbā'ī's view about the distinction of accidents into durational and durationless and Jubbā'ī's view about the destruction of durational accidents by their contraries.[8] Still this does not necessarily prove that Joseph al-Baṣīr and Jeshua ben Judah followed Abū al-Hudhayl and Jubbā'ī in affirming continuous creation and denying causality. From their contexts, these statements seem to have been used by Joseph and Jeshua only as empirical descriptions of two kinds of accidents, without any theological implication. It will be noticed that neither of them mentions Abū al-Hudhayl's created

[4] *Maḥkimat* I, p. 105a; *Ne'imot* I, p. 4a. Both passages are quoted in Schreiner, *Studien über Jeschu'a ben Jehuda*, p. 32, n. 2.

[5] *Bereshit Rabbah*, 74b; Schreiner, *op. cit.*, p. 46, n. 2.

[6] *Ne'imot*, p. 4a.

[7] *Bereshit Rabbah*, p. 74b; Schreiner, *op. cit.*, p. 46, n. 2.

[8] Cf. *Kalam*, pp. 538–540.

substratumless words "Endure" and "Perish" or Jubbā'ī's created substratumless accident of destruction in connection with their respective discussions of the durationalness and destruction of durational accidents. Nor does either of them express a belief in continuous creation in connection with their respective discussions of durationless accidents. Thus there is no evidence in what they say that they believed in continuous creation and denied causality. From the fact that they believe in free will it may be assumed that they believe in causality.

In this connection, the difference between the report by the Karaite Aaron ben Elijah of Nicomedia on the Muʿtazilite view about the durationalness of durational accidents and his report on the destruction of durational accidents and of bodies is significant. In the case of the former, he begins by stating that, with regard to what he subsequently describes as durational accidents, "the sect of Mu'tazilites say that, after one has brought an accident into existence, that accident of itself continues to exist, without there being any need on the part of the agent to bring it again into existence," [9] which is quite evidently the view of Jubbā'ī.[10] He adds: "So also have our sages, of blessed memory, said, namely, 'the agent has no influence upon that which is durational'," [11] which is a direct quotation from Jeshua ben Judah.[12] Subsequently, in describing the destruction of durational accidents and of bodies, he quotes the Muʿtazilites, by which again he means Jubbā'ī, as saying: "In the case of everything, there is a contrary which reduces it to nothing, so that when God wishes to destroy something [durational], He creates that which is contrary to it. Thus . . . when He wishes to destroy the world, He brings into existence a substratumless accident of destruction whereby the world is destroyed. By the same token, He destroys whiteness by a [substratumless] blackness which is

[9] *ʿEṣ Ḥayyim* 4, p. 16, ll. 7–9.
[10] Cf. *Kalam*, p. 537.
[11] *ʿEṣ Ḥayyim* 4, p. 16, ll. 9–10.
[12] *Bereshit Rabbah*, p. 64a; Schreiner, *op. cit.*, p. 29 and p. 32, n. 4.

its contrary." [13] Here he does not add that the Karaite sages are of the same opinion. Quite evidently he knew that no Karaite sage, even one who like Jeshua ben Judah believed in atoms, believed that durational objects are destroyed by God in the manner described and then recreated by Him.

5. IMPOSSIBILITIES

The view that despite His omnipotence God would not do certain things, which is to be found in the Hebrew Bible and in Philo, became, as we have seen,[1] a problem of impossibilities, which was discussed by the Church Fathers and the Mutakallimūn and other Muslim religious philosophers in its relation to the belief in the omnipotence of God. We shall now see how the same problem is dealt with by Jewish religious philosophers of the Arabic period.

Isaac Israeli, while not directly discussing impossibilities as a problem, shows that he was conscious of the existence of such a problem and tries to reconcile it with the belief in the omnipotence of God. He thus says: "There are many generations and ancestors between Adam and Moses, peace be upon him, but the fact that it was impossible for Moses, peace be upon him, to appear at the time of Adam is not due to the powerlessness of the creator to achieve that, but to the fact that such a thing would not belong to wisdom but to absurdity," and he goes on to explain that the only way God could have made Moses appear at the time of Adam was to have abolished "natural procreation" and to have created Moses directly without the intermediacy of parents, whereby "some of the characteristics and effects of wisdom would disappear." [2]

In Saadia, there is a direct discussion of the problem of impossibilities.

[13] *'Eṣ Ḥayyim* 4, p. 16, ll. 14–18.

[1] *Kalam*, pp. 578–589.

[2] "The Book of Substances," Fragment II, in Altmann and Stern, *Isaac Israeli*, p. 82.

First, he mentions certain things which he declares to be impossible. Thus, in one place, he repudiates those whose conception of the omnipotence of God has led them to the belief that God (1) "is capable of every absurdity, such as changing himself and whatever is connected therewith." [3] In another place, he enumerates the following impossibilities: (2) "to cause five to be more than ten without adding anything to the former"; (3) "to put the world through the hollow of a signet ring without making one narrower and the other wider"; (4) "to bring back the day gone by in its original condition." [4] All these examples of impossibilities reflect earlier literature. The impossibility of God's changing himself occurs in Plotinus [5] and pseudo-Dionysius.[6] The impossibility of making five more than ten is like Alexander of Aphrodisias' statement that it is impossible for God to make twice two equal five.[7] The impossibility of putting the world through a signet ring is like the statement in the Iḫwān al-Ṣafā that God is powerless to make a camel go through the eye of a needle.[8] The impossibility of bringing back the day gone by reflects Aristotle's approval of Agathon's saying:

> "Of this alone is Deity bereft,
> To make undone whatever hath been done." [9]

Second, Saadia tries to explain the compatibility of impossibilities with divine omnipotence. Thus, in answer to "certain heretics," of whom he says that they "often ask us about such matters," he says: "God is indeed able to do everything, but this thing that they ask of Him is not anything, for it is absurd (*muḥāl*: *hebel*)" and "the absurd is nothing, and so it is as though they were to ask, whether God is capable of doing what is nothing (*lā shay*: *lo kelum*), which is really what

[3] *Emunot* I, 3, 4th Theory, p. 48, ll. 9–10.
[4] *Ibid.*, II, 13, p. 110, ll. 5–7.
[5] *Enneads* VI, 8, 21.
[6] *De Divinis Nominibus* V, 6; cf. *Kalam*, p. 579.
[7] *De Fato*, 30.
[8] *Rasā'il Iḫwān al-Ṣafā'* 40, p. 358, l. 5; cf. *Kalam*, p. 582.
[9] *Eth. Nic.* VI, 2, 1132b, 9–11.

they are asking."[10] This passage reflects two statements. One of these statements is that of Aristotle, according to which one of the meanings of "the impossible" is that it is impossible that "that which cannot come to exist should come to exist,"[11] the implication of which is that the impossible is nonexistent. The second statement is that of the Kalam, which as restated by Maimonides reads that "an agent does not cause nonexistence (*al-ʿadam*: *ha-heʿder*), for nonexistence does not require any agent,"[12] and, as testified by Averroes, was generally accepted in the Kalam.[13] The use by Saadia here of the term *lā shay*, "nothing," for the term *al-ʿadam*, "nonexistence," in the Kalam statement is in accordance with his own view that "nonexistence" (*al-ʿadam*) is "nothing" (*lā shay*).[14]

In Joseph al-Baṣīr there is mention of one impossibility, and that is the division of an atom. Starting at first with the vague statement that the atom "cannot be divided either by ourselves or by anybody other than ourselves,"[15] he subsequently explains whom he has meant by "anybody other than ourselves" in his statement, which quite evidently refers to the atom, that it "cannot be divided either by ourselves or by God."[16] But evidently conscious of the apparent contradiction between the belief in the omnipotence of God and the belief in impossibilities, he immediately explains it in the following rambling passage: "When we say [with regard to the atom that] it cannot be divided by God, it is because it is not right that it should be divided. We did not say that this is because of a lack of power, that is to say, because God is powerless and unable to divide the atom; we said it only because it is not right that it should be divided, and God does not do that which is not right; He does only that which is right, for all His works are befitting, but this is not befitting, not because He is powerless

[10] *Emunot* II, 13, p. 110, ll. 7–11.
[11] *Phys.* VI, 10, 241b, 4–7.
[12] *Moreh* I, 73, Prop. 6, p. 140, l. 11.
[13] *Tahāfut al-Tahāfut* II, 24, p. 131, ll. 6–8.
[14] Cf. *Kalam*, p. 371.
[15] *Maḥkimat* 1, p. 105b, 4–5.
[16] *Ibid.* 21, 117b, 11–12.

and unable to do it. It was His decision that the atom should be indivisible [because its divisibility would be unbefitting] and since it is unbefitting, He will not divide it. Dost thou not see that if any one of us came to do something which is not to be done, he would be upbraided by the whole world for trying to do something which is not to be done. This being so, we have established our statement that [the atom] is divided neither by ourselves nor by God, for anything unbecoming is inapplicable to God, inasmuch as God has no desire for anything that is not done. Hence the atom is not divided either by ourselves or by God." [17] Probably this was also the justification used by the Muslim Mutakallimūn for the impossibility on the part of God to divide the atom.[18]

Abraham ibn Daud does not deal directly with impossibilities, but from his explanation why he believes that God has a foreknowledge of all possible future events, including future human actions, only as possibilities, without having a foreknowledge of the possibility that ultimately becomes realized,[19] it may be inferred that he includes this among those impossibilities which are due to the unfathomable wisdom of God in being unwilling to act contrary to certain laws of nature which He himself has established in the world.[20]

The Mutakallimūn's views on impossibilities is dealt with by Maimonides in two places of his *Moreh Nebukim.*

In Part I,[21] he first shows how, in contradistinction to the philosophers who maintain that it is for the intellect to decide whether that which is imaginable is possible or impossible, the Mutakallimūn maintain that everything imaginable is to be admitted by the intellect as possible, and this he illustrates by showing how certain things which the philosophers consider as impossible are considered by the Mutakallimūn as possible.[22] He then mentions four things which are admitted by all the Mutakallimūn as being impossible and one thing

[17] *Ibid.*, 12–21.

[18] Cf. *Kalam*, p. 470, 471.

[19] *Emunah Ramah* II, 6, 2, p. 96.

[20] Cf. *Kalam*, pp. 580–581.

[21] *Moreh* I, 73, Prop. 10, p. 144, l. 1 – p. 145, l. 5.

[22] *Ibid.*, p. 144, ll. 3–23.

which is admitted only by some of the Mutakallimūn as being impossible, the impossibility of all these things being due to their being not even imaginable.[23]

In Part III,[24] he starts out with a general explanation of the meaning of impossibility, concerning which he makes the following statements: (1) "the impossible has a stable nature . . . its change is in no way possible"; [25] (2) things impossible "are necessarily so"; [26] (3) the impossible "is not the work of an agent." [27] These three statements reflect respectively the following three statements in Aristotle: (1) one of the senses of "the impossible" (τὸ ἀδύνατον) is that it is impossible that "that which is incapable of changing should be in process of changing to that which it cannot change to"; [28] (2) "that which cannot be otherwise we say is necessarily so"; [29] (3) things which are necessary in this sense have no external cause of their necessity.[30] On the basis of this conception of the impossible, Maimonides concludes: "Hence God is not to be described as having power over it." [31] This statement he subsequently clarifies by explaining that it does not mean that God is actually powerless to change the impossible; it only means that God, in His wisdom, would not exercise that power of His.[32] This, as we have seen, is the explanation of impossibilities commonly used by all scriptural philosophers.[33]

Commenting upon this, Maimonides says in effect that, though the Mutakallimūn differ from the philosophers in maintaining that imaginability spells possibility, they are all in agreement with the philosophers that there are impossibilities, for they all admit that there are things which are not even imaginable, and that the only recorded difference of opinion among the Mutakallimūn themselves on the question of impossibilities concerns a thing which has only a slight sugges-

[23] *Ibid.*, ll. 23–28.
[24] *Ibid.* III, 15.
[25] *Ibid.*, p. 331, ll. 25–26.
[26] *Ibid.*, p. 332, ll. 28–29.
[27] *Ibid.*, p. 331, l. 25, and p. 332, l. 29.
[28] *Physics* VI, 10, 241b, 4–8.
[29] *Metaph.* V, 5, 1015a, 34–35.
[30] *Ibid.*, 1015b, 9–10.
[31] *Moreh* III, 15, p. 331, l. 26.
[32] *Ibid.*, p. 332, l. 28.
[33] *Kalam*, pp. 578–579.

tion of its being imaginable, whence the difference of opinion as to whether it should be included among the impossibilities or among the possibilities.[34]

Maimonides then mentions four things upon which, he says, all the Mutakallimūn agree that they are impossibilities. The first three of these impossibilities are the same as three of the four such impossibilities mentioned by him in Part I, so that with the addition of the fourth of such impossibilities mentioned by him in Part I, the five impossibilities agreed upon by all the Mutakallimūn are as follows: (1) "the concurrence of two contraries at the same instant in the same subject," [35] that is, the Law of Contradiction,[36] which is mentioned as an impossibility by the Iḫwān al-Ṣafā' [37] and Ibn Ḥazm [38] and Ghazālī; [39] (2) "the transformation of substances (*al-aʿyān*),[40] that is, for a substance to become an accident

[34] *Moreh* III, 15, p. 331, l. 27 – p. 332, l. 1.

[35] *Ibid.*, p. 332, l. 2; cf. I, 73, Prop. 10, p. 144, l. 24; II, 13, Second Theory, where it is attributed to the philosophers.

[36] *De Caelo* I, 12, 281b, 12–14, plus *Metaph.* IV, 6, 1011b, 15–22; cf. *Kalam*, p. 583.

[37] *Cf. Kalam*, p. 582.

[38] Cf. *Ibid.*, p. 585.

[39] Cf. *ibid.*, pp. 586–588.

[40] Cf. the Arabic term *al-a'yān* as it is translated into Hebrew by Judah Ibn Tibbon in the following places: (1) *Emunot ve-De'ot* III, 4, p. 120, l. 6: "to transform the substances (*al-a'yān*: *ha-'aṣamim*)"; (2) *ibid.*, l. 14: "a transformation of essence (*'ayn 'ayin*)"; (3) *ibid.*, p. 121, l. 7: "the essences (*al-a'yān*: *ha-'ayinim*)"; (4) *Cuzari* V, 6, p. 300, l. 5; p. 301, l. 5: "that which was transformed for them of the essences of substances (*al-a'yān*: *'ene ha-'aṣamim*)"; (5) *ibid.* V, 21, p. 354, l. 6; p. 355, l. 6: "the transformation of the essence of substances (*al-a'yān*: *'en ha-'aṣamim*)." Here Samuel Ibn Tibbon translates *al-a'yān* by *ro'shim*, which is accepted by Munk, who translates it by "*principaux*" and explains it as "les deux choses principales qui constituent le corps" (*Guide*, III, 15, p. 105, n. 4). Ḥarizi translates it by *ha-nir'eh le-'ayin*, which points to an Arabic reading *al-'iyān*, "the evident," "the distinct." Shem-Tob Falaquera in *Moreh ha-Moreh* III, 15 (p. 123), whose Arabic text must have read *al-'ayn*, the singular of *al-a'yān*, translates it by *ha-'eṣem*, "the substance." In the *Tahāfut al-Falāsifah* I, 9, p. 74, l. 11, the contrast between *al-a'yān* and *al-adhhān* is translated into Hebrew (Paris, Cod. Heb. 910, p. 13, col. 1) by the contrast between *ḥushim*, "senses," and *sekalim*, "minds," whereas the same contrasting Arabic terms in the *Tahāfut al-Tahāfut* I, 202, p. 110, l. 2, are translated into Hebrew (Paris, Cod. Heb. 910, p. 82, col. 3) by the contrast between *'inyanim*, "things," and *sekalim*, "minds."

and for an accident a substance," [41] which corresponds to what Ghazālī calls "the transformation of genera (*al-ajnās*)," described by him as the impossibility "for one thing (*al-shay*) to become another thing," as, for instance, for "blackness" to be transformed into "power"; [42] (3) "the existence of a corporeal substance without an accident in it"; [43] (4) "that God (a) should bring into existence someone like himself or (b) should annihilate himself or (c) should assume a body or (d) should undergo a change"; [44] (5) "that one body should penetrate another." [45] The point upon which there is a difference of opinion among the Mutakallimūn he says, is the question whether God "can bring into existence an accident that exists alone, not in a substratum," concerning which "a group from among the men of speculation, namely, the Muʿtazilites, took it to be imaginable and hence held it to be possible, whereas others declared it to be impossible." [46] The reference to the "Muʿtazilites" is to Abū Hudhayl and Jubbāʾī to whom Maimonides himself elsewhere refers as believing in the creation by God of a substratumless accident of destruction.

As for his own view on impossibilities, while it is from the philosophers' standpoint that intellect alone is to be the judge of possibility that Maimonides criticizes the Mutakallimūn's view that imaginability is the criterion of possibility, he openly disagrees with the philosophers' assertion that creation *ex nihilo* is an impossibility with reference to God [47] and, as

[41] *Moreh* III, 15, p. 332, ll. 2–3.

[42] *Tahāfut al-Falāsifah* XVII, 29, p. 294, ll. 4–6.

[43] *Moreh* III, 15, p. 332, ll. 3–4. The qualifying term "corporeal" is unnecessary here, for the mere term "substance" in the sense of "atom" cannot, according to the Mutakallimūn, as described by Maimonides, be devoid of accidents, even though, according to them, it is not a "body" and hence not "corporeal" (cf. *Moreh* I, 73, Prop. 5 and *Kalam*, p. 488). It will be noticed that in the corresponding passage in I, 73, Prop. 10, p. 144, ll. 25–26, Maimonides uses only the term "accident," without the qualifying term "corporeal."

[44] *Moreh* III, 15, p. 332, l. 5. For (a) cf. *Moreh* II, 13, Second Theory, p. 197, l. 16, and Iḫwān al-Ṣafāʾ, *Kalam*, p. 583; for (b) cf. Pseudo-Dionysius, *Kalam*, p. 579; for (c) *cf. Moreh* II, 13, Second Theory, p. 197, l. 16.

[45] *Moreh* I, 73, Prop. 10, p. 144, l. 28.

[46] *Ibid.* III, 15, p. 332, ll. 6–8.

[47] *Moreh* III, 15, p. 332, l. 11–12.

we shall see, he also disagrees with those who, on the ground of unintelligibility, include among impossibilities God's foreknowledge of future events, including future human actions.[48] In view of such exceptions to what the intellect, according to the philosophers, declares to be impossible, Maimonides begins to wonder whether intellect is really able to distinguish between what is intelligible and what is only imaginable and raises the question whether there is not something outside both the intellect and the imagination which alone is able to distinguish between those two and hence which alone is to be the criterion of possibility.

IX. Free Will

Free will as a doctrine was a religious heritage with all the Jewish philosophers of the Arabic period, both Rabbanites and Karaites. Shahrastānī's statement that, while the Rabbanites are like the Muʿtazilites on the question of free will, the Karaites are like the Compulsionists (*al-mujbirah*),[1] is based upon inaccurate information. So also not altogether accurate is Masʿūdī in singling out the Karaites as those among the Jews who believed in "unity and justice," [2] that is to say, who like the Muʿtazilites denied attributes and affirmed free will.

But while free will as a doctrine was with those Jewish philosophers of the Arabic period a religious heritage, free will as a controversial problem became known to them through their contact with Islam. In their own writings, therefore, dealing with free will, as they do in fact with all other religious beliefs, not assertively as a doctrine but dissertatively as a problem, they survey and critically examine all the various topics that are discussed in the Kalam in connection with the problem of free will. Of such topics dealt with by them I shall

[48] *Ibid.*, ll. 16–30.
[1] *Milal*, p. 164, ll. 16–18.
[2] Masʿūdī, *Kitāb al-Tanbīh wa'l-Ishrāf*, p. 112, l. 18 – p. 113, l. 1 (159).

present here the following two: (1) Maimonides' Restatement of the Mutakallimūn's Views on Predestination and Free will; (2) The Antinomies of Free Will.

1. MAIMONIDES' RESTATEMENT OF THE MUTAKALLIMŪN'S VIEWS ON PREDESTINATION AND FREE WILL

Maimonides reproduces the views of the Mutakallimūn on predestination and free will in two places of his *Moreh Nebukim*, in each of which he deals with both the Predestinarians and the Libertarians.

In Part I of his work, after stating that the multitude of the Mutakallimūn deny causality, he says that, "as for the actions of man, their views differ." [1] Taking up the Ash'arites first, Maimonides distinguishes within them between the view of "the multitude of the Ash'arites" [2] and the view of "one (*ba'ḍ*: *ḳeṣat*) of the Ash'arites" or, as it may also mean, "some of the Ash'arites." [3]

"The multitude of the Ash'arites," says Maimonides, "maintain that when a man wills a thing and, as he thinks, does it, the will is created for him, the power to do that which he wills is created for him, and the act itself is created for him — for man does not act by the power created in him, nor does the power have any influence on the action." [4] Maimonides quotes them as illustrating their view by an analysis of the act of writing. According to them, he says, the act of writing consists of four accidents each directly created by God and none of which is the cause of any of the others; the only relation between them is that of temporal coexistence. The four accidents directly created by God are as follows: first, man's will (*irādah*: *raṣon*) to move the pen; second, the power (*ḳudrah*: *yekolet*) to do so; third, the motion of the hand; fourth, the motion of the pen.[5]

[1] Cf. *Kalam*, p. 46.

[2] *Moreh* I, 73, Prop. 6, p. 141, l. 12.

[3] *Ibid.*, l. 20.

[4] *Ibid.*, ll. 16–19.

[5] *Ibid.*, ll. 12–16. Cf. Ghazali's analysis of the act of writing, *Kalam*, p. 704, 705.

As for the view of "one of the Ash'arites," Maimonides describes it briefly as maintaining that "this created power has a certain influence on the act and is connected with it." He then adds: "But they [the majority] regard this as abhorrent." [6]

Who this "one of the Ash'arites" was we are not told by Maimonides. The explanation generally given is that the reference is to one of the Ash'arites who was an Acquisitionist,[7] with the implication that "the multitude of the Ash'arites" were not Acquisitionists. But this is not so, for Ash'arī, according to his own statement,[8] and the Ash'arites, according to statements by Shahrastānī [9] and Averroes [10] and the Karaite al-Baṣīr,[11] were all Acquisitionists. Consequently the difference here between "the multitude of the Ash'arites" and "one (or some) of the Ash'arites" is not a difference between non-Acquisitionists and an Acquisitionist but rather a difference of opinion within the ranks of the Ash'arite Acquisitionists themselves as to whether acquisition has an influence on the action or not. Now we have seen how such a difference of opinion regarding the relation of acquisition to the action existed between the generality of the Ash'arites and Bāḳillānī.[12] We have further seen how Juwaynī, in his allusion to the view of Bāḳillānī, alludes to it not as the view of one man but rather as the view held by some Ash'arite teachers [13] and also how, in his rejection of it, he not merely expresses his disagreement with it but goes on to condemn it with such a vehemence as to give the impression that he was resounding the common sentiment of the Ash'arites.[14] We may therefore assume that, when Maimonides speaks here of "one" or "some" of the Ash'arites, the reference is to Bāḳillānī or to Bāḳillānī and his followers and also, when he says that the Ash'arites regarded this view as "abhorrent," the reference is to its con-

[6] *Ibid.*, ll. 21–22.
[7] Cf. Munk, *ad loc.* (I, p. 395, n. 1).
[8] Cf. *Kalam*, p. 684.
[9] Cf. *Ibid.*, pp. 692, 694–698.
[10] Cf. *Ibid.*, p. 688.
[11] Cf. *Ibid.*, p. 86.
[12] Cf. *Ibid.*, pp. 692, 693.
[13] Cf. *Ibid.*, 693.
[14] Cf. *Ibid.*

demnation by the generality of the Ashʿarites as resounded in the words of Juwaynī. Why Maimonides does not explicitly describe here the view of the "multitude" and the "one" of the Ashʿarites by the term "acquisition" is to be explained by the fact that already on a previous occasion he had dismissed "acquisition" as a meaningless term and as being only verbally different from "compulsion." [15]

In contradistinction to "the multitude of the Ashʿarites," who in their analysis of the act of writing maintain that the will to move the pen, the power (*ḳudrah*: *yekolet*) to do so, and the motion of the hand and the motion of the pen are all directly created by God, Maimonides says: "The Muʿtazilites contend that man acts in virtue of the power (*ḳudra*: *yekolet*) created in him." [16] The meaning of this statement quite evidently is that, according to the Muʿtazilites, neither the will nor the motion of the hand nor the motion of the pen is directly created by God in man. It is only the power to write and to perform all the preliminary acts necessary for the execution of the act of writing that is directly created by God prior to each act of writing, but once this power is created in man by God, it is man himself who by this power makes a decision of the will to move the pen and it is man himself who moves the hand and moves the pen.

In Part III of his work, under his discussion of the problem of divine providence — the problem which deals not only with the relation of God to what man does but also with His relation to what is done to man — Maimonides gives a complete and logically arranged outline of the predestinarian view of "the Islamic sect of Ashʿarites." [17] He begins with a general statement of (1) their denial of intermediate causes, so that every event in the inanimate part of the world, such as "the fall of a leaf," is directly caused by God.[18] This belief is extended by them (2) to "every motion and rest of animals" [19]

[15] *Moreh* I, 51, p. 76, l. 26 – p. 77, l. 2.
[16] *Ibid.* I, 73, Prop. 6, p. 141, ll. 19–20.
[17] *Moreh* III, 17, Third View, p. 336, l. 28.
[18] *Ibid.*, p. 336, l. 29 – p. 337, l. 6.
[19] *Ibid.*, p. 337, ll. 6–7.

and even (3) to the motion and rest of human beings, such as "Zayd's standing up and ʿUmar's arrival." [20] Moreover, this denial of human freedom is extended by them (4) to the performance of religious acts, so that man is not free "either to fulfill what he has been commanded or to avoid what he has been forbidden." [21] In consequence of this, (5) they believe that reward and punishment are not in accordance with one's actions, so that "it is possible that, on our having obeyed God's command, we should be punished and, on our having transgressed it, we should be rewarded." [22] Finally, they maintain that (6) "there is no injustice in this, for, in their opinion, it is permissible for God to punish one who has not sinned and to reward a sinner with benefits." [23]

In contradistinction to this view of "the Islamic sect of Ashʿarites," Maimonides mentions two libertarian views, of which he quotes one anonymously and the other in the name of the Muʿtazilites. Of the former he says that it is "the view of those who believe that man has capacity (*istiṭāʿah*: *yekolet*)"; [24] of the latter he says that "the Muʿtazilites are also of this view, though, according to them, man's capacity (*istiṭāʿah*: *yekolet*) is not absolute." [25] What the contrast is between the absolute and the non-absolute capacity is not explained. But in view of the fact that in his earlier restatement of the Muʿtazilite view on freedom Maimonides described it as maintaining that "man acts by a power created in him," the distinction here between the two views on freedom is to be taken to mean that, according to the Muʿtazilites, who are described here as holding that "man's capacity is not absolute," capacity is created in man by God before each act, whereas, according to "those" who are described here simply as holding that "man has capacity," capacity is something with which

[20] *Ibid.*, ll. 10–11.
[21] *Ibid.*, ll. 14–15.
[22] *Ibid.*, l. 17.
[23] *Ibid.*, ll. 22–23. For Kalam sources, see *Kalam*, pp. 607, 612, 616–617.
[24] *Moreh* III, 17, Fourth View, p. 337, l. 24.
[25] *Ibid.*, ll. 27–28.

man *qua* man is endowed by God. I have already discussed above these two conceptions of freedom among the Muslim Libertarians.[26]

2. THE ANTINOMIES OF FREE WILL

a. Free Will and Predestinarian Verses in Scripture

Believing as all the Jewish philosophers did in freedom of the will, they were faced by the same antinomies that the Muslim Libertarians faced, and directly or indirectly they tried to solve them.

First, there is the antinomy of free will and certain scriptural verses which seem to imply predestination. This antinomy is dealt with by Saadia, Ibn Ezra, and Maimonides. Of the various verses dealt with by them we shall select those which are analogous to the Koranic verses of the sealing of the heart and leading astray,[1] namely, the verses in Scripture with regard to Pharaoh, which, referring to God, says "I will harden" (Exod. 7:3) or "the Lord hardened" (Exod. 10:20) or "the Lord made strong" (Exod. 9:12) or "I will make strong" (Exod. 14:4) or "I have made heavy" (Exod. 10:1) the heart of Pharaoh; the verse with regard to Sihon, which says of God that He "hardened his spirit" (Deut. 2:30); and the verse "O Lord, why hast Thou made us to go astray from thy ways, and hardened our heart from Thy fear" (Isa. 63:17). It is to be noted that the rabbis have already tried to explain the statements with regard to Pharaoh by declaring Pharaoh to have been an exceptional case, because he was an exceptional sinner.[2]

Saadia classifies all the passages in Scripture which seem to be incompatible with the principle of free will into eight groups, of which the third consists of the verses dealing with the hardening of the heart of Pharaoh and Sihon[3] and the

[26] Cf. Munk, *Guide* III, 17 (III, p. 122, n. 2). Cf. *Kalam*, pp. 622–623.

[1] Cf. *Kalam*, pp. 601–602.

[2] Cf. *Exodus Rabbah*, 13, 3.

[3] *Emunot* IV, 6, p. 160, l. 16 – p. 161, l. 11.

fourth consists of verses which in various ways speak of God as leading men astray.[4]

With regard to the verses in the third group dealing with the hardening of the heart of Pharaoh, Saadia, without mentioning the rabbinic explanation, offers an explanation of his own. He takes the statements about God's "hardening" or "making strong" or "making heavy" the heart of Pharaoh not to mean that God caused him to disobey Him; they rather mean that God gave Pharaoh strength and fortitude so that he could withstand all the plagues "and remain alive until the rest of the punishment had been completely visited upon him." [5] Similarly Sihon needed such hardiness and fortitude "in order not to die from the terror inspired by the report about the children of Israel." [6] In their choice of action, however, both Pharaoh and Sihon were free agents.

Then, with regard to the verses in the fourth group which in various ways speak of God as leading men astray, such, for instance, as the verse: "O Lord, why hast Thou made us to go astray from Thy ways" (Isa. 63:17), he offers the same explanation which the Muslim Libertarians have given of similar verses in the Koran. Such verses in the Koran, as we have seen,[7] are explained by Muslim Libertarians not to mean that God actually causes men to go astray but rather to mean that God has found the wicked to have gone astray, "just as one says that so and so called so and so a coward because he has found him to be a coward." [8] So also Saadia explains all such verses as not meaning that God actually causes men to go astray but rather as meaning that God has found the wicked to have gone astray," just as we say that the judge made out Reuben to be a truthful man and Simon to be a liar or that he made out Levi to be just and Zebulun to be unjust." [9]

Abraham Ibn Ezra mentions three explanations of the hardening of the heart of Pharaoh. One explanation is like

[4] *Ibid.*, p. 161, l. 12 – p. 162, l. 20.
[5] *Ibid.*, p. 160, l. 16 – p. 161, l. 5.
[6] *Ibid.*, p. 161, ll. 6–11.
[7] Cf. *Kalam*, p. 656.
[8] Ash'arī, *Maḳālāt*, p. 261, ll. 15–16.
[9] *Emunot* IV, 6, p. 161, ll. 14–15.

that of Saadia, which, in one place, he attributes to "Rabbi Jeshua," [10] that is, the Karaite Jeshua ben Judah, but adds: "But he has not spoken what is right." In another place, however, he attributes the same explanation to "men of balanced judgment" (*anshe shikkul ha-da'at*),[11] that is, rationalists — a description under which elsewhere he is known to include Saadia.[12] Here, too, he adds: "As for my own explanation, you will gather it from my comment on the verse: "O that they had such a heart as this always, to fear Me and keep My commandments" (Deut. 5:26). In his comment on that verse he gives his own explanation. It is stated rather in his own peculiarly enigmatic and mystifying manner. What one may get out of it is this: God, who has singled out man from all other living beings and endowed him with reason, has also endowed him with freedom which is the good old theory of freedom as laid down by Philo and used by all scriptural philosophers, including Saadia. Pharaoh thus really hardened his heart by his own free will. But, inasmuch as it is God who has given him that freedom of the will by which he could choose to harden his heart, God is spoken of in Scripture as the one who has hardened the heart of Pharaoh.[13] A third explanation [14] is only hinted at by Ibn Ezra in his comment on the verse: "And the Lord hardened Pharaoh's heart, so that he would not let the children of Israel go" (Exod. 10:20), where he simply remarks that it is "in accordance with what our sages have said: 'To him who desires to contaminate himself doors are open [to go out and do according to his free choice]'." [15] By this, we take it, Ibn Ezra means to say that the verse should not be taken literally. It should be taken to mean that, because of his own free will Pharaoh chose to

[10] Longer Commentary on Exod. 7:3.

[11] Shorter Commentary on Exod. 7:3.

[12] Cf. Rosin, "Die Religionsphilosophie Abraham Ibn Esra's," *MGWJ*, 42 (1898), p. 28.

[13] Commentary on Deut. 5:26. Cf. Rosin, *op. cit.*, *MGWJ*, 43 (1899), pp. 175–178.

[14] Longer Commentary on Exod. 10:20.

[15] *Shabbat* 104a.

disobey the command of God to let the people go, he was allowed by God to follow the inclination of his own heart. It is in this sense that the expression "hardened Pharaoh's heart" is also interpreted by Tobiah ben Eliezer in his *Leḳaḥ Ṭob* (on Exod. 10:20) — a work mentioned by Ibn Ezra in his Introduction to his commentary on the Pentateuch. This, as we have seen, is also one of the explanations used by the Muʿtazilites for the expression "leading astray" in the Koran.[16]

Another verse, which Ibn Ezra tries to reconcile with the traditional Jewish conception of freedom, is that in which the Jewish people, in the Babylonian exile, are described as questioning God: "O Lord, why hast Thou made us to go astray from Thy ways, and hardened our heart from Thy fear?" (Isa. 63:17). He offers four explanations.[17]

First, as in his own explanation of the verse on the hardening of the heart of Pharaoh in Exodus 5:26 quoted above, he says that God is described in this verse as making us to go astray because He is "the highest cause, which is the first cause," by which he means that God is described as causing us to go astray only in the sense that He is the cause of the freedom which we possess to go astray by our own free will.

Second, having in mind the rabbinic saying that "to him who desires to purify himself assistance is given [from heaven]" [18] and having also in mind the rabbinic saying that "he who causes the multitude to sin will be given no opportunity to do repentance" [19] and taking the expression "will be given no opportunity" to mean "will be given no assistance [from heaven], he says that others explain this verse "in a sense similar to that of the statement of our ancients" with regard to a sinner of a certain type, that his sin is so grievous that "he will be given no opportunity to repent." [20] What he means to say is that God is spoken of here as causing men to go astray only in the sense that He does not think of them as

[16] Cf. *Kalam*, p. 656.
[17] Commentary on Isa. 63:17.
[18] *Shabbat* 104a.
[19] *M. Abot* V, 18.
[20] Cf. *Tosefot Yom-Ṭob* on *M. Abot* V, 18.

deserving to be assisted by Him in repenting from their evil ways. This is the same as his hinted-at third explanation of the hardening of the heart of Pharaoh quoted above.

Third, "some say that the verse expresses itself in accordance with the thoughts of man," that is to say, the verse makes the people address God in words which express their ordinary thought, and in their ordinary thought men attribute all their actions, including their evil actions, to God.

Fourth, "others, again, say: because we are in exile we cannot perform all those commandments which are made dependent upon the land." What this interpretation means is that the question raised in the verse is to be understood as follows: O Lord, why hast thou caused us to be exiled from our land so that we can no longer follow those of Thy commandments which can be performed only in our land?

Abraham ibn Daud follows Ibn Ezra's third explanation of the verses about the hardening of the heart of Pharaoh, taking them not to mean that God deprived Pharaoh of his free will but rather to mean that God did not think of him as meriting His auxiliary grace in assisting him to turn away from his free choice of his evil conduct.[21] Similarly he follows Ibn Ezra's second explanation of the verse "O Lord, why hast thou made us to go astray from Thy ways, and hardenest our heart from Thy fear?" (Isa. 63:17), taking it not to mean that the people are accusing God of depriving them of their free will but rather to mean that the people are questioning God why He does not think of them as meriting His auxiliary grace in assisting them to turn away from their free choice of their evil ways.[22]

Maimonides, in his *Shemonah Peraḳim*,[23] having in mind the common assumption that the drowning of Pharaoh and his host in the sea was a punishment for not letting the children of Israel go, raises the question that, inasmuch as Pharaoh

[21] *Emunah Ramah* II, 6, 2, p.98, ll. 3–5. [22] *Ibid.*, ll. 7–9.
[23] *Shemonah Peraḳim* 8, Arabic, p. 32, l. 24 – p. 34, l. 23.

refused to let them go because, as Scripture itself says, God hardened his heart, it was unjust on the part of God to punish him. In answer to this question, Maimonides makes two points. First, the sin for which Pharaoh was punished by drowning in the sea was not his refusal to let the people go, which, as said, was not an act of free will; it was rather his enslavement and oppression of those who were strangers sojourning in his land, which was a heinous sin committed by his own free will and without any compulsion. Second, what is meant by the hardening of the heart is that God deprived Pharaoh of the power of choosing by his own free will to repent of his sin and to let the people go and thus to escape his justly deserved punishment.

But here Maimonides seems to have become conscious of a difficulty. According to a statement by himself, while it is possible for God to deprive man of the power of free will with which He has endowed him, still, "according to the principles taught in Scripture, God never willed to do it, nor will He ever will it." [24] Is not there a contradiction between this statement of his and his explanation of the hardening of the heart of Pharaoh?

In anticipation of this difficulty, Maimonides says in effect that there is no generalization, by whomever and however formulated, to which there is no exception. The exception here, he goes on to say, is the case of one who by the exercise of his own power of free will has committed such a heinous sin that divine justice requires an irrevocable punishment for it. Inasmuch as repentance brings about a forgiveness of sin and hence leads to an escape from the punishment incurred thereby,[25] in order to make it impossible for a sinner to escape his well-deserved irrevocable punishment for a heinous sin committed by him through the exercise of his own power of free will, God deprives him of the power freely to will to repent of that sin. Such, concludes Maimonides, was not only

[24] *Moreh* III, 32, p. 386, l. 29 – p. 387, l. 2.
[25] *Pesiḳta de-Rab Kahana, Shubah* 38, p. 158b.

the sin of Pharaoh but also the sin of Sihon, king of Heshbon;[26] and in support of this explanation of his, he quotes scriptural verses in which he finds statements to the effect that the deprival of the power of repentance is used by God as a punishment for certain sins.[27]

Now, closely examined, what this explanation really amounts to is that one is to draw a distinction between man's power freely to choose between sinning and not sinning and his power freely to choose between repenting from sin and not repenting from sin. In the case of the former, God will never interfere; in the case of the latter, God may occasionally interfere. No reason is given by Maimonides why there should be such a distinction between the two cases of man's power of free choice. All he does is to quote scriptural texts in support of his present contention that God may sometimes deprive man of his power freely to choose between repenting and not repenting in order to harmonize it with another contention of his that on the basis of scriptural teachings God never deprives man of his power freely to choose between sinning and not sinning. Similarly in his *Mishneh Torah* all he does is to quote scriptural texts in support of his contention that God may sometimes deprive man of his power freely to choose between repenting and not repenting.[28] Should we therefore assume that the distinction between these two cases of freedom was arbitrarily made by Maimonides *ad hoc* in order to remove a contradiction between his explanation of the hardening of the heart of Pharaoh and his other statement about God in His relation to man's free will? But such an assumption would be inconsistent with all we know about Maimonides and his method of dealing with such matters. There must have certainly been in his mind some reason for drawing that distinction. What was that reason?

The reason, it can be shown, is another distinction which we may assume was made by Maimonides between God's

[26] *Shemonah Peraḳim* 8, Arabic, p. 34, l. 23 – p. 35, l. 7.
[27] *Ibid.*, p. 35, ll. 7–21.
[28] *Mishneh Torah*, *Teshubah* VI, 3.

endowment of man with the freedom to choose whether to sin or not to sin and God's endowment of man with the freedom to choose whether to repent or not to repent. The former was to him a matter of justice; the latter was to him a matter of mercy. Thus with regard to man's freedom to sin or not to sin, Maimonides argues, like many others, that, "if man were compelled in his actions, then . . . reward and punishment would be downright injustice." [29] More strikingly is this argument phrased by him in his statement that, if man were not free to obey or to disobey the divine commands, then "by what right and justice does God punish the wicked or reward the righteous? 'Shall not the judge of all the earth do right' [Gen. 18:25]?" [30] With regard, however, to man's freedom to repent or not to repent, Maimonides had before him some rabbinic statements that it was not a matter of justice but rather one of mercy. Thus, referring to the two contrasting ways in which God deals with men, that of the attribute of justice and that of the attribute of mercy, and having in mind the view that the divine name "Lord" (Jehovah) in the Hebrew Bible refers to the attribute of mercy and the divine name "God" (Elohim) refers to the attribute of justice, a certain rabbi, commenting on the verse "Return, O Israel, unto the Lord thy God" (Hosea 14:2), interprets it to mean, "Repent while He is still standing in the attribute of mercy," before He assumes the name "God" and deals with you in accordance with His attribute of justice.[31] So also certain other rabbis, similarly referring to the same two divine attributes, say that God accepts penitents "in opposition to the attribute of justice," [32] the implication thus being that He accepts them by His attribute of mercy.

We may thus conclude that it is because of his belief that man's endowment by God with the freedom to choose between repenting and not repenting, unlike his endowment by

[29] *Shemonah Peraḳim* 8, p. 27, ll. 26–34.
[30] *Mishneh Torah, Teshubah* V, 4.
[31] *Pesiḳta de-Rab Kahana, Shubah* 142, p. 164a.
[32] *Pesaḥim* 119a; *Sanhedrin* 103a.

God with the freedom to choose between sinning and not sinning, was not a matter of justice but one of mercy that Maimonides has arrived at the view that, while God never deprives man of his freedom to choose between sinning and not sinning, He may, in the case of certain sins, deprive man of his freedom to choose between repenting and not repenting. What sins, besides those mentioned in the texts quoted by him from Scripture, are punishable by depriving the sinner of his freedom to repent Maimonides does not say either here or in his *Mishneh Torah*. Here he only makes the following statement: "It is not incumbent upon us to have such a knowledge of the wisdom of God as to be able to know why [in the cases mentioned] He punished [the sinners] with such a manner of punishment as He did and did not punish [them] in another manner, even as it is not incumbent upon us to know for what reason He has made a certain species to have such a kind of form as it has rather than to have another." [33] In the *Mishneh Torah*, where he has a list of twenty-four sins, subdivided into five types, all of which are described as sins which in various ways "hinder (*me'akebin*) repentance," [34] he expressly says that they are not those which "make repentance impossible (*mone'in*)." [35]

Prefatory to his explanation of the verse about the hardening of the heart of Pharaoh, Maimonides, as is his wont, calls attention to the novelty of his forthcoming explanation, in the following words: "This presents a topic of discussion, wherefrom there results an important principle (which has never occurred to any of the commentators). Reflect upon what I am about to say on this matter, set thy mind upon it, compare it with what has been said on it by others, and choose for thyself that which is the best." [36] Whether the words enclosed within parentheses existed in the original Arabic or whether they were added by the Hebrew translator, the term

[33] *Shemonah Peraḳim* 8, p. 34, ll. 5–8.
[34] *Mishneh Torah*, *Teshubah* IV, 1–5.
[35] *Ibid.*, IV, 6.
[36] *Shemonah Peraḳim* 8, p. 32, ll. 24–28.

"commentators" undoubtedly refers to Saadia and Ibn Ezra, whose interpretations of the verse we have reproduced above. It is, however, to be noted that the two points made by Maimonides are partly found in the Midrash. Thus, commenting on the verse, "but I shall harden his heart, that he shall not let the people go" (Exod. 4:21), the Midrash says that the hardening of the heart was "in order to punish them." [37] Inasmuch as this verse occurs prior to Pharaoh's refusal of letting the people go, it is quite evident that, like Maimonides, the Midrash takes the hardening of the heart which ultimately led to the drowning in the sea as a punishment for the enslavement and oppression of the children of Israel. Again, commenting on the verse, "and the Lord hardened the heart of Pharaoh" (Exod. 9:12), which occurs at the sixth plague, and evidently having observed that in the case of the first five plagues Pharaoh's hardening of the heart is ascribed not to God but to Pharaoh himself (cf. Exod. 7:22, 8:11, 8:15, 8:28, 9:7), the Midrash says, as does Maimonides, that its meaning is that Pharaoh will not be allowed to repent.[38]

So much for Maimonides' explanation of the verses about the hardening of the heart of Pharaoh.

As for the verse "O Lord, why dost Thou make us to go astray from Thy ways, and hardenest our heart from Thy fear?" (Isa. 63:17), Maimonides explains it as follows: [39] "The prophet is disturbed here over our exile, our expatriation, our decline, and the ascendancy of nations over us, and so he exclaims prayerfully: O Lord, when the children of Israel see this condition of the ascendancy of disbelievers, they will go astray from the way of truth and their heart will turn away from fearing Thee, and Thou wilt be the cause, as it were, of those silly persons' relinquishing the truth, as Moses has said: 'Now if Thou shalt kill these people as one man, then the nation which have heard the fame of Thee will speak saying: Because the Lord was not able to bring this people into the

[37] *Exodus Rabbah* 5, 7. [38] *Ibid.*, 4, 6.
[39] *Shemonah Peraḳim* 8, p. 35, l. 21 – p. 36, l. 2.

land which he swore unto them, therefore He hath slain them in the wilderness (Num. 14: 15–16)." This is like one of the explanations mentioned by Ibn Ezra, though it is presented by Maimonides somewhat differently.

b. Free Will and God's Foreknowledge

All the Jewish philosophers except one solved the antinomy of free will and God's foreknowledge by declaring that God's foreknowledge is not causative.

Saadia, after setting up an objector who raises the question with regard to the antinomy of God's foreknowledge and man's free will, says: "The person who raises the question cannot really prove that the Creator's foreknowledge of things is the cause of their coming into being." He then goes on to prove the non-causativity of God's foreknowledge by the following argument: "If God's foreknowledge of anything could be the cause of its coming into being, then all things would have to be eternal, having existed always since God has always known of them."[1] It is to be noted that his argument for the non-causativity of God's foreknowledge is exactly the same as Hishām b. al-Ḥakam's argument for the denial of God's foreknowledge quoted above.[2]

Hai Gaon says briefly that "God's foreknowledge is not the cause for the coming of a thing into being."[3]

Judah Halevi states the problem and its solution as follows: "There is still another objection, namely, the belief in freedom implies that those free actions are outside the foreknowledge of God, for that which is absolutely possible is by its own nature something unknown. The Mutakallimūn have dealt with this matter in detail and have arrived at the conclusion that the knowledge of that which is possible is accidental, so that the knowledge of such a thing is not the cause of the

[1] *Emunot* IV, 4, p. 154, ll. 14–17.

[2] Cf. *Kalam*, p. 661.

[3] See G. Weil, "Teshubato shel Rab Hai Gaon 'al ha-ḳeṣ ha-ḳaṣub la-ḥayyim" in *Sefer Asaf* (1953), Arabic, p. 264, ll. 1–2; Hebrew, p. 266, l. 11.

generation of that thing. Accordingly, God's knowledge does not compel things yet to be generated — they are, despite His knowledge of them, possible either to be generated or not to be generated, for the knowledge of that which may be generated is not the cause of its being generated, just as the knowledge of that which has been generated is not the cause of its having been generated." [4]

Abraham Ibn Ezra says: "God's [fore]knowledge does not cause man to choose good and forsake evil, seeing that He has placed in his hand self-control and power." [5]

Maimonides deals with this antinomy in three of his works. In his *Shemonah Peraḳim*, after stating the problem, he goes into a lengthy discussion to show how God's knowledge, like all His other attributes, is identical with His essence and therefore, like His essence, it is incomprehensible. On the basis of this he then argues that in some incomprehensible way God's foreknowledge of man's future actions is compatible with man's free choice of his actions.[6] Similarly in his *Mishneh Torah* he solves this antinomy simply on the basis of our inability to comprehend the nature of God's knowledge.[7] In neither of these places is there any mention of the principle of the non-causativity of God's foreknowledge. In his *Moreh Nebukim*, however, in his attempt to explain why our intellects are incapable of comprehending the true nature of God's knowledge, he enumerates five ways in which God's knowledge differs from ours, the fifth of which he describes as follows: "One of the things that have become clear to me by the texts of the Torah is that His knowledge that a certain possible thing will come into existence does not in any way make that possible thing quit the nature of the possible. On

[4] *Cuzari* V, 20, p. 340, ll. 20–26; p. 341, ll. 17–23. In my translation, the term "compel" in the expression "accordingly, God's knowledge does not compel" is based upon the term *takriaḥ* in the Hebrew version, which quite evidently reflects the Arabic term *tajbur* (or *tujbir*) used instead of the Arabic term *tankur* of the printed edition.

[5] Shorter Commentary on Exodus 23:26.

[6] *Shemonah Peraḳim* 8 toward end (p. 36, ll. 22 ff.).

[7] *Mishneh Torah*, *Teshubah* V, 5.

the contrary, the nature of the possible remains with it; and [God's] knowledge concerning what possible things will be produced does not entail one of the two possibilities becoming necessary." [8] Again: "It is in accordance with the opinion of our Law that God's knowledge does not bring about the actualization of one of the two possibilities even though He knows perfectly how one of them will come about." [9]

It will be noticed that, while Halevi describes this as a view of the Mutakallimūn, neither Saadia nor Hai nor Maimonides mentions the Mutakallimūn in this connection. Saadia treats it as a view so well known generally that he challenges any person who questions it to prove its contrary and, when he himself tries to prove this generally well-known view, he proves it by argument used by somebody else in denying God's foreknowledge. Hai's statement quite evidently reflects that of Saadia; and Maimonides describes the view as being derived from "the texts of the Torah" and as being in accordance with the opinion of our Law." As I have already mentioned above,[10] this principle of the non-causativity of God's foreknowledge had been enunciated long before the rise of the Mutakallimūn in Judaism by Rabbi Akiba and in Christianity by John of Damascus and Abucara.

The principle of the non-causativity of God's foreknowledge is also implied in statements by Joseph al-Baṣīr, Joseph Ibn Ṣaddiḳ, and Abraham Ibn Ezra, all of which reflect the Mu'tazilite view quoted above that a man foreknown by God not to believe has the power to become a believer.[11] As phrased by Joseph al-Baṣīr, it reads in part that "God's knowledge that a man will not believe does not prevent his believing." [12] As phrased by Joseph Ibn Ṣaddiḳ, it reads: "A man is not under necessity to provoke God to anger on account of God's foreknowledge that he would provoke Him to

[8] *Moreh* III, 20, p. 349, ll. 2–5.
[9] *Ibid.*, ll. 16–17.
[10] Cf. *Kalam,* p. 663.
[11] Cf. *Ibid.*, p. 662.
[12] *Muḥtawī*, p. 108a; *Ne'imot*, p. 47b.

anger." [13] As phrased by Abraham Ibn Ezra, it reads: "God's foreknowledge does not cause man to choose evil and forsake what is good, forasmuch as He has committed rule and power into his hand." [14]

The exception to which I have referred is Abraham Ibn Daud. He solved the antinomy of free will and God's foreknowledge by denying that God foreknows any future human action, maintaining that what God foreknows is only that a certain man will be faced with the possibility of choosing between two modes of action, but He does not foreknow which particular mode of action the man will choose.[15] From his explanation of this view of his it is clear that he placed this lack of knowledge on the part of God among those impossibilities which are due to the unfathomable wisdom of God by which He is unwilling to act contrary to certain laws of nature which He himself has established in the world. We have already met with such a view among the Muslim Libertarians.[16]

c. Free Will and the Appointed Term (ajal).

The conception of an appointed term of life and the antinomy arising from it is dealt with by Jewish philosophers of the Arabic period either in the form of a discussion of its technical Arabic term *ajal* or in the form of a discussion of its corresponding conception in Judaism.

Saadia, in that part of his *Emunot ve-De'ot* in which he deals with what he describes as "the essence of the soul and death and what comes after death," after he has completed his discussion of the essence of the soul, says: "Now let me discuss the matter of the *ajal* (*ḳeṣ yeme ha-hayyim*; *ḳeṣ*; *ḳeṣ ha-yamim*)." [1] He first tries to show, on the basis of scriptural

[13] *Olam Katan* IV, p. 63, ll. 7–8.
[14] Shorter Commentary on Exodus 23:26.
[15] *Emunah Ramah* II, vi, 2, p. 96.
[16] Cf. *Kalam*, p. 580.
[1] *Emunot* VI, 6, p. 203, l. 5.

verses, that in the Holy Writ there is a conception of an appointed term of life. Then he goes on to describe two main characteristics of the scriptural conception of the appointed term, evidently selected by him for their contrast with the two corresponding characteristics of the Muslim conception of the *ajal*.

First, evidently being aware that in the Muslim Kalam, with its denial of causality, the belief in the *ajal* means that God decrees directly each man's span of life, he asserts that in Judaism, with its affirmation of causality, the appointed term of life is brought about by that complexity of intermediate causes which constitutes the order of nature. He thus says: "There can be no doubt that the body is provided by God from the very beginning of its creation, with a certain built-in power, either great or small, and it is the extent of the duration of this power that is called the appointed term of life." [2] What that "power" is we are not told by Saadia. But from what we find in other Jewish philosophers, whom we shall quote soon in the course of our discussion of this topic, we may gather that what Saadia means by it is the amount of moisture and heat which, according to Aristotle, determines the length of one's life.[3] That Saadia had knowledge of this view of Aristotle can be shown by the fact that Aristotle elsewhere in his works describes this heat as the "innate natural heat" (σύμφυτος θερμότης φυσική) which together with the soul has its seat in the heart,[4] and Saadia elsewhere in this work of his similarly speaks of that which he describes as "the innate or natural heat" (*al-ḥarārah al-gharīziyyah*; *ha-ḥom ha-ṭibe'i*) and of which he says that together with the soul it has its seat in the heart.[5] Since this "power" is thus conceived of by Saadia as something corporeal, we may assume that, like anything corporeal, it is considered by him as being subject to all the vicissitudes of nature

[2] *Ibid.*, ll. 13–15.
[3] *De Longitudine* 5, 466a, 17–32.
[4] *De Vita* 4, 269b, 7–17.
[5] *Emunot* IV, Exordium, p. 146, ll. 6–7.

brought about either by the fortuitous concourse of causes or by the free actions of man, such, for instance, as death brought about by "cold and heat," which, according to the teaching of the rabbis, is outside "the power of Heaven." [6] Accordingly, when in proof of the existence of such an appointed term of life he quotes the verse reading "The number of thy days I will fulfill" (Exod. 23:26),[7] he takes it to mean only a promise for the completion of the term of life warranted by the particular "power" with which one is endowed from birth.

Second, in the Muslim Kalam, as maintained by Saadia's own contemporary, Ash'arī, on the basis of Koranic verses, the *ajal* is inexorable.[8] It is in contradistinction to this, we may assume, that Saadia declares: "I say, furthermore, that God may either increase this span of life or diminish it," but this increase or diminution is not due simply to "God's knowledge of how long He will allow the soul to remain within the body, . . . for God's knowledge exercises no direct influence on the reality of a thing"; it is rather due to God's increasing or diminishing "the extent of the power with which the body has been endowed." [9]

"But," asks Saadia, "what are the causes of this increase and diminution?" [10] and thereupon he goes on to state what he thinks these causes are. The very fact that Saadia introduces his own view on the question why God changes one's appointed term by specifically raising this question would seem to indicate that he knew of some other view on the same

[6] *Ḳiddushin* 30a. See Rashi *ad loc.* and Tosafot on *Baba Batra* 144b, and also Abraham ibn Daud, *Emunah Ramah* II, vi, 2, p. 96. I take it that Saadia (as well as Ibn Daud) took the Talmudic terms *ṣinnim paḥim* to mean "cold and heat," even though the same terms in Prov. 22:5 are translated by Saadia in his Arabic version of the Book of Proverbs by *masāll wa-fiḫaḫ*, "large packing-needles and snares," for so also Rashi, who takes these two terms in Prov. 22:5 to mean "thorns and snares," takes them in the Talmud to mean "cold and heat."

[7] *Emunot* VI, 6, p. 203, ll. 6–7.

[8] Cf. *Kalam*, p. 657.

[9] *Emunot* VI, 6, p. 203, ll. 9–13.

[10] *Ibid.*, l. 20.

question, one from which his own view was to differ. Now a view on the question why God should change one's appointed term which Saadia could have known and from which his own view differs is, we may assume, that which is implied in the Muslim tradition "which mentions the fact that some actions of obedience increase one's span of life." [11] Now this tradition implies that from eternity God had decreed about a certain man both that he should perform certain actions of obedience and that his *ajal* should accordingly increase over what it would have been had God not decreed that the man should perform those certain actions of obedience.[12] In contradistinction, Saadia maintains that, according to the Hebrew Scripture, the increase and the diminution of the appointed term are not concomitant respectively with eternally decreed actions of obedience and actions of disobedience but rather come respectively as a reward and as a punishment for righteous actions and wicked actions performed freely during one's lifetime.

This view is supported by Saadia in three ways.[13] First, in support of his view that increase is a reward for righteousness and diminution is a punishment for sin, he quotes the verse "The fear of the Lord prolongeth days but the years of the wicked shall be shortened" (Prov. 10:27). Second, in support only of his view that increase is a reward for righteousness, he quotes the verses in which man is urged to perform certain acts of righteousness by the promise "that thy days may be long" (Exod. 20:12; Deut. 25:15). Third, in support only of his view that diminution is a punishment for sin, he quotes two kinds of verses. (a) He quotes verses which contain two concrete cases, one of which is the case of the plague (*maggefah*) inflicted upon the children of Israel for the sin committed by them in Shittim, where twenty-four thousand

[11] Taftāzānī, p. 108, ll. 13–14. Elder (p. 94, n. 9, of his translation) gives reference to Ibn Ḥanbal's *Musnad*, III, 229 (ed. Cairo, A.H. 1313).

[12] This is practically also Taftāzānī's interpretation of this tradition (p. 109, ll. 2–4).

[13] *Emunot* VI, 6, p. 204, ll. 1–9.

died before the plague was stayed by the zealous act of Phinehas (Num. 25:7–11). (b) Then, wishing to show that the death of so many people by the plague in Shittim, which came as a punishment for sin, occurred at a time which did not coincide with what would have been the time of the normal deaths of those people, he says: "The prophet has already indicated that *al-maggefah* [that is, the plague in Shittim, expressed here by the Hebrew *maggefah* prefixed by the Arabic definite article *al*] is other than *al-ajal* [that is, the appointed term of life]," and thereupon he quotes the verse in which David, after restraining his followers from killing Saul, says: "The Lord shall smite him; or his day shall come to die; or he shall go down into battle and perish" (1 Sam. 26:10), in which he quite evidently takes the possibility of the Lord's smiting of Saul to be as a punishment for some sin. It is to be noted, that nothing is said by Saadia about the death of many people not in a plague brought about by God as a punishment for sin but in an epidemic brought about by natural or accidental causes; nor is any comment made by him on the last statement in the verse, namely, "or he shall go down into battle and perish."

Toward the end of his statements that increase and diminution of one's appointed term come respectively as a reward for righteousness and as a punishment for sin, Saadia became conscious of the traditional Jewish belief that the ultimate reward and punishment for one's deeds are in the world to come [14] and especially of the rabbinic interpretation of the promise of long life for certain righteous acts in the verse "that thy days may be long" quoted by himself as referring to its fulfillment "in the world which is everlasting." [15] He therefore concludes: "However, let me say that not every righteous man has his life increased, nor is every sinner's life diminished. Everything depends rather upon the choice of the Creator and upon what is salutary in each case. Those

[14] *Ta'anit* 11a; *Ḳiddushin* 40b.
[15] *Ḳiddushin* 39b.

righteous individuals, therefore, whose life is not increased, can look forward to reward in the world to come. Again the wicked who have not been cut off before their time in this world have punishment awaiting them in the world to come." [16]

With his belief in an appointed term of life subject to change by the various vicissitudes of nature, Saadia was not troubled by the antinomy of free will and the appointed term of life for which those Muʿtazilites who believed in the Koranic inexorable *ajal* sought a solution.[17] Still, the antinomy is raised by him in connection with the following special case. Suppose God has decreed that a man is to die prior to the time of his normal death either as a punishment for some sin or for the purpose of trying and testing him,[18] and suppose that a murderer by the exercise of his free will murdered that man, "what shall we think of that act or to whom shall we ascribe it?" [19] Saadia's solution of this antinomy reads as follows: "The cutting off [decreed for the victim] is the act of God, but the manner of the slaying is an act of the evil-doer. For as long as [divine] wisdom demands the extermination of the individual in question, even if the actual slayer should not in his malice slay him, the victim might perish by some other means." [20] In this closing remark, Saadia has reference to the Talmudic maxim, quoted by him a little later,[21] which says in effect that, when it is decreed by God that someone should die, He has at His disposal many agents of death.[22]

The next important discussion of the *ajal* in Judaism is that by Hai Gaon.

Hai Gaon,[23] on being questioned whether an appointed

[16] *Emunot* VI, 6, p. 204, ll. 9–12.
[17] Cf. *Kalam*, pp. 657–660.
[18] *Genesis Rabbah* 22, 3.
[19] *Emunot* IV, 5, p. 156, ll. 17–20.
[20] *Ibid.*, p. 156, l. 20 – p. 157, l. 2.
[21] *Ibid.*, p. 157, ll. 6–8.
[22] *Ta'anit* 18b.
[23] See G. Weil, "Teshubato shel Rab Hai Gaon," *Sefer Asaf* (1953), 261–279; David Kaufmann, "Ein Responsen des Gaons R. Hāja über Gottes

term of life, designated by the Arabic word *ajal*, is subject to increase and diminution, answers that an *ajal* in its Muslim sense of a term of life preordained by God and inexorable is alien to Judaism. But then he goes on to add that, with regard to the question whether God has a knowledge of how long a man will live, his view is that "God has a knowledge of what will come to be, but this knowledge of God is not the cause of a thing's coming to be." [24] As for the verse reading "The number of thy days I will fulfill" (Exod. 23:26), he says, "it is not impossible that its meaning is [a promise of] death by old age and length of life." [25] By the same token, the verse in which David says, with regard to Saul, "or his day shall come to die" (1 Sam. 26:10) is to be taken to mean "the day on which God knows that Saul will die a natural death," [26] that is to say, and not the kind of death which is described in the first part of the verse as that by which "the Lord shall smite him." Thus, while denying the Muslim conception of a preordained *ajal*, he believes in an individual term of life for each human being, one which is foreknown to God, but not caused by that knowledge, that is to say, not decreed by God, and which also ends in a natural death and not in a death by which God smites one.

Now Hai does not explain what the cause is of that term of life of which God's foreknowledge is not the cause. Saadia, however, as we have seen, explains that the cause of that term of life, which he similarly describes as being foreknown to God but not caused by His foreknowledge of it, is a "power" with which the human body is endowed from birth.[27]

Vorherwissen und die Dauer des menschlischen Lebens (Agal)," *ZDMG*, 49 (1895), 73–84.

[24] Weil, in *Sefer Asaf* (1953), Arabic, p. 264, ll. 1–2; Hebrew, p. 266, ll. 16–18.

[25] *Ibid.*, Arabic, ll. 7–8; Hebrew, ll. 16–18.

[26] *Ibid.*, Arabic, ll. 8–9; Hebrew, ll. 18–19. It is to be noted that the underlying Arabic for "natural" in the expression here "natural death" is not the technical term *ṭabīʿī*. The Arabic expression *sayamūtu ḥatfa anfihi* used here literally means "he will die the death of his nose."

[27] Cf. above, p. 218.

We may, therefore, assume that it is similarly (1) with such a "power" that Hai would identify the cause of every human being's term of life; (2) that that "power" would be conceived of by him as something corporeal, such as the Aristotelian "moisture" and "heat" which are said to determine one's length of life; and also (3) that, like anything corporeal, that corporeal power would be considered by him as subject to the effects of all kinds of causes, including death from heat and cold.[28] Moreover, despite the difference in the phrasing of his interpretation of certain verses of the Scripture from the phrasing of Saadia's interpretation of the same verses, Hai maintains, like Saadia, that God may increase or diminish that term of one's life which is foreknown to Him but is not caused by His foreknowledge of it and that that increase or diminution is in accordance with one's righteousness or wickedness during his lifetime.[29]

Hai then discusses three questions. Weil in his exhaustive study of Hai's Responsum [30] has shown how his three questions and answers are based upon similar questions and answers quoted in the name of various Mutakallimūn in Arabic sources, mentioning Ash'arī's *Maḳālāt* and Ḥillī's *Kashf al-Murād* in connection with the first question and answer and Ījī's *Mawāḳif* in connection with all the three questions and answers. Of these three works only the first dates from a time prior to Hai; the other two are later works, which, however, are based upon works earlier than Hai. I shall re-examine Hai's three questions and answers with a view to finding out whether Weil was right in making them based exclusively upon the sources he mentioned.

The first question, as phrased by Hai, reads as follows: "The question arises with regard to someone who was assailed by an assailant and was killed, whether, if the murderer had not killed him at that particular time, you would say that the

[28] Cf. above, pp. 218–219.

[29] Weil, in *Sefer Asaf* (1953), Arabic, p. 263, ll. 1–25; Hebrew, p. 265, l. 8 – p. 266, l. 8.

[30] *Ibid.*, pp. 273–274.

victim would have died anyhow or you would say that he would have remained alive." In his answer, Hai says: "We may assume that he would die at the same time, even if the murderer did not kill him, but one may also assume that, according to the principle laid down by us, God knew that, if the murderer did not kill him he would continue to live for some time." [31] This answer, according to Weil, is the same as the answer to the same question ascribed by Ashʿarī to some Muʿtazilites [32] and by Ḥillī to those referred to by him as most of the Verifiers.[33] But in my comment above on the answer ascribed to those two different groups of authors, I have shown how the premises underlying this answer differ with each group of its authors, for with those "some Muʿtazilites" to whom it is ascribed by Ashʿarī its underlying premises are (1) the affirmation of an inexorable *ajal*, (2) the affirmation of free will, and (3) the denial of foreknowledge on the part of God, whereas with those most of the Verifiers to whom it is ascribed by Ḥillī its underlying premises are (1) the same affirmation of an inexorable *ajal*, but (2) the denial of free will and (3) the affirmation of causative foreknowledge on the part of God.[34] Now the underlying premises of the same answer as used by Hai are (1) the denial of an inexorable *ajal*, (2) the affirmation of free will, and (3) the affirmation of non-causative foreknowledge on the part of God. And so, while his answer is the same as that ascribed to some of the Muʿtazilites and to most of the Verifiers, the reasoning by which he has arrived at that answer differs from that by which either one of those two groups of Muʿtazilites and Verifiers has arrived at its answer.

Hai's second question reads as follows: "It may also be asked: Often a great multitude of people are killed at once in a violent disaster. Are you to believe that the entire multitude

[31] *Ibid.*, Arabic, p. 264, ll. 9–13; Hebrew, p. 266, ll. 20–25.
[32] *Maḳālāt*, p. 257, l. 3. Cf. *Kalam*, p. 659.
[33] Weil, p. 274, n. 50.
[34] Cf. *Kalam*, p. 659.

of people would have died anyhow at the same time?" [35] Here, too, Hai's answer differs from Ījī's answer to the same question. Ījī, according to whom the Mu'tazilites believe in a divinely decreed *ajal*, but that it could be upset by the free acts of men,[36] ascribes to these Mu'tazilites the view that, in the case of a great multitude of people who were killed at once in a battle, it cannot be assumed that they would have died anyhow at the same time,[37] and this is their answer to the question. Hai, however, with his denial of a divinely decreed *ajal*, disagrees with them; and, evidently having in mind not only the question as raised by the Mu'tazilites but also the question as dealt with by Saadia, he divides his answer correspondingly into two parts.

In the first part of the answer, he addresses himself to the question as dealt with by the Mu'tazilites, according to which the great multitude of people were killed in some accidental or natural manner, such, for instance, as being killed in battle, which is mentioned by the Mu'tazilites, or in an epidemic (*waba*) or by the collapse of a building or in the sinking of a ship, which are mentioned here by Hai himself. In such cases, he says, it is conceivable that, if the great multitude of people were not killed, they would either die anyhow at the same time or live until their natural end.[38]

In the second part of the answer, he addresses himself to the question as dealt with by Saadia, according to which the great multitude of people died as a punishment for some sin, such, for instance, as in the case of the plague in Shittim (Num. 25:7–11), which is mentioned by Saadia, or as in the same case of the plague in Shittim and in the case of the plague following the sedition of Korah (Num. 16: 46–50), which are mentioned here by Hai himself. In such cases, he says, if the

[35] Weil, Arabic, p. 264, ll. 13–15; Hebrew, p. 266, ll. 26–27.

[36] See Jurjānī, *Sharḥ al-Mawāḳif* VIII, p. 170, ll. 13–15 (ed. Cairo, A.H. 1325); ed. Sorensen, p. 125, ll. 10–12; cf. *Kalam*, p. 658.

[37] *Ibid.* (Cairo), p. 171, ll. 4–6; ed. Sorensen, p. 127, ll. 19–20; Weil, Arabic, p. 275, ll. 14–15; Hebrew, p. 277, ll. 9–10.

[38] Weil, Arabic, p. 264, ll. 15–18; Hebrew, p. 266, ll. 27–31.

great multitude of people did not die as a punishment for their sin, they would not die at the same time.[39]

Hai's third question is presented as follows: "Someone may ask: If you assume that, if the murderer had not killed him, the murdered man would have died anyhow by the act of God, then how could the murderer be considered as the one who committed the violence on the man and why should he be sentenced to death?" [40] It is to be noted that no explanation is given here of what is meant by the phrase "by the act of God" by which Hai is assumed to believe that the murdered man would have died anyhow. Certainly it could not refer to the appointed team, for the appointed team, according to Hai, as we have seen, is not inexorable and may be increased or diminished. Inevitably this question reflects the question raised by Saadia, which, as we have seen, deals with the special case of a man who, having been decreed by God to die prior to his natural death, either as a punishment for some sin or for the purpose of trying and testing him, was killed by a murderer also prior to his natural death.[41] Accordingly, the phrase "by the act of God" used here means by the decree of God that the man should die prior to his natural death either as a punishment for some sin or for the purpose of trying and testing him.

Hai's answer is like that of Saadia. It reads as follows: "The murderer had no right to perpetrate his assault on the victim, so that, despite the assumption that, even though he had not slain him, the victim would have died anyhow, the murderer is not exempt from the blame of his having done what he should not have done and hence he deserves the sentence that is justly to be passed on him." [42]

[39] *Ibid.*, Arabic, p. 264, ll. 18–23; Hebrew, p. 266, l. 31 – p. 267, l. 6.
[40] *Ibid.*, Arabic, p. 264, ll. 23–25; Hebrew, p. 267, ll. 7–9.
[41] Cf. above, p. 222.
[42] Weil, Arabic, p. 264, l. 25 – p. 265, l. 2; Hebrew, p. 267, ll. 9–12. In the opening statement of the answer, I have adopted the reading *lam yakun* as in the Arabic text printed in Wertheimer's *Kohelet Shelomoh* (1899), p. 76, l. 13, in preference to the reading *lu lam* as in the text printed by

Abraham Ibn Ezra discusses the problem of the appointed term of life in his comment on the verse, "The number of thy days I will fulfill." (Exod. 23:26) in both his Longer and his Shorter Commentary on the Book of Exodus. In its shorter version the comment is almost a restatement of the view of Saadia, and in its longer version, it reads like an elaboration on it. In the shorter version, Ibn Ezra begins with the statement that "the meaning of this verse is that God has endowed each body with a power by which it is to exist a certain time." In the longer version, his comment reads as follows: "We know that for each man there is a fixed and foreknown measure of time during which he may continue to live, and this is determined by the amount of the innate heat and moisture in him in preponderance over the foreign heat and alien moisture which are in opposition to the innate." [43] In this version, it will be noticed, the term "power" of the shorter version, which seems to be a quotation from Saadia, is explained by the terms "innate heat and moisture." From the phrasing of his statement we may gather that the source of his knowledge about "the innate heat and moisture" was not only Aristotle, quoted above in connection with Saadia, but also Avicenna, who explicitly states in his *Ḳānūn* that the cause of death is the diminution of the "innate heat" and the loss of "moisture." [44] Then, like Saadia, he says in his Shorter Commentary that, "although God knows even before one has grown to young manhood [45] what way he will choose,

---

Derenbourgh in *REJ*, 22 (1891), p. 206, l. 1, and by Weil, *op. cit.*, p. 264, l. 26.

[43] Literally, "during which he may continue to live in accordance with the greatness — or the greater portion — of the innate heat and moisture, not the foreign heat and alien moisture . . ."

[44] *Ḳanūn*, Lib. I, Fen III, Cap. 1, p. 149, ll. 18–23 (ed. Bulak, 1877). Cf. Taftāzānī, p. 109, ll. 9–10, where he says that the view of al-Nasafī is "unlike the position of the philosophers, who asserted that a living being has a natural appointed time, which is the time of its death through the dissolution of its moisture and the extinction of its heat."

[45] Literally, "before the coming to be of the young man (*ha-na'ar*)." The use here of the term *na'ar* as a designation of one who has reached the age of discretion reflects the verse, "Wherewithal shall a young man

that knowledge of God does not cause man to choose good and forsake evil, seeing that He has placed in the hand of man self-control and power." Again, like Saadia, he shows how this appointed term of life is not inexorable. In the Shorter Commentary, he says that "if man cleaves unto the Lord, by whom actions are weighed, the Lord will bring about causes to preserve his body by the strengthening of his sustaining spirit, and the opposite of this will He bring about in the case of man's straying away far from the source of life." Similarly in the Longer Commentary he says: "He who cleaves unto the Lord will have the heat and the moisture in him strengthened by the power of the soul and he may then live longer than his appointed term; it is thus written, The fear of the Lord prolongeth days, but the years of the wicked shall be shortened (Prov. 10:27) and it is written, [He that getteth riches, and not by right], shall leave them in the midst of his days (Jer. 17:11)".

Then in the same Long Commentary there comes a passage which I take to mean as follows: "And it is written, Nay, but the Lord shall smite him [with a plague]; or his day shall come to die; [or he shall go down into battle and perish]" (1 Sam. 26:10). He who dies in battle or by a plague does not die on 'his day,' that is, at the time appointed in accordance with the innate heat and moisture, for from without befall him happenings (*miḳrim*) [like these]. But the Lord, unto whom he cleaves, will preserve him from all of them."

This passage calls for the following comments. (1) The Hebrew term *yiggefenu* in the first part of the verse, which is usually translated by "shall smite him," is taken here by Ibn Ezra, as may be seen from his subsequent comment, in the sense of "shall smite him with a plague," as so also is the term *va-yiggof* in Exod. 32:35 explicitly said by him to be taken in the sense of "and He smote with a plague." (2) When he says that both he who dies in battle and he who dies by having

(*na'ar*) keep his way pure? By taking heed thereto according to Thy word" (Ps. 119:9).

been smitten by God with a plague, quite evidently as a punishment for some sin, do not die on the day that would be the day of their natural death, he means thereby that, while the deaths of both of them do not have to synchronize with their natural deaths, in the case of the former, where the death comes as a divine punishment for a sin, it will never synchronize with his natural death; in the case of the latter, where the death may come about by accidental causes, it not only may not synchronize with his natural death, but it also may synchronize with it. (3) The Hebrew term *miḳrim*, applied by him to both one who dies by having been smitten by God with a plague as a punishment for sin and one who dies in battle, is quite evidently not used by him in its technical sense of "accidents" as things which happen without design and purpose; it is rather used by him in the general sense of disastrous events which may be caused even by agents acting with design.

Maimonides, in a letter addressed by his pupil Joseph ben Judah, was solicited for an opinion with regard to the preordained span of life, as designated by the Arabic term *ajal* and as conceived of in Islam.[46] Maimonides answered categorically: "According to our opinion [that is, as Jews], there is no preordained span of life (*ajal*)." He then goes on to say that "any living being is kept alive as long as it is indemnified for whatever is dissolved of its substantial moisture, so that it remains in its state uncorrupt, as Galen has said: the cause of death is the destruction of the equilibrium of the innate heat."[47] This is followed by a long discussion of the causes of the destruction of this equilibrium. All this agrees in a general way with the view which we have already met with in Saadia and others concerning the cause of one's appointed term of life.

Then from statements in his other works about God's fore-

[46] Cf. Gotthold Weil, *Maimonides über die Lebensdauer*, 1953.

[47] *Ibid.*, Arabic, p. 12, ll. 8–12; German, p. 16. Reference to Galen is to *De Historia Philosophica* XXXVII (Opera, ed. Kuhn, vol. XIX, p. 339).

knowledge of future events and that His foreknowledge is not the cause of those future events it is quite evident that, like Saadia and Hai and Ibn Ezra, Maimonides held that God has a foreknowledge of one's appointed term of life but that His foreknowledge of it is not the cause thereof.

Then also, like Saadia and Hai and Ibn Ezra, he tries to show, on the basis of scriptural proof-texts, that the days of man's life may be either lengthened or shortened by God in accordance with the man's deserts.[48] Among the verses quoted by him are some of those quoted by Saadia and Ibn Ezra, among them the verses "The fear of the Lord prolongeth days; but the years of the wicked shall be shortened" (Prov. 10:27).[49]

d. Free Will and the Provision of Sustenance (rizḳ)

While the general statement in the Hebrew Scripture that God it is "who giveth food to all flesh" (Ps. 136:25) could not give rise to an antinomy of free will and the *rizḳ* like that for which the Muʿtazilites sought a solution,[1] the Talmudic statement that "the entire sustenance of a man [for the year] is fixed for him [during the period extending] from New year to the Day of Atonement"[2] could have given rise to such an antinomy; but, as far as I know, it did not. Such an antinomy, however, is raised by Saadia in connection with the following special case. Suppose God has decreed that a man is to lose some of his property either as a punishment for some sin or for the purpose of trying and testing him, and suppose that a thief by the exercise of his free will stole that property from the man, "shall this act be considered as an act of God?"[3] Saadia's answer reads as follows: "The [decree

[48] Weil, *Maimonides,* Arabic, p. 14, l. 18 to end; German, p. 19, bottom, to end.

[49] *Ibid.*, Arabic, p. 15, ll. 14–15; German, p. 21.

[1] Cf. *Kalam*, p. 660.

[2] *Beṣah* 16a.

[3] *Emunot* IV, 5, p. 157, ll. 2–4.

concerning the] loss of the property is an act of God but the theft is an act of man, for as long as [divine] wisdom demands the loss of that particular object, if the thief were not to steal it, it might be destroyed by other means,"[4] and thereupon he quotes the Talmudic maxim, which says in effect that, whenever God decrees something, He has at his disposal many agents to carry out His decree.[5]

e. Free Will and God's Power

The solution of the antinomy of free will and God's power offered by Jewish philosophers of the Arabic period, or provided by them in anticipation of such an antinomy, is like that advanced by all scriptural philosophers before them: Philo, the Church Fathers, and the Muʿtazilites. Briefly stated, it is the affirmation that free will is a special gift by God to human beings. This explanation, it can be shown, is common to all these Jewish philosophers. Here I shall quote those of them who express themselves explicitly on this point. Thus Saadia, starting out by showing that there is a gradation in the order of beings and that man, who is "the intended purpose of creation,"[1] has been endowed by God with "freedom of choice,"[2] concludes that this gift of free will to man is "in keeping with the justice of the Creator and His graciousness (*ra'fatuhu*: *ḥemlato*) to man."[3] Similarly Baḥya explains man's free will as being due to "the great solicitude (*ʿināyat*: *ḥemlat*) of God for His creatures."[4] So also does Maimonides say that, according to Scriptural teaching, man possesses free will because "God has willed it so,"[5] that is to say, because God, who acts by will and design and for the good of His

[4] *Ibid.*, ll. 4–6.
[5] *Ibid.*, ll. 6–8; cf. *Taʿanit* 18b.
[1] *Emunot* IV, Exordium, p. 146, ll. 12–13.
[2] *Ibid.* IV, 1, p. 147, l. 2.
[3] *Ibid.* IV, 3, p. 150, l. 19.
[4] *Hobot* II, 5, p. 117, ll. 3–4.
[5] *Moreh* III, 17 (5), p. 338, ll. 24–27.

creatures,[6] has singled out man for that special gift of free will. This explanation is more fully expressed by him as follows: "Just as the Creator willed that fire and air should move in an upward direction and earth and water should move in a downward direction and the celestial sphere should move round in a circle, and that similarly all the other things in the world should follow their customary way as He had willed it, so also did He will that man should be in the possession of his own power to act and that all his actions should be left to his own discretion." [7]

Had these Jewish philosophers known the works of Philo, they would undoubtedly have quoted his statement that "of that free will which is His own most fitting and proper possession God gave to the human mind such a portion as it was capable of receiving," [8] with the result that the human mind "is in this respect made like Him." [9] Centuries later, Descartes, who could have known this statement of Philo, for Philo's *Quod Deus Immutabilis Sit* had been available in print both in its original Greek and in a Latin translation ever since 1613, says free will "in a certain sense renders us like God," [10] and Spinoza, in his rejection of the particular conception of free will as it was first formulated by Philo, argues that those who endow the human mind with freedom "make it out to be a God." [11]

[6] *Ibid.* III, 25.
[7] *Mishneh Torah, Teshubah* V, 4.
[8] *Quod Deus Immut.* 10, 47.
[9] *Ibid.*, 48.
[10] *Les Passions de l'Âme* III, 152.
[11] *Tractatus de Intellectus Emendatione* 60.

Inasmuch as most of the bibliographical data needed for citations in this book is available in *The Philosophy of the Kalam*, no new bibliography has been provided here. Aron Zysow supplied and checked cross references in the footnotes and prepared the index.

Index